Critical Masses

GEORGE D. MOFFETT

Critical Masses

The Global Population
Challenge

VIKING

VIKING
Published by the Penguin Group
Penguin Books USA Inc., 375 Hudson Street,
New York, New York 10014, U.S.A.
Penguin Books Ltd, 27 Wrights Lane, London W8 5TZ, England
Penguin Books Australia Ltd, Ringwood, Victoria, Australia
Penguin Books Canada Ltd, 10 Alcorn Avenue,
Toronto, Ontario, Canada M4V 3B2
Penguin Books (N.Z.) Ltd, 182-190 Wairau Road,
Auckland 10, New Zealand

Penguin Books Ltd, Registered Offices:
Harmondsworth, Middlesex, England

First published in 1994 by Viking Penguin,
a division of Penguin Books USA Inc.

1 3 5 7 9 10 8 6 4 2

LIBRARY OF CONGRESS CATALOGING IN PUBLICATION DATA
Moffett, George D.
Critical masses: the global population challenge /
George D. Moffett III.
p.   cm.
Includes bibliographical references and index.
ISBN 0-670-85235-X
1. Overpopulation.   2. Population forecasting.   3. Environmental degradation.
4. Birth control.   I. Title.
HB871.M57   1994
363.9'1—dc20   94–11798

Printed in the United States of America
Set in Janson Text

To Martha

Acknowledgments

During one of my several trips to research this book, I drove past the great pyramids of Egypt. It was a warm evening in May, and it occurred to me then how alike are building Egypt's great monuments and writing a book: Neither task could ever be accomplished without the support of countless people who will never get the full credit and recognition they deserve. A large number of scholars, demographers, economists, journalists, government officials, and practitioners in the field of family planning gave freely of their time and expertise during the year this book was being written. I am profoundly grateful for their generosity. This book, very simply, could not have been written without them.

The idea for the book was originally presented by Paris Wald, my first editor at Viking-Penguin. I am indebted to her for setting the project in motion, as I am to my two current editors at Viking, Michael Millman and Kristine Puopolo, and to my production editor, Robert Castillo, for the support and wise counsel that have helped see the book through to its conclusion.

Along the way numerous others have made indispensable contributions. Richard Cattani, my editor at the *Christian Science Monitor*, graciously granted me permission to take a leave of absence to undertake the project. Charles Blitzer provided the extraordinarily hospitable and supportive environment of the Woodrow Wilson International Center for Scholars, which he directs. Four others at the Wilson Center also deserve special mention for their support and assistance: Samuel Wells and Dean Anderson, deputy directors of the Wilson Center; Robert Litwak, who directs the Center's international division, where I wrote the book as a visiting scholar; and Ann Sheffield, who directs the Center's fellowship program. I am deeply indebted to each of them. Unsung heroes at the Wilson Center also include my three tireless research assistants, Chad Bryant, Kristin Jentsch, and Jonathan Stanger.

The needed financial support to write the book was generously provided by the Rockefeller Foundation and the Charles Stewart Mott Foundation. I am particularly indebted to Steven Sinding at the former and William White at the latter for the strong vote of confidence their financial backing represented. The project could not have been undertaken without their assistance.

The following people provided invaluable help during my country visits: Carol Berger and Hisham Kassem in Egypt; Donald Thomas and Gideon Mutiso in Kenya; Vida Amor de la Paz, Alfredo Mendez, and Norman Schwartz in Guatemala; Debbie Romero and David Clark Scott in Mexico; and John Knodel and Anthony Pramualratana in Thailand.

My gratitude goes also to those who performed the unglamorous service of reading and commenting on chapters in draft form: Ghaleb Abdul-Rahman, Joseph Chamie, Aziz Fahmi Farag, Jane Friedman, Carl Haub, Dennis Hodgson, Jodi Jacobson, Eileen Kennedy, Frances Kissling, John Knodel, Cynthia Lloyd, Sylvia Marcos, Father Francis Murphy, Samuel Preston, Gabrielle Ross, Saskia Sassen, Sallama Shaker, Donald Thomas, Joachim Von Braun, and Bruce Wilcox. Their suggestions have all been invaluable.

Vital support has also come from an institution that I have come to know well during the course of writing this book and that has won my deep admiration: Population Action International. At the start of the project J. Joseph Speidel, PAI's president, and Sharon L. Camp, then PAI's senior vice president, generously offered to provide research support for the book. Since then I have drawn on the formidable talents of a number of PAI's staff. Joseph Speidel, Catherine Cameron, Shanti Conli, Robert Engelman, Pamela LeRoy, and Patricia Sears read and reread the evolving manuscript, providing insightful comments that have been indispensable to the work. Elsewhere at PAI, librarians Ann Marie Amantia and Susan Spence performed heroically, tracking down books and documents; and Patricia McGrath provided valuable help with the business end of the project. My debt to these dedicated professionals can never be repaid. And of course, any errors herein are my own and not attributable to PAI.

Four other individuals need to be singled out for special recognition: Sally Ethelston, media director of PAI, whose wise counsel, extraordinary good humor, and unbelievable patience with my endless questions have earned my boundless respect and gratitude; Rushworth Kidder of the Institute for Global Ethics, whose faith in the project and constant encouragement have been a great moral support; Peter Grier, an extraordinary writer and extraordinary friend, who helped me think through the hard parts and whose editorial support has made an indispensable contribution; and finally Martha, my wife, whose devotion to the book and its author, whose cheerful forbearance through endless late nights and long journeys away from home, have been the most cherished contribution of all.

To these valued people and others here unmentioned, I owe a profound debt of gratitude.

Contents

Acknowledgments   vii

INTRODUCTION   1

ONE "Crowds, O World, Crowds":
      The Explosion of Cities   25

TWO "A Place at the Banquet": Feeding the World   61

THREE "The Limits to Growth": Environmental
      Degradation and the Multitudes   97

FOUR "Fewer Is Better": A Model of Family Planning   136

FIVE "A Woman's-Eye View": Redefining
      the Approach to Population   184

SIX "Go Forth and Multiply": Faith and
      Family Planning   224

SEVEN "A World Population Plan of Action":
      The International Policy Response   262

EPILOGUE   292

Notes   298
Suggestions for Further Reading   335
Index   343

Critical Masses

Introduction

There are two ways to view the extraordinary growth in human numbers that has occurred during the last half of the twentieth century. One is with trepidation. The other is with hope. During a recent three-year tour of duty as a newspaper correspondent in the Middle East I found abundant cause for both.

Trepidation comes more easily in a region where continuing high rates of population growth have contributed to a visible array of political, economic, and social problems. It is an emotion evoked merely by walking down the street in a city like Algiers. The vacant stares of the joyless, jobless men who wile away long hours on street corners and in coffeehouses because they have nothing else to do tell a disturbing story. These poor are part of an army of unemployed men and women that includes three quarters of Algerians between the ages of sixteen and twenty-nine.[1] Their circumstances are bleak for many reasons. An inefficient socialist economy and thirty years of increasingly corrupt one-party rule have made their contributions. But there is something else at work, and it bears down more heavily each year on Algeria's future. It is the relentless onrush of humanity that has magnified inefficiency and mismanagement, that has swelled the ranks of the joyless and jobless, and that has led even hard-core optimists to wonder whether this once proud nation can ever regain its footing. The despair expressed on the faces in Algiers tells one side of the population story.

It is reflected in the pessimism of a recent report issued by the august Council on Foreign Relations: "No government, no academic expert, has the faintest idea of how to provide adequate food, housing, health care, education, and gainful employment to such exploding numbers of people, particularly as they crowd into megacities like Mexico City, Cairo, and Calcutta. . . . Can anyone doubt that even if [the United Nations' medium population projections for the twenty-first century] are realized, our children and grandchildren will witness unprecedented misery, worldwide violence, and a tidal wave of unwanted immigration coming their way?"[2]

But there is a more hopeful side to the subject of global population as well. I discovered it one day while responding to a request from my editor at the *Christian Science Monitor* to report on the consequences of rapid population growth in Egypt. After interviewing the usual government officials and population experts, I was directed to a small family planning clinic located near Cairo's infamous "City of the Dead," a sprawling group of cemeteries that is now home to half a million living Cairenes who have nowhere else to reside. It was there that I met Aziza.

Until three years before, Aziza had been one of the majority of Egyptian women who, according to one Egyptian public-opinion poll, wanted to stop having children but did not know how. Just how to use the birth control devices passed out by a local government clinic was a mystery. Family and friends warned her of grave side effects if she tried. Meanwhile the children, five born into the squalor of her teeming Cairo neighborhood, kept coming. At the clinic she finally found what she needed: a sympathetic doctor named Mawaheb el Mouelhy who took the time to provide advice that cut through the layers of fear, ignorance, and suspicion that attend the use of contraceptives in much of the developing world. Three years later, when I met her, Aziza's children still numbered five.

One of the privileges of being a foreign correspondent is access: A trip to a city like Cairo usually means interviews with high-ranking officials and local elites. The thought that occurred to me as I left el Mouelhy's clinic was that my usual government sources were mostly in the business of *managing* problems. What was different about el Mouelhy was that she was one of the few people I had met in the region who was actually *solving* problems, by getting at one of the roots of the poverty, joblessness, and environmental decay that are on the verge of overwhelming any number of poor nations. Though largely unknown outside her own impoverished community, el Mouelhy is one of the people on whom Egypt's future largely depends. She is one of the thousands worldwide who are helping to give courage to women who, although committed in theory to having smaller families, are constrained from using modern contraceptives by ignorance, prevailing cultural and religious values, the disapproval of family members, or the limited accessibility of family planning services. Their unheralded work has injected an element of hope into sometimes desperate circumstances. This book will seek to elucidate that hope as well as the desperation that persists in the midst of the daunting reality that a quarter of a million people are added to the global community every day.

This is not a book strictly for experts. Hundreds of specialists in the fields of demography, economics, and environmental science have performed the serious, state-of-the-art research required to understand the demographic trends now at work in the world and their implications for the future of humankind. I have attempted to translate their necessarily technical findings into language that, I hope, will be both understandable to the serious layman and helpful to the policymaker.

While I hold these scholars and practitioners in the highest regard, I have not relied exclusively on their work. I have ventured beyond the library stacks to search out real people around the world who are grappling firsthand with the daily reality of the subject, either as victims of rapid population growth, as unwitting exponents of the environmental degradation it contributes to, or as enlistees in the army of men and women seeking to help humanity slow population growth or cope with its consequences. These are voices of living, breathing people—an Egyptian pensioner, a Kenyan farmer, a Mexican priest, a Thai housewife, a rural villager in Bangladesh. I intend that their experiences will take the subject out of the purely academic realm and enable readers to connect intellectually and emotionally with the challenging circumstances created by rapid population growth in the developing world.

More than most people realize, the subject of population growth and its consequences is immensely complex and highly nuanced, the more so because the field of population studies lies at the intersection of so many different disciplines. My task has been to simplify the subject without oversimplifying, to distill without losing essence. My most fervent hope is that this work has been done with the accuracy and fairness intended.

Beyond the nuances, there are the minefields. The issue of global population is intensely controversial. This should come as no surprise since it touches virtually every aspect of the human experience, from the intimate to the cosmic. Mighty debates rage among experts over whether economic underdevelopment is the cause or consequence of rapid population growth; whether family planning or economic and social development is the best way to slow population growth; whether population growth is a crisis or a blessing in disguise; whether forests and croplands, fisheries and the earth's atmosphere are on the verge of destruction, and, if so, whether population growth plays a role. No one can be entirely neutral when dealing with such provocative issues. Even though my own biases may be evident in the pages that follow, the book is not intended as a piece of special pleading. On the contrary, its primary purpose is to define the large measure of common ground that exists among experts with respect to two critical points—points that policymakers, above all, need to understand.

The first concerns what *needs* to be done: However sharply they may disagree about the long-term implications of rapid population growth, the vast majority of experts believe that any prudent strategy for dealing with the future must include measures to slow projected population growth. The second point concerns what *can* be done: Despite disagreements over tactics, broad strategic agreement exists among population experts that slowing population growth requires a combination of effective family planning and development plans that include, but are not limited to, increased educational opportunities for girls. If both of these steps were taken with dispatch, the population problem could be solved within the lifetime of today's children.

Because the poverty and environmental degradation to which rapid population growth has contributed are so unpleasant to come face to face with; because the population issue is too often presented as a statistical rather than a deeply personal matter; because long-term demographic trends are often underreported in a media environment in which breaking or sensational news is favored—for all of these reasons there is a high level of public ignorance about the population problem and thus little pressure on policymakers to move it to the top of the agenda, where it belongs. There are three reasons why breaking through the barriers of misinformation and apathy are especially crucial now. The first is that population growth is one of the global problems that will bear most heavily on the peace and prosperity of the international system during the next few decades. The second is that the end of the Cold War offers an unprecedented opportunity for policymakers to accelerate the dramatic progress that has already been made during the past three decades in reducing global birthrates. The third is that unless policymakers seize that opportunity during the decade of the 1990s, it will be far harder in the next century to stabilize population growth at a sustainable level. This book is intended largely to call attention to this opportunity and to point to the consensus for action that already exists.

Thousands of books have been written on the subject of population, and virtually all of them have something to do with a dramatic historical trend that began around the turn of the seventeenth century and that will probably end sometime during the twenty-second. Through most of human history the world's population remained below 300 million, capped by birth- and deathrates that were locked in a seemingly permanent equilibrium. But sometime after the year 1600, the line demographers use on graphs to plot population growth began to stir, and then took an unexpected—and until now permanent—turn upward. The ascent was slow at first. The line probably crossed the half billion mark sometime during the seventeenth century. Nudged along by improvements in agriculture and public health and then by the industrial revolution, it climbed higher through the eighteenth century. After the turn of the nineteenth century it reached a milestone, passing the one billion mark for the first time in human history. That was around the year 1800, not long after the English economist Thomas Malthus penned his famous essay warning that such growth would outpace food supplies and hold mankind in the grip of poverty.

The line continued upward into the present century and began its steepest ascent in the years after World War II, when two developments sent deathrates plummeting in the poor nations of Asia, Africa, and Latin America. One was the introduction of antibiotics and the advent of public health programs that led to mass immunizations and improvements in sanitation and water supplies. The other was an agricultural revolution based on chemical fertilizers, irrigation, and improved seed strains that dramatically expanded food supplies. The combined effect was to reduce mortality rates.

But with no corresponding drop in birthrates the population line was propelled into the demographic stratosphere. By the 1960s the *rate* of population growth reached 2.1 percent globally and 2.5 percent among developing countries—the highest ever recorded— and then dropped off. But, driven by the disproportionately large percentage of young people in the nations of the "third world," the line plotting the *actual growth in human numbers* continued its upward course. Several decades of the fastest population growth in human history still lie ahead, according to the United Nations. If fertility declines fast enough the line will level off sometime after the middle of the twenty-first century. If it does not, its ascent will continue into the twenty-second. Its long upward journey will then, finally, be at an end.

Over the years demographers have groped for ways to convey some sense of what this extraordinary growth in human numbers means. The sheer speed of population growth is suggested by this simple comparison: It took eighteen centuries from the time of Christ for the earth to reach its first one billion inhabitants but only *one* century to reach its second and only one *decade* to reach its latest billion. Or by this one, invoked by United States president Bill Clinton: It took 10,000 generations to reach the first two billion (in 1930) but only one lifetime to reach the next two (in 1980).[3] Or by this projection: Ninety-six hours from now the earth will have one million more inhabitants, which translates into (at 1990 population levels) a new Pittsburgh or Boston every two days, a new Germany every eight months, a new Mexico or two new Canadas every year, a new Africa and Latin America *combined* during the decade of the 1990s alone. Or by this graphic analogy, invoked by the British medical journal the *Lancet*: If an atomic bomb as destructive as the one that destroyed Hiroshima had been dropped every day since August 6, 1945, it would not have stabilized human numbers.[4] Indeed, two bombs per day would not offset today's net daily global population increase of 250,000.

The world's population now stands at about 5.6 billion, on its way to 6 billion by the turn of the century. At current growth rates it will double by the year 2035, while in Africa, where growth rates remain the highest in the world, population will double in just over half that time, from 670 million today to 1.4 billion by about 2015. Exactly when and at what level global population growth will finally peak is extremely difficult for demographers to predict. The precondition to an eventual leveling is getting "fertility"—that is, the average number of children a woman has during her reproductive years—down to "replacement" level, or the two children a couple needs to replace itself. While a number of industrial democracies and a handful of developing nations have reached or even dipped below replacement fertility, for the world as a whole it stands at nearly four children per family. Not counting China, which has a fifth of the world's population and its most aggressive program to curb birthrates, fertility in the developing countries averages 4.4 children per family.

One problem that makes the task of projecting ultimate population levels so difficult is that even if replacement fertility were reached overnight it would be years before the world's population would stop growing, mainly because of a phenomenon called "population momentum." About 40 percent of the population of developing countries is under the age of fifteen. With so many just entering their reproductive years, population is destined to increase for decades more. If Mexico, for example, were instantly to achieve replacement fertility, its population would still double over the next fifty years.[5] Japan, which attained replacement fertility in 1957, will not reach zero population growth until 2006.[6] Thus, as demographers analogize, stopping population growth is like stopping a speeding train: There is a long delay between putting on the brakes and coming to a full halt.

The range of theoretically possible population futures is suggested by the UN, whose periodic projections have long been a standard reference point for demographers. If fertility declines to replacement level immediately, population could level off at

around 8.5 billion by the middle of the next century. If fertility remains at today's level indefinitely, the world's population could pass the 700 billion mark by the middle of the twenty-second century. More realistic estimates are based on the assumption that fertility will gradually decline to around replacement level. Depending on how fast that happens, the world's population will peak somewhere between 6 (if fertility dips *below* replacement) and 21 billion, according to 1992 UN projections—a range that is up substantially from the world body's 1980 low-to-high projections of 8 to 14 billion. Under the UN's 1992 "medium" projection—the number regarded as the most probable maximum—population would reach 10 billion around the year 2050 and peak sometime during the twenty-second century at about 11.5 billion. The projection is based on educated guesses that replacement fertility will kick in at different times in different countries or regions: by 2030 in India, for example, but not until 2050 in Africa.[7]

Another way to understand such growth is to measure the annual additions implied in such estimates. The world's population is now growing by close to 93 million per year, a figure that may rise slightly before it starts to decline, according to the UN. The figures have greater impact when demographers get down to specific cases. By way of comparison, consider the population increase experienced in the United Kingdom during its period of maximum growth. It swelled from about 10 million in Malthus's time to about 40 million by World War I, a span of a century. Now consider the African nation of Nigeria. In 1985 Nigeria had a population of 83 million. According to the World Bank, it will be double that size by 2010 and triple that size by 2035. By then it will be 250 million people larger than it was in 1985 and will be the fifth- or sixth-largest nation in the world, up from tenth place today.[8] Some experts doubt that there will be a "by then" for Nigeria, meaning that before the country's population reaches its projected ultimate figure, massive deaths will begin occurring from famine and want, slowing population growth on nature's grim terms.

Demographers explain that developing nations like Nigeria are just at the beginning of a four-stage demographic transition that most of the countries of Western Europe and North America began in the nineteenth century and completed several decades ago. Stage one begins in pre-industrial societies, where both birth- and deathrates are high, producing the kind of population stability that characterized much of human history before the seventeenth century. In the second stage of the transition, improved living conditions, sometimes produced by industrialization, reduce deathrates, but birthrates remain high because children are still needed in pre-modern rural societies to provide farm labor and eventual old-age security for their parents. In stage two, the benefits of having children continue to outweigh the costs. In the third stage of the transition, improved living conditions, urbanization, and the upgraded status of women reverse the calculus of childbearing. As a family's dependence on children decreases and as the need to educate children increases, the cost of rearing children begins to outweigh the benefits, producing a desire for smaller families. In the final stage, a new parity is attained between low birth- and deathrates, which once again produces population stabilization, though at a much higher aggregate level of population.

Thanks to economic growth and comprehensive family planning programs, a small number of developing nations—Thailand and South Korea, for example—have already completed the transition, nearing or reaching replacement fertility in a few short decades. Many more, including a number of Latin American countries, are progressing through stage three. But another group of nations, mostly African, lingers in the perilous realm of stage two, where declines in birthrates trail declines in deathrates. Some demographers are worried that without the impetus of industrialization and economic development, the factors that helped lower birthrates in Europe and East Asia, the poorest countries could get stuck at stage two, with catastrophic results. In this worst-case scenario, population growth would reach a point at which demand would exceed sustainable yields of farmland, forests, and aquifers. As a result, deathrates would rise and the transition would be reversed, with poor nations thrown back into the first stage of high birth- and high deathrates.

Fortunately, one development is likely to minimize the prospect that developing countries will fall into this "demographic trap": the contraceptive revolution that began sweeping the developing world in the late 1960s and extended family planning services into the remotest corners of the globe. The conventional wisdom has long been that, because it spurs urbanization, reduces dependence on children, and creates opportunities for women outside the home, economic development is the best and perhaps only contraceptive. It was a logical assumption, since it was based on the European and North American experience. But the extension of family planning programs has made an independent contribution to reducing the birthrates, usually in tandem with social and economic development, as in East Asia, but occasionally alone, as in the case of Bangladesh. Bangladesh is one of the poorest and most densely populated nations on earth, where a rural lifestyle still makes large families a logical choice. Even so, two decades after the government and various private organizations began aggressively promoting modern contraceptives, fertility has declined from 7 to 4.9 children per family, while contraceptive use has risen from 3 percent of women of reproductive age to over 40 percent. Under the more controlled conditions produced in the Matlab region of southern Bangladesh, where infusions of outside aid have sustained a large experimental program, contraceptive prevalence now exceeds 60 percent.[9] In Bangladesh and elsewhere, researchers have found that the existence of family planning programs has not only helped to satisfy the existing demand for the contraceptives needed to space pregnancies and limit family size but, by legitimizing the idea of smaller families, has actually created new demand.

A further variable that could affect population projections is the AIDS pandemic, the impact of which has been greatest in regions of the world where the fastest population growth is occurring. According to the World Health Organization (WHO), 40 million people worldwide could be infected with the HIV virus by the turn of the century.[10] Some two-thirds of AIDS cases are believed to be concentrated in sub-Saharan Africa, with HIV prevalence estimated at nearly 25 percent among adults in urban areas in the worst-hit countries, including Uganda, Zaire, and Tanzania. The epidemic will take its heaviest toll among infants and among young adults in their prime productive and reproductive years.

Most demographers doubt that AIDS will lead to negative population growth since birthrates still far exceed current and projected AIDS deathrates even in the worst-affected countries. Even with the projected losses, population growth rates will remain high and population doubling times will be increased by only a few years.[11] "The view held by some people that 'AIDS will take care of the population problem' is completely erroneous," one group of experts concluded in 1993.[12] At the same time, experts are worried that the AIDS epidemic could hasten the spread of other diseases, including tuberculosis, and thereby increase deathrates. A more pervasive worry is that crowded and unsanitary conditions, to which rapid population growth has contributed, could provide a hothouse environment for the spread of antibiotic-resistant strains of other infectious diseases and exact a high toll in third world mega-cities.

Paradoxically, the AIDS cloud that hangs heaviest over Africa and South and Southeast Asia could have a silver lining. If AIDS education programs succeed in convincing large numbers of adults to limit the number of their sexual partners and to use condoms regularly, the result could be a decrease not only in HIV infections but in population growth.[13]

Behind the stark reality that the world's population now surges by 11,000 people every hour of every day, there are hopeful considerations.

One is that the astronomical population growth that has occurred since the start of the seventeenth century is a historical
anomaly and not, as one United Nations study notes, a natural,
normal, or, in all likelihood, permanent feature of human history.[14]
The factors that caused it are unlikely to be repeated, since gains
in development, public health, women's rights, and contraceptive
technology are likely to bring four centuries of accelerating
growth in human numbers to a gradual end. The runaway population growth of the past several centuries is thus a unique chapter in
demographic history. Most experts believe that it will end sometime late in the twenty-first or early twenty-second century when
one of two possible states is reached. One is a new balance in the
world as a whole between births and deaths, stabilizing global population for the first time in over four centuries. The other is more
likely and less tidy: a continuation of differential growth rates, with
population declining in most areas while still growing, though at
slower rates, in others.

Another heartening fact is that because of the combination of
family planning programs and improving economic conditions
that exists in many developing nations, the demographic transition
that took a century to achieve in the West has been telescoped in
much of the developing world. The circumstances that have enabled countries like Thailand to reach replacement fertility within
a mere generation are likely to be duplicated in other countries as
information on how to manage successful family planning programs is more widely disseminated and as command economies
give way to free market systems and thus to the faster economic
development that will hasten the transition to lower fertility.

Some economists have also taken heart from the fact that the
biggest population explosion in history is occurring in the context
of the most sweeping technological changes in history, changes
that could well mitigate the worst affects of population growth.
The communications revolution has extended the reach of family
planning messages into the homes of vast numbers of third world

poor, legitimizing the small-family norm and influencing family size preference. Agricultural technologies have revolutionized farm production, resulting in quantum leaps in output. A combination of market mechanisms, conservation, and substitution techniques has stretched available supplies of mineral resources despite unparalleled increases in population. Combined with intelligent public policies, these economists argue, technologies that can expand freshwater supplies, reduce atmospheric pollution, or coax more food from fixed quantities of arable land can make the concept of limits obsolete, no matter what the ultimate size of the earth's population.

But when it comes to weighing a future that will have to accommodate double or triple the world's present population, even with the family planning revolution, caution should outweigh optimism. To understand the reasons why, consider that in most of sub-Saharan Africa the demographic transition has barely begun, much less progressed toward replacement fertility. Despite notable increases in contraceptive prevalence and decreases in fertility in a few African nations, the continent as a whole is an anchor that the rest of the world is dragging on its voyage toward population stabilization. Or consider that some of the nations long heralded as family planning success stories have faltered on the road to replacement fertility. In India, the country that launched the family planning revolution but which has been anything *but* a success story, fertility has plateaued at just under four children per family. As a result, India could well overtake China as the world's most populous country before the middle of the next century. Temporary stalls have been recorded in other countries, with huge numerical consequences. Even though fertility has dropped off sharply in Indonesia since the early 1960s, to three children per couple, its population is still growing at an annual rate of 1.7 percent. In the unlikely event that it remains that high, the country with the most successful family planning program in the Islamic world will be twice its current size of 188 million in a mere forty-two years. In all, sixty-three countries with a total of 850 million people still average more than five children per family.

What is true in individual countries has also been true globally. After declining during the 1970s, the global population growth rate lingered at 1.7 percent during the 1980s. If the rate had continued its decline through the 1980s and beyond—a hypothetical but suggestive calculation—a zero growth rate would have been attained by around 2025, with a peak population of perhaps no more than 7 billion. If the growth rate of the 1980s continues into the future, on the other hand, the world's population will double to 10.7 billion by 2030 and continue its upward climb thereafter.[15]

The main reason so many demographers are worried is that population growth is concentrated in the very regions of the world least able to cope with it. Ninety-five percent of future population growth will occur in the developing nations, where three of every four people now live and where nine-tenths of humanity will live in the near future. And most of them will live in the most vulnerable areas of the developing world: cities. A few statistics provided by the U.S. National Academy of Sciences hint at why this particular *distribution* of population growth poses problems: Less developed countries generate only 15 percent of the gross world product; they are home to less than 7 percent of the world's active scientists and engineers; they have a net outflow of tens of billions of dollars per year because of trade imbalances and obligations to foreign lenders; they are already struggling to retrieve one billion people from absolute poverty and another 600 million from the brink of starvation.[16] Into this arena of lack and deprivation, between 3 and 7 billion more people will be introduced within the next sixty years, according to the UN's most likely scenario. On average, each of the countries in the third world will grow between 200 and 300 percent before population stability is reached, while their rich neighbors to the north will increase by a mere 10 to 15 percent.

But it is not this skewed distribution alone that concerns many experts but the breakneck speed with which population growth is likely to take place, a speed so far out of balance with rates of economic and social advancement that it imposes heavy penalties on nations and families alike. Jessica Tuchman Mathews, a senior fellow at the Council on Foreign Relations, spells out the implications: "A government that is capable of providing food, housing, jobs and health care for a population growing at one percent per year, therefore doubling its population every seventy-two years, could be completely overwhelmed by an annual growth rate of three percent, which would double its population in twenty-four years."[17]

It is hard to imagine that governments in at least some developing nations will not be taxed to or beyond what they can bear just to keep up with the relentless demands such fast-growing populations will make on jobs and housing and social services. Difficult economic conditions, exacerbated by rapid population growth, have already prompted millions of rural poor to migrate to cities and millions more—at a rate of 10,000 per day, according to the UN High Commissioner for Refugees[18]—to cross international borders in search of a better life. Those who stay behind will press upon surrounding farmland and intensify pressure on ecological systems.

"The problem is not population growth per se," explains Bruce Wilcox, a biologist who heads the Institute for Sustainable Development, in Menlo Park, California. "It's when the rate of population growth exceeds the rate at which technology and social change can compensate. When that happens, the result is environmental damage and human suffering. The real issue is thus not whether Earth can sustain 10 billion people or 100 billion people, but how much damage will be done between now and when humanity comes to terms with the constraints of the global environment."[19]

Although many experts believe that rapid population growth is a root cause of economic underdevelopment, political instability, and environmental degradation, the population issue has not evoked much public concern in the United States since the late 1960s and early 1970s, when books like Paul Ehrlich's *The Population Bomb* and the Club of Rome's *The Limits to Growth* created a stir with projections of famine and economic collapse.[20] Nor, curiously, has it assumed among recent American policymakers the kind of priority given to it by one secretary of state of the 1960s, Dean Rusk, who warned that getting nuclear weapons and high global population growth rates under control were the two greatest challenges facing mankind.[21] But neither ignorance nor apathy will spare Western nations from the implications of the growing body of evidence that population expansion, alone or in conjunction with other factors, is having significant and adverse consequences, and not just in poor nations.

In the United States, which has a population growth rate five times that of Western Europe and four times that of Japan, immigration and natural population growth are occurring so fast that the U.S. Census Bureau was recently forced to revamp its longterm projections.[22] In the late 1980s the Bureau projected that the U.S. population would peak at just over 300 million before the middle of the next century. New projections issued just four years later put the 2050 total at between 383 and 500 million, with continuing increases projected through the twenty-first century. In communities all across the United States, citizens are already grappling with increasing traffic congestion, a shortage of landfill space, and worsening air and water quality—all problems to which population growth makes a significant, if not exclusive, contribution.[23] Their children could end their lives in a country twice as crowded, and probably more polluted, than it is now.

Elsewhere, the effects of rapid population growth are far more severe. In the developing world, population growth has magnified the adverse effects of bad government policies and social inequities, contributing to extensive deforestation, land degradation, overcropping, urban overcrowding, and, in countries like Algeria, worrisome political trends. Among the wealthy industrial nations of Europe, meanwhile, population growth lies behind significant new social tensions and the growth of pernicious right-wing political movements. The cause: a continuing flow of humanity across the Mediterranean in search of the jobs that North Africa's inefficient economies are unable to generate fast enough to keep up with population growth. The region with the world's lowest population growth is bracing itself for worse to come from the region with the world's highest. Africa, which today has about as many inhabitants as Europe, could have three times Europe's population within a generation.[24] Europe's immigration laws are already tightening as millions of dispossessed Africans are knocking on its doors. In the future national budgets in Europe will be stretched to provide the resource transfers needed to help African nations provide for their own. The implied threat to European nations, explains the Rand Corporation's Marten Van Heuven, is that "either you visit the problem where it is or the problem will visit you."[25] If a blow-up occurs or if Islamic fundamentalists take control of a country like Algeria, a million or more refugees, including European expatriates, could head for Europe seeking asylum, according to European estimates.[26]

Population issues should command the attention of the public and policymakers for another reason: Demographic change is contributing to political and social dislocations that could put the most serious strains on the international system in the post–cold war era. Future threats to global security are likely to be highly decentralized—what Harvard government professor Stanley Hoffman calls an "epidemic of local chaos"[27]—as population growth contributes to domestic instability in the developing world and to interstate competition for resources, including the land and water needed to grow food. The potential consequences of such competition are certain to be magnified as small states increase their stockpiles of sophisticated weapons.

"Population projections out to 2050 are dramatic and have dramatic implications. We're going to have to begin to deal with these implications, and that will change the content of security issues dramatically," says John Steinbruner, who directs foreign policy studies at the Brookings Institution in Washington. "Along with the internationalization of the economy and the information revolution, population creates an entirely new set of circumstances, altering the character of what we understand to be security. We have a major story on our hands here, and people will have to notice eventually."[28]

Rapid population growth can affect security in various ways. In rural settings, competition for land, intensified by rapid population growth, could be a catalyst to conflict between large landholders and impoverished peasants. In urban areas the combination of crowded conditions, pollution, crime, lack of sanitation, shortages of public services, and the frustration of expectations raised by broader exposure to the media, produce a considerable potential for violent upheaval, according to one group of scholars who recently reported on the implication of demographic trends on U.S. security.[29] All around the developing world, meanwhile, governments are struggling to counteract the downward tow exerted by rapid population growth on economic growth and, in particular, on the potential for job creation. Some 500 million people are already un- or underemployed in developing countries, and 30 million more are entering the job market each year, according to the United Nations Population Fund.[30] By the International Labor Organization's calculations, 350 million jobs will have to be created in less developed countries during the 1990s alone.[31] Many experts doubt that capital and technology can be created fast enough in poor countries to keep up with the demand. If they are correct, welfare costs and political discontent could escalate. Simultaneously, authoritarian rule could be imposed or strengthened as governments hard pressed to provide the health, housing, employment, and education needs of swelling populations seek to retain control. As one political leader warns in Mexico, a country that particularly worries U.S. policymakers: "The consequences of not creating [at least] 15 million jobs in the next fifteen years are unthinkable. The youths who do not find them will have only three options: the United States, the streets or revolution."[32]

Rapid population growth can have other important, if less direct, consequences when it is linked to competition for scarce resources. In 1990 the American Academy of Arts and Sciences and the University of Toronto assembled a group of thirty experts to evaluate the connection between environmental degradation and conflict.[33] The panel reported that deteriorating environmental conditions, which are partly the result of population pressures, have already contributed to dislocations and violent conflicts in many parts of the third world. Unless broad social, economic, and technical reforms are instituted in time, the panel concluded, such conflicts could foreshadow an upsurge of violence induced or aggravated by environmental decline.

In the worst case, such violence could take the form of interstate strife. The most serious threat concerns control of rivers and watersheds. Experts predict that the intensification of competition for diminishing water supplies in regions like the Middle East, fueled in part by rapid population growth, will lead either to unprecedented cooperation or lethal conflict.[34] Conflict could also result as millions of "environmental refugees" abandon overworked, worn-out land in search of a better life. In one troubling precedent, population pressures have prompted an estimated 10 million Bengalis to quit Bangladesh since the 1970s and to migrate to the Indian states of Assam and Tripur, with their more favorable growing conditions. This surge of humanity has disrupted landholding patterns and economic relationships and engendered ethnic conflict.[35]

Experts agree that coping with the threats posed by rapid population growth, among other factors, will require a radical restructuring of American foreign policy, away from the unilateralism of the cold war era and toward closer coordination with the Western industrial democracies. In lieu of containing and deterring the Soviet Union, U.S. policy will have to be dedicated to careful monitoring of environmental and economic conditions around the developing world. The United States will also have to harness its multibillion-dollar intelligence-gathering network to the task of providing early warning of regional conflicts and military applications of high technology by less developed countries. The United States and its Western allies will also have to be more attentive to inequities in the international economic system that exacerbate population-induced instability, perhaps by channeling more foreign investment to the third world, reconfiguring overseas development assistance, and equalizing the terms of trade between rich and poor nations.

"In the end we're going to have to take equity very seriously," says Brookings scholar John Steinbruner. "One way to do that is with a macro-economic policy that succeeds in getting the globalizing economy to extend rather than restrict the participation of poor nations."

Given the technological achievements of the past two centuries as well as the grim, mostly localized examples of the contribution rapid population growth has made to poverty and environmental decay, it is hardly surprising that experts view the future through radically different lenses. The optimists, endowed with faith in science, technology, and the free market, see open-ended possibilities for mankind. The most extreme pessimists foretell a future of demographically driven privation, environmental overshoot, and economic collapse. In fact, both futures are possible.[36]

The experts who worry that the population bomb has not fizzled have a point. When people began talking about the population explosion twenty-five years ago the world was growing by 50 million people every year. Today the annual addition is nearly twice that number and still increasing, despite lower rates of population growth. If birthrates decline no faster in the future than they did in the 1980s, the world will at least triple in size before population is stabilized. Few could gainsay that such growth poses an unprecedented challenge to mankind.

The experts who herald mankind's past achievements and perpetual ingenuity have a point as well. Despite unprecedented increases in population growth, the world is better off in many quantitative respects, if not always in terms of quality of life, than ever before. In the aggregate, if not in some individual countries, infant mortality is lower, literacy rates are higher, and prosperity is more widespread. It is true, meanwhile, that the pressures of rapid population growth have sometimes been the mother of invention, spurring scientists and engineers to come up with solutions to the very problems such growth has created. It is true as well that smarter government policies could go far toward alleviating the effects of rapid population growth, as one team of population experts meeting under UN auspices in 1988 concluded: "Even under conditions of rapid population growth, soundly conceived and efficiently implemented institutional changes and public policies in the fields of agriculture, employment, education, health, resources, international trade and finance, income distribution, urban development, environmental protection, and natural resource management could successfully surmount most of the economic challenges facing developing countries."[37]

One thesis of this book is that the future does not *have* to be one of population-induced scarcity and environmental decline but that it *may* be, and for the very reason that the "soundly conceived and efficiently implemented" policies needed to redeem the future are in such short supply in the countries that need them most. The pages that follow provide a few examples of a well-documented phenomenon: that governments frequently act in ways that are inimical to their own long-term best interests. The British ecologist Norman Myers refers to the phenomenon as the "Barbara Tuchman factor," after the late American historian who chronicled examples of governmental "folly" from Troy to Vietnam.[38] Such folly bears heavily on any assessment of whether the doubling or tripling of the earth's population will be accompanied by prosperity or deprivation.

The task of accommodating the kind of population growth expected in dozens of the world's poorest countries would tax the capacities even of the richest. Without the benefit of prosperity, the crucial requirement will be to do "most things right most of the time," according to one UN study. But as the same study suggests, hundreds of case studies, including those cited in these pages, serve "to give warning rather than inspire hope."[39] In Egypt, urban housing for lower-income families is in short supply partly because of anachronistic rent-control laws. In Africa, food supplies are inadequate partly because of government policies that discriminate against farmers. In Guatemala, forests are felled partly because of inequitable land distribution. In none of these countries is population growth the main culprit. But in each, population growth has exacerbated the negative effects of shortsighted policies, and it will likely do so to a greater degree in the future. To say that matters need not be this way is perfectly true but largely meaningless, since matters *are* this way in many countries and are likely to remain so in the foreseeable future for reasons ranging from political opportunism to bureaucratic incompetence to a fundamental failure to comprehend the consequences of inappropriate policies.

Thus high political and institutional barriers separate what *can* be done to mitigate the effects of rapid population growth—implementing enlightened agricultural policies, for example—from what is *likely* to be done in all too many countries. As the experience of nations like South Korea demonstrates, bleak futures are not inevitable. But until there are more Koreas than Algerias in the world, more Singapores than Pakistans, policymakers will need to anticipate the likelihood that continued rapid increases in population will be attended by social tensions, political instability, and environmental disruption, and they must therefore give the highest priority to measures to lower population growth. As the team of population experts meeting in 1988 concluded: "Successfully meeting the challenges posed by rapid population growth . . . will require that technical and institutional adjustments be implemented and human and financial resources be mobilized at rates that are unprecedented in all of human history."[40]

Unless such dramatic steps are taken, and soon, it will be almost impossible to prevent the world's rendezvous with the UN's medium projection of 10 billion by 2050. If no steps are taken, it's a safe bet that a doubling or tripling of the world's present population or more will be in the offing for humanity, with whatever risks such numbers imply.

ONE

"Crowds, O World, Crowds": The Explosion of Cities

Egypt

Mohamed Sid-Ahmed says the thing he misses most is the green. Decades ago his upper-class Cairo neighborhood of Zamalek was an oasis of gardens and trees and birds, a magic place in the magic city on the Nile. Now the trees and growing plants are mostly gone, crowded out by endless blocks of nondescript buildings. "They're mediocre," he says. "It's as if they're barracks."[1]

Sid-Ahmed is sixty-six now, still one of Egypt's leading intellectuals. Sitting in the high-ceilinged library of his comfortable flat, he looks the part: bespectacled, a man of thoughtful pose. He grew up a favored son of the governor of Suez and Port Said, and in those years Cairo was his dream city. He believed its reality would be like the fiction of Lawrence Durrell's romantic tales of Alexandria—only better.

For a while it was. Those were his years of energetic political engagement, when his involvement with Egypt's communist party landed him prison terms under both King Farouk I and the man who led the 1952 revolt that deposed him, Gamal Abdel Nasser.

He laughs softly: "I was too much on the left for both, even though I'm from the upper classes."

But around the time that Nasser took over, the dream city began to change. Cairo experienced a sudden spurt of growth that turned it into one of the most densely populated urban areas in the world. Now as many as 160,000 residents per square mile are jammed into the confines of some of the city's older districts (Manhattan, by contrast, has 68,000 people per square mile).[2] From the window of a high-rise apartment, the capital of the Arab world seems on all but the clearest days a vast stretch of brown, a mass of pollution, poverty, and crumbling sandstone buildings.

Today Cairo is like an aging woman, Sid-Ahmed says. It is better to see it at sunset, when the soft orange light does not highlight its flaws. "There's still a lot of beauty in Cairo," he says. "There's experience and there's authenticity. But there are so many people now."

When Napoleon led his legions into Egypt in 1798, the country's population was under 4 million. As late as the mid-1930s it was only 16 million. Then it doubled, and doubled again; now there are over 60 million Egyptians. About 13 million of them live in greater Cairo. To walk the streets of the city is to think they are all there in front of you, blocking the sidewalk with their old chairs, hawking produce or fish or whatever comes to hand.

Sid-Ahmed says that he does not know where these people sleep, eat, wash, and carry on other basic functions of existence. He wonders if having so many people in such a small place is turning human relations "bestial." Beyond the physical hardships of poverty, he worries about the identity crisis that now afflicts the masses of rural immigrants. These Egyptians are becoming "disembedded," a term coined by British sociologist Anthony Giddens.[3] Before, they were "embedded," linked to a given place, a given time, a given status, a given history. But the migration to Cairo has severed such links, leaving millions of newcomers disconnected and rootless.

"No other identity has replaced the first one. That's the big story here," says Sid-Ahmed. For millions of rural Egyptians transplanted to the city, there's a sense of in-betweenness. "You are no longer in your home village. You're neither where you were, nor are you going anywhere. You belong to nothing. There's so much ambivalence about who you are."

The things that worry Sid-Ahmed most are the deep divisions the population crush has helped create. On one level the divide is physical, between old Cairo and a poverty belt of hastily built immigrant communities that have sprung up around it. Cairo still symbolizes expectation for poor rural Egyptians, and it pulls in tens of thousands of them every year. They inevitably end up in the squalid shantytowns that have sprouted overnight in "megacities" like Cairo all over the developing world. There are whole regions around the city now where middle-class Cairenes don't go, where the authority of the government doesn't exist. These pockets of poverty are where resurgent Islam has flourished to the point that it dares to challenge secular authority. "It's a growing phenomenon, not a marginal thing now," claims Sid-Ahmed. "It's an expression of a tear in society."

On another level the tear is economic, a growing chasm between the vast number of impoverished and the few of unprecedented and ostentatious wealth. Under Nasser there were certain proportions: The rich were less rich and the poor less poor. The rich were keen to play by the rules. But the new rich who came after the upheaval of the Nasser years, especially under Nasser's successor, Anwar Sadat, have less care for tomorrow, says Sid-Ahmed. They are pretentious, arrogant, vulgar, out to get what they can by any means they can get it. There's a new attitude in the city, says the veteran Cairene: "Everyone for himself and to hell with all the rest."

The new attitude is evident in the city's infrastructure. Inside, apartments are well-kept, sometimes luxurious; outside, the buildings are shabby, unkempt, the new ones built for fast profit and not posterity, the old ones too decayed to be retrieved.

"People no longer spend money with a civic sense. There's no public order or public requirements. All of this has to do with population, with a style of behavior that is shaped by the phenomenon of overcrowding."

All of which plays to the advantage of the Muslim fundamentalists. Sid-Ahmed sighs. "Now you can bribe your way through anything. The Islamists respond by saying the rich have no legitimacy because their well-being is built on our poverty. So if one man becomes rich because of bribes while the other man remains poor, the other man says it's okay to resort to the gun."

Thus are corruption and terrorism linked. First there is the will to violence. Then there is the ideology that justifies violence. Thirty years ago that ideology was communism. Today it is radical Islam, and it capitalizes on what Sid-Ahmed calls the "eruption of animosity" spawned by widening social inequities.

"It is irresistible and growing, and I fear the government hasn't the means to deal with it," says Sid-Ahmed.

It is becoming more and more difficult for the unhappy coexistence between rich and poor to work in Cairo, warns the highly respected writer. For even as the psychological barriers between them have gone up, the physical barriers have come down because of the press of population. He says the result is analogous to the construction of a nuclear bomb: The weapon explodes when masses that are separate are thrown together, creating an unstable, critical mass.

"I fear that we're getting close to critical mass," he says. "At a given critical point the whole thing will blow up. I don't know what that means. It's difficult to foresee how that explosion will happen. But it's obvious that we're going in that direction. We're heading for a difficult future. I don't see any way out."

Cairo is just one example of the explosive urban growth that has led the world to the brink of a historic turning point. Demographers calculate that sometime around the turn of the century a majority of the world's population will be packed into urban areas like Cairo for the first time in human history.

"Barring the unpredictable or unthinkable," writes Robert Schiffer in his book *The Exploding City*, "a new urban world will come into being when the new millennium dawns."[4]

The development is as sudden as it is dramatic. Cities first appeared 10,000 years ago, after the advent of herding and cropping made a sedentary, non-nomadic lifestyle possible. But they were few, far between, and, for the most part, small. Until modern times only one, Changan (now called Xian), the imperial city of the T'ang Dynasty in China, ever reached a population of one million. It was only with the coming of industrialization during the eighteenth century that large cities like London, the first outside of China to reach the one million mark, became common. Even then, at the dawn of the twentieth century, 86 percent of the world's population remained rural.

Next to population growth itself, the dominant demographic trend of the late twentieth century has been urbanization.[5] It began in earnest after the Second World War. On the eve of the war, most of the twenty-six urban agglomerations with populations of 2 million or more were in the developed world. After the war the balance began to change, as falling deathrates and a massive migration from rural to urban areas produced an urban explosion in developing nations. Hundreds of millions more residents of developing countries are expected to gravitate to urban areas before global population growth levels off at the end of the twenty-first century or beyond. By then nearly 70 percent of the world's population will live in cities that will occupy only about 2 percent of the earth's surface. As the authors of a survey of a hundred urban areas concluded in 1988, the problems associated with this massive ingathering constitute "one of the great issues of humanity in the twentieth century."[6] The speed of urban growth is suggested by a UN Development Programme projection that between 1990 and

1995, 320 million people—the equivalent of eighteen cities the size of New York—will be added to the world's urban areas. A small portion of this growth will occur in the cities of the industrialized world. The lion's share will take place in the third world, where an average population growth rate of 2.0 percent (2.3 percent without China) translates into an average doubling time of 36 years.

One extreme example of the relentless mathematics at work is greater Lagos, the capital of Nigeria, which now has a population of nearly 8 million. In 1950 Lagos had just 288,000 inhabitants. At the current growth rate it will have 13.5 million by century's end, 21 million by 2010. Cities like Sao Paulo, with 18 million now and swelling by half a million residents each year, do not lag far behind.

By the year 2000 a total of 3 billion people will live in urban areas, three-fourths of them in the developing world. Another billion—or the equivalent of about sixty more cities the size of New York—will be added by the year 2025. New York itself, the city that in 1950 topped the list of the ten largest cities, may not even make the list by 2025, as it is overtaken by swelling third world capitals like Jakarta and Manila.[7]

Such dramatic growth has given rise to a whole new vocabulary. In 1950 there were only two mega-cities of 8 million or more, neither of which was in the developing world. By the year 2000 there will twenty-eight such megacities, only six of which will be in the developed world, according to the UN.[8]

As for super-cities or hyper-cities of 15 million or more, the UN estimates that there will be half a dozen by the year 2000. The largest will be Tokyo-Yokohama. One of the largest will be Mexico City, which by then will have half the population of Canada. If UN projections hold true, the combined population of the ten largest cities at the end of the century—163 million—will equal that of the twenty-six smallest countries.

"In Sao Paulo, in Djakarta, in Kinshasa, in Lagos, in Calcutta—in virtually every third world city—statistics once thought spectacular, if not unbelievable, are now routine," writes Schiffer.[9]

Demographers estimate that about 60 percent of recent urban growth has resulted from high birthrates in the cities themselves. The rest derives from internal migration, the huge influx of rural residents pulled into cities by the lure of better jobs and schools and pushed by rural poverty, unemployment, and the exhaustion of agricultural land. The combined effect has been to translate regions that were once largely rural into bastions of urbanization. Latin America, for example, is already 70 percent urban. By 2025, it—along with Europe and Asia—will approach an urbanization rate of 85 percent. The trend has even reached Africa. Before 1960 only three cities in Africa (Cairo, Alexandria, and Johannesberg) had a population of a million or more. By 2025, with twenty-five or more cities over a million, even Africa will be approaching an urban majority.[10]

The astonishing speed with which mega-cities have grown has created mega-problems, for most urban governments have had neither the money nor the management and technical skills to keep pace. It took London 130 years to climb from one to 8 million residents. Mexico City covered the same distance in just thirty years, between 1940 and 1970. Sixteen years later the city's population had doubled to 16 million. Faced with vast numbers of jobless and dispossessed, urban areas like Mexico City around the world are sagging under the weight of overwhelming demands for sanitation and water supplies, housing and employment, transport and public safety. Such problems prompted one city—Sao Paulo, Brazil—to resort to an unusual tactic. In an effort to discourage more rural immigrants, it produced a series of TV spots bearing the message that life will be worse in the city.

Poignant evidence that urban governments are failing to keep up can be found in squatter communities that have sprung up in cemeteries in Cairo, garbage dumps in Mexico City, dry riverbeds in Karachi; in the tens of thousands of illegal, unsafe housing units that have cropped up in Sao Paulo; in the 4,000 tons of trash that accumulate daily in Manila;[11] in the air pollution that has condemned 60 percent of Calcutta's residents to breathing disorders;[12] in wastes that wash out of an overloaded sewage system onto the streets of Alexandria; in the 20 million homeless—the equivalent of the combined populations of London and Paris— who wander the streets of Latin America's cities.[13]

Most of all, poverty can be found in the shantytowns—the "misery villas," or "lost cities," or "mushroom communities," as they are variously known—that have cropped up around the periphery of most third world metropolises, cut off from roads, electricity, health services, clean water, and sanitation. Half the populations of Delhi, Nairobi, and Manila are slum dwellers. Slum rates are almost as high in Casablanca, Calcutta, Bogota, and Kinshasa, according to a 1990 Population Action International study that ranked cities according to ten indicators ranging from pollution to housing.[14]

"It is clearly impossible for these sprawling metropolitan areas—many located in the world's poorest countries—to keep pace with the need for transportation, sanitation, utilities, schools, and hospitals, as long as their populations double every twelve to twenty years," says the report.

The rural immigrants who populate these mushroom communities have been hard for urban experts to categorize. "The fact that you have these massive agglomerations of people doesn't necessarily mean that they are urbanized," says Saskia Sassen, an urban affairs specialist at Columbia University. "The fact is that they are merely de-ruralized."[15]

"We say cities are growing but we need to qualify that," Sassen continues. "Many squatters are profoundly connected to the rural areas. Their livelihoods, their conception of who they are, are connected to those rural areas. So the city becomes like it was in Europe in the Middle Ages, where lots of people lived who weren't necessarily urban people. We don't have a name for this new third space. It's neither rural nor urban in the way we've normally thought of those terms. It's something in between that has emerged at the edges of the urban structure."

In all, one quarter of the urban populations of Africa and Asia do not have enough money to finance a permanent home, according to World Bank estimates.[16] Fewer than 60 percent of urbanites living in developing countries have access to sanitation, and only 30 percent are connected to sewer systems, adds the World Health Organization.[17]

As Paul Kennedy notes in his book *Preparing for the Twenty-First Century*, the phenomenon of runaway urban growth in poor nations has changed the whole meaning of cities.[18] For thousands of years, great urban centers like Rome and Paris, Vienna and London, have been associated with wealth and creativity, culture and economic opportunity. "By contrast," writes Kennedy, "Asian, Latin American, and Central American mega-cities of 20 million inhabitants have become increasingly centers of poverty and social collapse."

The good news associated with this explosive urbanization is that it encourages smaller families. The bad news is that with population-doubling times in the third world so short, it will take a long time for the good news to have much of an impact. Until it does, national governments will have to face excruciatingly difficult choices as they seek to balance the needs of urban and rural populations. The "urban bias" demonstrated in many poor nations has helped keep food prices low for city dwellers. But in the process it has depressed agricultural production, creating an expanded need for food imports, which have to be purchased at the expense of domestic economic development. Low farm prices have also forced farmers off the land and into the city, even as urban growth consumes valuable farmland. The result: As the need for food has grown, the capacity to produce it has diminished.

But tilting too far the other way—often under pressure to implement structural reforms imposed by international lenders—can have equally serious consequences, as riots over hikes in food, transport, and gas prices in cities from Cairo to Bangkok have demonstrated. Indeed, as resources decline in relation to expectations, the stage is set in third world cities for what many demographers and urbanologists fear could be a wave of violence. Saskia Sassen agrees that urban poverty is an explosive issue but doubts that the total collapse of a major city is in store.

"In the past when there's been the collapse of civil order it always happened at the macro level: the masses bringing down the king. Now what we're running into is the fragmentation of civil order to the point where any collapse is also likely to be fragmented—epidemics of drugs, crime, and so forth.

"There probably won't be a mega-collapse because cities have built-in protective mechanisms. Some are institutional, like police and security systems. Some are geographical, like the citadels where the rich live. Some are ideological, like the promise of the good life that can be gained by staying within the law. It's like the mechanisms that were built into the financial system to deter a repetition of the 1929 crash."[19]

A World Bank official issues a more apocalyptic prediction: "Urban poverty will become the most significant and politically explosive problem in the next century."[20]

Dar Es Salaam has long had the reputation of being one of Cairo's worst neighborhoods. For forty years villagers have streamed into its fetid blocks, seeking to escape rural poverty. The slum is now so densely packed that to the rest of the city it is known simply as "China."

As far as the eye can see, rows of five- and six-story cinderblock apartment buildings rise above Dar Es Salaam's teeming, unpaved streets. Everywhere there is litter and animal dung. Exposed sewer pipes parallel the sidewalks—belated contributions to the neighborhood by a government that is barely able to cope with urban growth. On side streets drying laundry cascades down from balcony to balcony.

Four flights up a narrow, unlit concrete stairwell is Farag's apartment. It is impossibly tiny by Western standards, though by the standards of Cairo's poor there are worse. Farag, his wife, and four children are crammed into three tiny rooms, appended by a four-by-five–foot kitchen and a minuscule water closet.

Farag sports a three-day beard and has a bandage stretched across his forehead. He too migrated to Cairo to find a job, in his case from a village in the Nile delta. Like most men in a country where unemployment is epidemic, he survives on odd jobs, laying pipes and carrying bags of sand at a local factory for two or three dollars a day, two or three days a week. He gets by because of a small inheritance from his parents, which he has used to buy four apartments, including his own. He rents out the others for about six dollars a month each. Even with this added income, there are nights when he goes to bed hungry.

"We're just surviving," Farag says. "Certain days we don't eat, and sometimes we stretch one day's food into two. If I don't have enough to eat I close my door and go to sleep. I don't understand how people with seven and eight children survive."

He laughs when asked what Cairo will be like with another 6 or 7 million people, the number demographers project will be added to the city's population within twenty years. "There's no way we can add that many people. We'll eat each other because there's no food. I'm not eloquent, but common sense tells me that if we double in size we can't survive."

Cairo is a city with a long history. It was founded over one thousand years ago, after the Muslim conquest of Egypt. Since then it has been occupied by Turks, French, and British. In terms of its influence in the Arab world, as Egyptian sociologist Sa'ad Eddin Ibrahim notes, it is as important as Paris, the Vatican, Oxford, Hollywood, and Detroit combined.[21]

But today it is in danger of becoming a city of Farags, of hard-pressed, hopeless men and women with no steady jobs and few prospects. Cairo's unremitting growth has created massive congestion, environmental degradation, and poverty. It is a combustible mix that, in the opinion of some Egyptian experts, poses real risks of political and social collapse.

"To say that Cairo has overwhelming problems is extremely stating the obvious," writes Ibrahim.[22]

To be sure, not everyone waxes apocalyptic about Cairo's future. Ask Cairenes to comment about what their city will be like with nearly half again as many people within a generation—the government's own projection—and they invariably respond in two ways. First they heave a long, audible sigh, followed by an exclamation that usually comes down to something like "Incomprehensible!" Second, they take refuge in history. "Cairo has survived for a thousand years," comes a typical response. "It will survive this crisis as well."

Indeed, Cairenes are among the most resourceful of urban dwellers. And economic growth could help the city weather the thirty years that remain before its population is expected to peak. But in the view of many long-time residents, the city's problems have already reached tragic proportions. One such resident is Naguib Mahfouz, Egypt's eighty-five-year-old Nobel laureate and one of the capital's best-loved citizens. He says that population growth has taken a major toll on the city he loves: "Cairo has changed very much. It was little, quiet, clean, and very beautiful and pure. Perhaps now it is the contrary in everything. As for Cairenes, today they seem not as good as they were. A quiet city makes quiet people. Crowded cities make what you call 'lost people.' "[23]

For those who are well enough off to live in what one long-time resident journalist calls a "zone of humanity"—one of the nicer neighborhoods like Zamalek, for instance—life is still bearable. But for those who live in slums like Dar Es Salaam or Imbaba, the intensity of the population squeeze makes even clear thought difficult.

"This is not survival, it's slow suicide," says the journalist, Mohammed Auda, of the conditions in Cairo's slums. "It destroys people's humanity, their self-respect, their dignity."[24]

For its first 900 years Cairo was a city of manageable proportions. In 1900 it had only 600,000 inhabitants; a mere 3.7 million as late as 1960. The city's first official master plan, prepared in 1953, projected a population of 5.5 million by the year 2000; the UN now says 17 million is likely. In some individual neighborhoods, the population density is three times greater than in the infamous slums of Calcutta or Jakarta.

After being confined for centuries to the east bank of the Nile, Cairo, like a dormant beast, stirred, then prowled far beyond its original borders. Swelled by over 300,000 new residents a year, it now sprawls westward into the endless neighborhoods of Giza. Northward, it has devoured rich agricultural land as far as forty miles from the center city.[25] It now reaches into three of Egypt's forty-two governorates, consumes nearly half the country's food and drinking water, and threatens to surround and isolate the great pyramids of Giza—like the Acropolis in Athens—in a sea of humanity. Such explosive growth has intensified the competition for working and living space in Cairo. As the case of Leila illustrates, the results have not always been satisfactory.

Leila was thirty-eight when her husband died eight years ago. Since then she has carried on his business, if it can be called that, catching a few Nile fish each day and selling them for sixty or seventy cents at a fish market downstream.

Leila lives on the river where she works. Her home consists of two battered green fishing boats tied together a few feet off a stretch of garbage-strewn Nile shoreline. The boats are thirteen feet long. They arch out to a five-foot width, then narrow quickly toward the bow and stern. As living space goes it is cramped, even by Cairo standards. It would be tolerable but for one thing: She shares the space with eight children. Four sleep in one boat, five in the other. Five were born on the boats, which bob within sight of Cairo's glamorous riverfront hotels.

The boats are littered with rags, tin cans, and pots. A torn canvas tarp provides the only cover against Cairo's infrequent rains. Leila cooks on a tiny gas stove nestled into the hold of one of the boats. For a playground the children wade through the debris that floats along the shoreline. Three or four times a week, she and the older boys row one of the boats into deeper waters for the fishing expeditions that provide the family income. Every day she looks longingly up the stone embankment toward the modest apartments that line the river above her boats.

"People come with projects on how they will help find housing for us, but nothing happens." She sighs. "What's in one's own hands? We can do nothing else. God has ordered this situation."

Even from a vantage point higher than Leila's water-level view, Cairo appears less as something God has ordered than something God has forgotten. The effects of rapid population growth are everywhere. Cairo's streets, for example, are choked with some of the worst traffic on earth, with the number of private vehicles in the city increasing by 17 percent per year. Here as elsewhere in the developing world, traffic snarls have increased tensions and decreased productivity. According to a Mexican government study, the traffic jams caused in Mexico City by 2.6 million private cars are responsible for an average daily loss of 1.3 million man-hours of productivity.[26]

But traffic is only one of the population-related problems that afflict a city like Cairo. The air in the Egyptian capital is clogged with a toxic cocktail of auto exhaust and noxious emissions from nearby iron, steel, and cement factories that blankets the city nearly every day. Its river and lifeline, the Nile, is egregiously polluted.[27] Vast outlying areas lie beyond the reach of the city's sewer system, the main part of which was constructed seventy years ago to accommodate a city of a million. Now at least three times as many Cairenes live in unsewered areas, a number dwarfed by a few other third world cities, including Manila, where only one-tenth of a population of nine million is served by sewers. Even the open space that remains in Cairo is fast disappearing. According to Sa'ad Eddin Ibrahim, the Egyptian sociologist, Cairo had slightly more than one square yard of green per capita twenty years ago. The figure now is less than seven square inches. In Europe, by contrast, the average is nineteen square yards of green space per person.[28]

"The existing size of the population of Cairo is far beyond the available infrastructure and services," says Egypt's minister of local affairs, Mahmoud Sheriff. "So we are really very much worried about the availability of water, good sanitary conditions, and services."[29]

Jostled by crowds and choked by pollution, Cairenes are worried about the shortages of other necessities—like jobs—which have been exacerbated by rapid population growth. Almost nobody seems to be working full-time. The majority of Cairenes are reduced to odd jobs: hawking cheap papyrus scrolls, washing cars, acting as impromptu tour guides, collecting recyclable trash. Along the corniche, near the city's five-star hotels, the friendly "You 'merican? Welcome Cairo" is the invariable prelude to an invitation to take a felucca or taxi ride that a simple "no thank you" is rarely sufficient to shake off. Though no one knows for sure, unemployment in third world mega-cities like Cairo and Mexico City is estimated to be at least 25 percent, and millions of additional jobs will be needed to keep up with future demand. One result: Child labor appears to be on the increase throughout the developing world, as families attempt to supplement incomes to keep up with rising costs.

Housing is also scarce in a city where ten people can often be found living in one room. Though most of the funds earmarked by Egypt for public housing are spent in Cairo, the government—like urban administrations in other developing countries—has been unable to keep up with the swelling demand. The result has been an explosion of illegal, low-standard houses that, according to the UN, has accounted for nearly 85 percent of all new units constructed in the city during the 1970s.[30]

One popular method of "informal" construction is to cram new floors or additions onto already overloaded buildings. It is a strategy that has provided Awad a home.

Along with hundreds of thousands of other Cairenes, Awad, his wife, and six children live on a rooftop. Their building is a twelve-story downtown office whose fin de siècle elegance, ordered up by one of the city's leading manufacturers and bankers, is a fading reminder of Cairo's better days. Awad's quarters were once storage rooms for the tenants below. They are cramped, but they have the redeeming feature of one of the city's better views.

"Every rooftop in sight is occupied," he says, gesturing to the dozens of makeshift living quarters perched atop the buildings of central Cairo. "If you don't see someone on the roof, don't be fooled. It probably means someone's in the basement."

The best estimates are that Cairo has half a million roof dwellers. In a city where living space is at a premium, many people are only too happy to claim such jerrybuilt quarters as home. Landlords, for their part, can use the extra income provided by a small rent. In Awad's case the contribution is labor: He works as the building's night watchman.

Awad and his family have lived within the pink and green plaster walls of their three small rooms for ten years. It is comfortable enough, by Cairo standards, and represents the opportunity he emigrated from Aswan years ago to claim. But for Awad and tens of thousands of roof dwellers like him, there is no security of tenure. Despite a decade of service, he will be forced out, with no income and nowhere to go, when he is too old to make his nightly rounds.

Ironically, the numbers alone say that Cairo has more than

enough housing to go around. According to the 1986 census—
Egypt's latest—the city has 11.3 million dwelling units and only
9.7 million households. Since then the number of dwellings has actually increased faster than the number of families.

Thus Cairo faces what Cairo University economist and housing
specialist Milad Hana calls "the paradox of the housing problem:
houses without tenants and people without houses." In fact, says
Hana, Cairenes do not have enough places in which to live. The
statistical surplus is accounted for by higher-income units and the
fact that many wealthy Egyptians own more than one home.[31]

The result has been a housing crisis for the poor, linked to
housing laws of the Nasser era that have frozen rents at rates so
low that landlords find it impossible to make a profit. With no incentive to build new rental housing, developers have plowed
money into high-income condominiums. With no incentive to
maintain existing rental buildings, landlords have allowed them to
deteriorate. Indeed, the evidence for this can be seen on many
Cairo streets, where block after block is lined with old yellow-gray
sandstone buildings that are visibly crumbling.

The laws have been a boon for renters, who can still obtain a flat
for as little as four dollars a month. But they have led to a serious
shortage of low-income housing. The problems for landlords are
exacerbated by the fact that leases can be bought and sold by tenants, preempting opportunities for increases that might otherwise
be imposed. The situation is so serious that landlords often pay
tenants "key money" to evacuate so that rents can be raised.

"The result," says Hana, "is that for the past fifteen years nobody has built for rent. Everyone is building for condominiums.
Any good housing policy should have two feet: one is rental units;
one is condos. The existing housing policy is suffering infantile pa-
ralysis, since one leg is limping and the other leg is strong.

"Anybody who is rich can buy a number of flats without government controls; but young couples without savings can afford
nothing. So slums are created. Slums are a threat because they are

breeding grounds for fundamentalism, so the government has taken the stand that living conditions must be improved. But slums will continue because market forces are not allowed to operate."

The government is caught in a catch-22, Hana adds. Preserving the existing rent laws will ensure shortages in low-income housing for the foreseeable future. But any changes that would ensure a reasonable profit for builders would price most Cairenes out of the market. Many have balanced their lives on low rents. Some 63,000 low-income families are without housing altogether, acknowledges Mahmoud Sheriff; unofficial estimates put the figure much higher.

Shelter is not the only necessity of life that is now lacking in Cairo. The supply of food has been affected by rapid population growth as well. The quality of diet is falling as the prices of meat and staple provisions rise beyond the reach of many poor residents.

Food is a problem throughout Egypt. Wheat production has tripled since the early 1970s, with about 7 million acres now under production. But the country is still falling short—nearly $2.5 billion short, which is the amount Egypt spends each year on imported food, most of it wheat. Egypt now produces less than half of what it consumes. And this food deficit has been growing steadily for at least two decades. One reason is the encroachment of urban areas onto agricultural land, a pattern common to other third world cities. Bangkok, for example, has devoured an area of farmland half the size of Manhattan,[32] while African cities drove 10 million African farmers off the land during the first half of the 1980s alone.[33]

Although the reclamation of desert lands has eased the pressure somewhat, tens of thousands of acres of farmland are still swallowed up each year by squatters or developers seeking living space for Cairo's fast-growing population. Between 1980 and 2000, a total of 10 million acres of land could be lost to urbanization.[34] Land reclamation could partially offset that loss, but the feasibility of such conversion is questionable because of the huge costs involved. Desert land, meanwhile, produces smaller yields than the rich farmland lost to housing. So Egypt's food gap continues to widen each year.

Besides land, the other major constraint on agriculture is water, which flows into Egypt in fixed and limited quantities. "There's no hope of reaching self-sufficiency in food because we are limited to the Nile water and the underground waters in the desert," says Cairo University demographer Sobri Abdel Hakim.[35] Official efforts have shifted away from a goal of Egypt meeting all its own food needs in favor of import. Instead of self-sufficiency, "now we are talking about self-reliance," says Hakim.

Overall, "this is not a country that can feed itself," adds one Western diplomat in Cairo. "They might come close to feeding the current 60 million if bread subsidies [which keep farm prices artificially low] are removed but not much more."

With basic needs in increasingly short supply, the social fabric of Cairo is showing signs of fraying. Overcrowding has weakened the cherished tradition of extended families living together. Housing shortages have forced thousands of couples to delay marriage, sometimes for years. Economic deprivation has increased both petty and violent crimes, turning some cities into murder capitals. In Sao Paulo, nearly 5,000 murders were committed in 1990, while armed robberies soared to over 170,000.[36]

"When you open the newspapers and read about crimes that happen now in Egypt you shudder," says Mohammed Auda. "A young man kills his mother for about three dollars. Another man kills his grandfather for five dollars. You never heard about such crimes before. It was not a perfect society before but this kind of violence is very alien to Egypt."[37]

Even civility, long the trademark of this gentle, sophisticated city on the Nile, is being taxed. Traditional hospitality among neighbors has given way to what one Cairo doorman calls "boatsman's invitations."

"You're on shore and someone passing on a boat invites you to join him for tea. Obviously you can't do it. People still say it, but it's not sincere. The generous spirit is not as strong as it used to be," the doorman laments.

Tahseen Basheer exemplifies the genteel and considerate Cairo of the past. He is a diplomat of the old school, a former ambassador to Canada and the Arab League and a spokesman for former Egyptian presidents Gamal Abdel Nasser and Anwar Sadat. In the lobby of a downtown hotel he reminisces about the Cairo of his youth.[38]

"If you came here in the 1930s, you would have found a Cairo that was very urbanized and very urbane," he says. "The wealthy used to copy the European nobility by imitating French country houses."

Since then two things have happened that he thinks have changed Cairo's character. For one, the city's aristocracy has been replaced by what he terms a "petty bourgeoisie" dedicated to getting rich by quick fixes. Meanwhile, there has been a massive influx of rural migrants whose mentality has been shaped in the villages of the Nile delta and upper Egypt. In the dust and garbage of Egyptian villages, cleanliness can be meaningless, he says. The houses are made of clay. People share their living quarters with chickens. It does not bother them. "Now that mentality has been brought to the city and we have a phenomenon: the ruralification of the urban," says Basheer.

One result is that public space in Cairo has deteriorated. While Cairenes have a sense of cleanliness in their own apartments, the buildings themselves are dirty. "You look in the alley between the best buildings and it's a dump. People don't care what happens. Civil habits of cleanliness and beauty have changed to become just a matter of the inside, which means we have a very ironic kind of urbanization in Cairo." The "quick, massive, uncharted urbanization" of the past twenty years has also distorted Cairo's sense of space, he says. Early neighborhoods of the city, such as Heliopolis, were laid out in human proportions. They extended horizontally into the desert but were linked to the center city by good roads and a trolley system. The latest development has exploded into the sky and onto the Nile's rich agricultural lands.

Cairo has now sprawled far beyond a single jurisdiction, and the result has been an invitation to disorderly growth, corruption, and inadequate regulation. The city has grown haphazardly and illegally. "It's become an institution of disorder," says Basheer. "Zoning laws are not implemented. The money power of the builders outweighs the resistance of the poorly paid government architects and engineers who have to give out the building permits and zoning licenses. So they bribe them. Now the whole country is run by a myopic bourgeoisie with a mentality that does not care for the people. The banks of the Nile have been taken over by developers for the rich. Meanwhile we have a massive cement jungle, with no parks, no space. The children are becoming alienated because all they have to look at is cement."

This oppressive cityscape is robbing Egypt of its smile, charges Basheer. People are becoming self-centered, apartment-centered. Psychiatrists are overloaded with patients whose problems reflect the increased pressures of city living. "We're getting sick psychologically from building a city without space. But nobody seems to care about it," he says.

In the old days—of only a few decades ago—people used to say *malesh*, "never mind," all the time. The elevator breaks, and passengers waiting in the lobby would say *malesh*. People would be stuck in a traffic jam for an hour and write it off with *malesh*. Cairenes claim that word is heard far less often now. People seem to be on edge and less forgiving. They don't react with as much equanimity to adversity.

Meanwhile, society is beginning to polarize between haves and have-nots, between those with a stake in the government and the status quo, and those who feel that the current order ignores their aspirations. Through the 1970s the Egyptian state was seen as a provider. Society seemed reasonably equitable. People had jobs; basic needs were met. Now the masses are beginning to feel that the state has broken the social contract. Many Cairenes no longer identify with a common cause or a sense of participation. As a result, say some Cairenes, the country is splitting into two camps: the state, and the mass of people.

"In this climate it's not a surprise that even fanatics, if they care for the group—let's forget how illogical some of the teaching— have prospered," says Basheer.

The signs of their prospering are evident in the vast social network that has sprung up outside official channels and which is paid for and controlled by Islamists. In many Cairo neighborhoods Islamic schools, clinics, and hospitals rival or substitute for their government counterparts. The phenomenon was highlighted in the aftermath of an earthquake in 1992, the worst to hit the city in decades. Within hours the Islamists were on the streets providing food and blankets, alternative housing and tents, while the government was nowhere to be seen.

Performing this role—the "new religiosity," as Basheer terms it—is a positive force in Egyptian life, filling a gap in a society that has become atomized, and responding to the frustrations of large numbers of Cairenes who have been alienated by the growing disparity between rich and poor.

"They are answering a need for social order and values because the government and society and the bourgeoisie no longer care," says Basheer. "In this context their role is not negative, even though you get a bag of nonsense with that good service. What the Islamic extremists are doing is creating a new family. They are creating self-support, even psychological support."

If the "new Islam" is a protest against the status quo, it is also the most visible expression of the fact that a vast new underclass has emerged in Cairo that has neither a stake in the society nor a disposition to abide by its rules. "I don't like terrorism," says

Basheer. "But the terrorism and killings are signposts telling us of the danger."

The drawing power of Muslim fundamentalism is best understood by studying the faces of the jobless. They stand on nearly every Cairo street corner, watching the traffic and staring into space. The deep desire among them for change represents a force that many experts fear could end decades of rule by secular, socialist-style governments. The government's failure to respond to their needs has heightened the attraction of radical Islam and by extension produced an increasingly vengeful conflict between security forces and Muslim militants. Fueled by terrorist attacks by Muslim extremists who are seeking to overthrow the government and by the alleged brutality of government forces, the war has left nearly 400 dead since the beginning of 1993.[39] The state has unleashed force on a scale unprecedented since the assassination of President Anwar Sadat. Homes, mosques, and entire villages have been raided and thousands of arrests have been made. A new antiterrorist law prescribes the death penalty for receiving military training abroad or even planning a terrorist attack.

"The government can't meet the problem at its source," one Western journalist observes. "So it reacts the only way it can, by cracking down—producing more support for the fundamentalists."[40]

Yet despite the state's intense struggle for its own security, the signs of Islam's growing appeal—and thus its growing threat—are everywhere in Cairo. Far more Egyptian women are wearing the Islamic head covering, called the *higab*. There is more religious programming on television, while what one disgruntled street vendor calls the "good parts" of old movies are now usually excised. At noon at the bazaar at Khan al Khalili, a cassette tape of a hot Algerian pop star is switched off in favor of Friday prayers.

The link between unemployment, hopelessness, desperation, and fundamentalism seems clear.

"When you face problems that are beyond the scope of what you can deal with, you seek the refuge of religion," observes one Western diplomat in Cairo. "When you seek the refuge of religion you don't seek a moderate one. The fundamentalists are saying, work hard, be born again, you can go to heaven. They're offering something the state has long since ceased to offer: hope."[41]

"So where does someone like this go?" asks Egyptian journalist Mohammed Auda in concurrence. "He goes to the mosque. He joins people who believe this is a society that must be destroyed because it can't be changed. And population is one of the main causes."[42]

Fundamentalism is in fact alien to Egypt's traditional sense of religion, claims Auda. While religious tension has ebbed and flowed in the past, it has rarely been as extreme as the current trend seems to be.

Auda, for one, believes radical Islamists won't be able to threaten the current political system. Members of the moderate Muslim Brotherhood comprise up to a quarter of Egypt's parliament, but the radical Islamic underground, the Gam'a Islamiyya (Islamic Group), though a strong cultural influence, has eschewed traditional politics. "Whatever happens we will not have a religious government in Egypt. That would be completely contrary to the nature, the history, the heritage of Egypt." But he feels that the vicious cycle—rapid population growth which contributes to poverty which contributes to religious radicalism which provokes government crackdowns—is likely to continue so long as rapid population growth continues.

Some see the hand of foreign agents in Egypt's religious revival. According to this theory, Iranian mullahs are the culprits, fomenting unrest in Egypt to destabilize an old regional rival and to gain influence in the Arab world. In his gravelly voice, Tahseen Basheer disagrees. "To think that terrorism came out of the sky through a conspiracy fostered by Iran, aided and abetted by Sudan, is humbug," he says. "I'm sure there is some Iranian input but I wouldn't give it more than five percent."

Marginalized people are simply creating their own society, says the retired diplomat. Their views may not always fit Islam, but Islam fits their social predicament and gives them a reason for existence: They are poor because they are clean and virtuous. "And the rich are damned because they make all this money illegally," says Basheer. "Islam gives me a definition why I am poor and why all these thieves are rich."

Even as the architects of the new Islam have given meaning to the lives of poor Cairenes, they have fundamentally changed the character of Islam itself, Basheer says. By accentuating "negative virtues, worry, and sadness," he says, they have darkened the normally bright outlook of millions of Cairenes. Islam advocates enjoying life within the limits of virtue, says Basheer. "The new Islam is the Islam of a depressed people, and that is different from the Islam of happiness and laughter, and it has left young Egyptians with few hopes or dreams.

"Nasser embodied the dreams of my generation," he says of the Egyptian leader who galvanized Egyptian and Arab nationalism. "The fact that he failed is not the point: If our dream does not exceed our grasp, what is life for? So we forgave him a lot. He suppressed political freedoms for a dream. Now we have to suppress a lot without a dream. Now the only dream we have is figuring out how to live with the little we have."

Yet Basheer says he is not entirely pessimistic about the future. "I see the problems of today as the bell ringing to tell the keeper of the gate in Egypt that his policy is bunk."

Basheer finds hope in unexpected places, like Boulak El Kakrour. Boulak El Kakrour is one of the hard-pressed communities of once-rural dwellers on Cairo's periphery. It was years before the city got around to providing services there. But long before then, the residents of the sprawling new neighborhood had seized the initiative, improvising new sewage systems, rigging homemade pumps to get water to the upper floors of hastily erected apartments, creating social order. This survivalist instinct is one reason why Egypt has managed since 1981—the year Egypt's current president, Hosni Mubarak, took office—to absorb as many people because of population growth as now populate Israel, the West Bank, Gaza, Jordan, and the Palestinian diaspora combined.

"If Israel wants a million more Russian Jews, America has to put up $10 billion in loan guarantees. We did it ourselves, without having civil wars. We did it without killing each other," says Basheer. "Who in the world has managed in the past to absorb in a small country with a small [per capita] income not reaching $800 per year 15 million people? The achievement is tremendous because the society is vibrant."

While Egypt may not have received U.S. loan guarantees, its vibrancy has not been without outside help. Japan contributed Cairo's gleaming new opera house, France its subway system, and Britain and the United States the money to revamp the city's aging sewage system. The United States, Egypt's largest benefactor, has given over $2.5 billion a year in economic and military aid since the 1978 Camp David treaty was signed. Still, it is the adaptability of Cairenes themselves that has made much of the difference. Life in Cairo often manages to work even under the oppressive conditions of poverty and rapid population growth.

Just why and how are sometimes suggested by small things. On Cairo's streets, for example, red, green, and yellow lights are, at best, suggestions. If the cross street is empty, drivers go, even if the light is red. If it's crowded, policemen make them stop, even if the light is green. To the extent that traffic flows at all in this clogged city, says Bashir, it is "not because of Western rules but because of the rules of survival."

Cairo's adaptability has mostly to do with its resource-less but resourceful multitudes, including Hassan, who lives in a neighborhood that gives new meaning to the term "ghost town." Hassan is a former policeman and one of the estimated 500,000 Cairenes who have taken up residence in a group of adjacent cemeteries in the eastern reaches of Cairo known as the "City of the Dead."

Forty years ago only a small community of caretakers, watchmen, and stonemakers lived among the tombs and monuments that house the remains of the peasants and pashas whose sepulchers now crumble in disrepair. Forty years ago it began to attract squatters who could not find cheap housing elsewhere. Today, with nearly 5 percent of Cairo's population, the cemetery is one of the largest squatter communities in the world, complete with its own thriving commercial life, small industries, and even bus service.

Like most of the cemetery's residents, Hassan lives in a tiny mourning room adjacent to a tomb. He has seen the mourners, his landlords, only twice. They have never asked for rent, only for upkeep on the tomb, the final resting place of the corpse with whom he shares his home.

"Please come in," Hassan says to a stranger, whose unexpected arrival startles his wife and four small children. A fifth, a newborn, sleeps under a shawl to protect her from swarming flies attracted by the cool dampness of the room.

Hassan did not move to the "City of the Dead" by choice. But with his tiny pension, earned during twenty-three years of service as a Cairo policeman, he could not afford to rent an apartment. Like millions of other Cairenes, he has made the best of difficult circumstances. Inside the green plaster walls of his eight-by-eight–foot "apartment," he has managed to cram the necessities: two beds and a small table. A tiny anteroom houses a portable gas stove. The apartment is small by most standards. By the standards of Cairo, where 12,000 people are crammed into every square mile (upwards of 60,000 in some neighborhoods), Hassan's living quarters are not so bad.

He pays no rent or taxes to the government. But his pension provides his only income—about fifty-five dollars per month. And with no government-provided services, most of it is spent to survive. Hassan has to buy gas cylinders to light the stove and the two small lamps that light his apartment. He gets his water from a public tap a quarter of a mile away. The toilet, in a nearby tomb, is one of his biggest expenses: Every three months Hassan pays a private company six dollars to pump the cesspool. Even the TV, which incongruously broadcasts a speech by President Clinton, is run with batteries that Hassan has had to purchase himself because he has no electricity.

As a teenager Hassan decided to quit school to fight in the guerrilla war against British rule over Egypt. He later fought in the 1956 Arab–Israeli war. Others may be worse off in Cairo, but Hassan wishes for better.

"I've earned a palace, not this," he grumbles.

Hassan El-Geretly has a theory about Cairo's adaptability in the face of overcrowded conditions. "In Egypt there is a kind of space which is not physical," he says. "There is an allowance for other people that I have not seen anywhere else."[43]

El-Geretly is one of his country's most respected young theatrical directors. In 1987 he founded Al Warsha (The Workshop), the first theater group in Egypt not officially recognized or funded by the Ministry of Culture. Bearded, he dresses with a casual elegance that reflects a privileged upbringing. His father was a distinguished academic who served briefly as finance minister under Nasser.

"Often you're in the most crazy, overpopulated situations, with hundreds of thousands of people on the street or in a bus in Cairo. It's sardines. I know all the theories about rats and violence, but there's such a gregarious tendency in Egypt that you feel less crowded here. It's because people are letting other people into the space that we seem to need. The closer you come the better it is here. I think it's a fantastic phenomenon."

He tells the story of a waiter in a downtown hotel in which a population conference is being held. A conferee asks him how many children he has.

"Six," he answers.

"Why do you have so many children?" asks the conferee.

"By adding water to the sauce there's enough sauce to go around," he responds, with a logic that is purely Cairene.

"There's a different kind of reality about the population issue here," explains El-Geretly. "People have a whole concept of the tribe, of the other, of being together. It's not tolerance. It's not togetherness in the sense of being gregarious. It's *samaha*. It's not making allowances; it's allowing. It's making space for other people. It has a lot to do with not making a necessity of limiting family size. This is why people are happy. We're not talking about solving the population problem anymore, just living with it. But I believe there is hope. Somehow Egypt works in spite of itself."

He tells another story—it may be apocryphal, he acknowledges—about a German expert who went up into a skyscraper above the swirling bazaar of Khan al Khalili in central Cairo.

"He made drawings and schemes trying to solve the problem of traffic in Ataba Square," says El-Geretly. "Finally he looks down and says, Don't touch it. It shouldn't be working, but it is. Don't spoil it."

A German traffic expert in Egypt would not be unusual. Around the globe, the richer nations have made easing the overcrowding of third world cities a top aid priority. The industrialized world now contributes about $1 billion per year through bilateral aid programs to relieve urban congestion. The major source of relief is the World Bank, which since 1972 has spent between $30 and $40 billion financing urban programs in 10,000 third world cities. Compared to the total estimated value of urban housing and infrastructure in developing nations ($3 trillion), the amount seems small. But much of the Bank's money has been devoted to helping cities manage their own problems. "We provide in a catalytic way by supporting sound policy and strengthening the local capacity to solve problems," says Michael Cohen, who heads the Bank's urban development division.[44]

Supporting sound policy has meant, to choose one example, dissuading some cities from investing huge sums in subway projects in favor of improving the capacity of existing road systems for a fraction of the cost. The Bank has also helped urban governments assess and collect taxes more efficiently to raise the revenue needed to build houses and roads and to upgrade sanitation systems. The United Nations Development Programme, which has also made urbanization a high priority, teaches urban administrators how to manage land and plan and maintain city infrastructure.[45]

Still, urban problems intensify, as the example of Cairo makes plain. Even the traditional tolerance of Cairenes seems unlikely to retrieve their city from a difficult future. Like Egypt as a whole, its economy rests heavily on three shaky legs: tourism (until recently, $3 billion in annual foreign currency earnings), oil ($1 billion), and the Suez Canal ($1.8 billion). Taken alone, these three sources of income are insufficient to pay for Egypt's imports, much less to finance improvements in Cairo's economic infrastructure. To make matters worse, in the opinion of some Western diplomats, these sources could actually shrink. Tourism, which has dropped by at least half from its 1991 level, could drop further if terrorist incidents perpetrated by extremist Islamic groups continue. Canal revenues could decline if higher tolls divert more traffic around the African Horn. The price of oil could sink further.

As for Cairo itself, one solution to the city's woes is to prod the process of physical decentralization. Cairo's overcrowding has already caused authorities to develop what the UN calls "one of the most ambitious physical planning efforts in the developing world."[46] To make the desert bloom and attract Cairenes away from the city, the government has constructed free-standing new towns and satellite cities in the desert. This enterprise has so far fallen far short of its targets, but it remains a high priority. Experts point to

Aswan in the south and the Mediterranean and the Red Sea coasts of the Sinai—a potential home for 3 million Egyptians—as the most promising areas to create communities and jobs.

"We need to create opportunities to live in communities outside the [Nile] valley, on sand instead of on mud," says Cairo University's Sobri Abdel Hakim.[47]

Nor is Egypt alone in its determination to decentralize its population. Over the past three decades, dozens of countries in Africa, Latin America, and Asia have articulated a desire in national development plans to limit the growth of their largest metropolitan areas.[48] With mixed success, many have followed through. Since 1950, for instance, eleven countries have relocated their national capitals to less-populated areas, leading to the rise of entirely new cities such as Brasilia.[49] Many governments have strived to make existing towns and provincial capitals more attractive places in which to live and invest by providing tax incentives and infrastructure improvements. India has created nearly 500 industrial "estates" with good transportation and communications facilities to lure businesses away from big cities.[50] In the 1970s Korea used a similar approach to disperse industries from Seoul, then complemented the policy with new zoning laws and permit requirements that have made it harder for industries to locate in the capital.[51] Brazil has used financial incentives to entice millions of citizens to settle in the frontier of the Amazon basin.[52] Governments have even compelled decentralization. In 1970 Jakarta limited migration by decree. Any rural Indonesian who wished to move to the Indonesian capital had to obtain a six-month permit, which cost a substantial sum of money. The money was refunded only when proof was provided that the migrant had found a job.[53] China is the most extreme example of forced dispersion. Since the Great Leap Forward of the 1950s, millions of young and unemployed people have been sent to the countryside.[54]

If Egypt is to provide for its growing urban population it will also need to redouble its efforts to increase agricultural output. In theory, it is possible for the country to produce more food, since agricultural conditions (year-round sunshine, no frost, and water flows regularized by the Aswan Dam) are favorable and new crop options (rice and horticulture) are marginally promising. But even the most optimistic experts are not overly optimistic. The pessimists, on the other hand, are very pessimistic. "Egypt doesn't have a prayer of feeding itself," concludes one, a Western agronomist who has worked for years in the North African nation. Any potential for increased farm production has to be weighed in the balance against stubborn facts. The amount of farmland available to feed Egypt is shrinking. Much of it is waterlogged and increasingly salinated. Water is in short supply, dimming the promise of rice cultivation, which is highly water-intensive. Meanwhile, even though horticultural exports could generate hundreds of thousands of dollars, that amounts to little against the country's $2.5 billion food-import bill.

Of course, overall economic growth would be the most effective way to deal with Egypt's fast-rising numbers—assuming it could be distributed equitably, which it hasn't been in the past. The irony is that population growth itself eats away at development potential. It places the nation on a hamster's wheel: No matter how hard it runs, it never seems any closer to greater prosperity for its individual citizens. "If Egypt had been able to control population growth, then income, living standards, the quality of life would be a lot better today," says Heba Handoussa.[55]

Handoussa is a professor of economics at the American University in Cairo. A specialist on industrial policy and an adviser to the Egyptian government, she has a broad view of the country's economic and social problems. Population pressures worry her. She says they have eaten away at Egypt's potential for development during the past forty years. But other things worry her more. "Economic policies generally, the maldistribution of resources," have all contributed to Egypt's state of stagnation, she says. As she speaks she is sitting in her own spacious apartment, one floor up in an upscale building overlooking the Nile. Her huge dining-room/ library serves as her office. Although it is late at night books are strewn everywhere, and the space hums cheerfully with phone calls and visitors.

The employment picture in Egypt is not cheerful, she says. There are 450,000 entrants into the labor force each year but only 200,000 jobs created, in roughly equal amounts, by the public and private sectors. Efforts to bridge the 250,000-job gap have been hindered by a four-year recession. The employment picture is so bleak in Egypt that the government has fallen far behind in its commitment to find jobs in the public sector for every high school and college graduate. Recent graduates now go to the bottom of a seven-year waiting list. To make matters worse, each of the three main job-creating sectors now appears saturated. Agricultural employment, once the country's largest employer, is shrinking fast, partly as a result of mechanization. Meanwhile, a 1991 structural adjustment program imposed by international lenders has forced Egypt to slash public investment by half, which has also slowed private investment. Nor is the future promising in the third sector: jobs abroad that employ about 2 million Egyptians in countries like Saudi Arabia, Jordan, Iraq, and Libya.

Undaunted, Handoussa points to the good news that rates of rural migration to urban areas dropped sharply between censuses conducted in 1976 and 1986. One reason was an upward trend in nonagricultural rural employment between the two dates, from 15 to 34 percent. "That gives hope that if we could just keep up the momentum and encourage more and more of that kind of activity you'd get a multiplier effect," says Handoussa. That would encourage rural Egyptians to feel comfortable where they are, with cheaper land, a job, and a future. Fewer of them would take the risk of heading for Cairo, where they could easily end up beggars or vendors on the street.

Handoussa points to other steps Egypt can take to create the jobs needed to keep up with population growth. The first is an export-oriented strategy for industry. This macro-economic approach has worked famously for the so-called "Tigers" of East Asia. South Korea, Taiwan, and Hong Kong have all acquired a measure of prosperity by developing export industries, erecting high tariff walls, and focusing on labor-intensive employment. To a lesser extent, Latin America has had success with the same policy. Yet Egypt has barely scratched the surface of its own potential with such goods as textiles, furniture, and leather. High Egyptian export tariffs have led many Egyptian manufacturers to be content with selling at home. But the home market has a limited absorptive capacity. "Once trade restraints are removed," says Handoussa, "that will prompt the fast growth of manufactured exports."

Another measure that could boost employment is the encouragement of small-scale business enterprises. Since the Nasser era large industries have enjoyed favored treatment, including access to cheap credit. "Small businesses are starved for credit. Ninety percent of their finances come from their own savings, their own networks, their own families," says Handoussa. Yet small-scale enterprise accounts for 90 percent of the employment in the Egyptian private sector, excluding agriculture. Right now each small business employs 2.1 people, on average. Upping that statistic by just one would create hundreds of thousands of new jobs. "If you had anything like 5–6 percent growth in the informal sector and small-scale enterprises you would solve the employment problem," she says.

In the 1950s and '60s Egypt could have set policies to encourage slower population growth. It didn't. In the intervening decades income growth did not make population increases irrelevant, as government officials had hoped. It was not until the Mubarak period that officials concluded that they would have to spend large sums on population awareness and family planning. Egypt then established a Supreme Council for Population and Family Planning but did not concentrate on providing contraceptives and training service providers until the 1980s.

"The people who are going to enter the labor force for the next twenty years have already been born. We know who they are, where they are, and how many there are. So there's no point crying over spilled milk." But there is also no point in being overly pessimistic, Handoussa says. It is true that the country is unlikely to add the estimated 9 million new jobs needed to keep unemployment at a natural level through the 1990s. "But I still think we can do a lot more than we're doing. The potential is there for creating more than twice as many jobs as we're creating."

"I'm convinced that the key to the future is rebuilding the private sector that existed before the Nasser years," adds Ali Shulkani, a prominent lawyer whose life in Cairo has spanned seven decades. He says it is not too late for the remnants of an aging capitalist class to re-create a private economy that could be the country's salvation. "Either the private sector wins or the fundamentalists win," he says. "The fundamentalists are going back to what happened in Iran. That would be a catastrophe for Egypt."[56]

With a stronger private sector, a more vital ethic of self-help might also emerge. Around the world locally motivated, small-scale projects have led to some of the most impressive improvements in living conditions. For the past twenty years, for example, a local nongovernment organization in San Salvador has offered loans for construction materials and technical training to help people build their own homes.[57] In Jakarta, the government gives squatters title to their plots in return for help in building footpaths and improving drainage.[58] In Dhaka, volunteer groups distribute packets of oral rehydration solution in neighborhoods where diarrhea is prevalent, reducing the incidence of hospitalization.[59] In Delhi, an International Labor Organization–backed pilot program gives instruction on how to rehabilitate discarded shoes. The program has created scores of jobs and put 10,000 shoes a month back on people's feet.[60] Even food production can be boosted by grassroots urban projects, which in various cities have taught urban dwellers how to utilize waste water and solid waste as agricultural inputs. In Kenya and Tanzania, two out of every three urban families now grow at least part of their own food. Ninety percent of the vegetables consumed in some big cities in China are grown within urban limits.[61]

As for Cairo, it will take such innovation and much more to enable Africa's most populous city to keep its head above water. Greater Cairo now has an estimated 13 million inhabitants. It is growing by at least 300,000 per year—as fast as Tokyo, which is over twice its size. How will Cairo cope with this onrush of humanity? Contemplating the future of Cairo, a name as resonant as Athens and Rome, Damascus and Nineveh, there is a nearly irresistible temptation to be apocalyptic. But Cairo will survive, if on a different, far grimmer, basis. Successive generations will probably have living standards lower than those enjoyed by their parents. The city's social fabric will be tested, social traditions will be altered. But, as a different kind of city than ever before, it will survive.

For now the city's mood is captured in a popular song, *Zahama Ya Dunya* ("Crowded, O World"):[62]

> I go this way, crowds
> This-a-way, that-a-way, crowds
> I go this way, crowds
> Crowds, O world, crowds.

TWO

"A Place at the Banquet":
Feeding the World

Kenya

During the long dry season, the steep hills of the Machakos district of eastern Kenya exhibit a kind of sullen beauty. The dominant motif is the vibrant red of the iron-rich soil derived from rocks formed by metamorphic action half a billion years ago. Superimposed is a blanket of faded green provided by the eucalyptus, acacia, and mango trees that cascade down hillsides gashed by erosion.

In a blink of geologic time, the region has undergone an extraordinary transition. Less than a century ago, elephants, giraffes, and wildebeest roamed this sparsely settled area, drawn by abundant water and vegetation. By the 1940s, two decades before Kenya gained its independence from Britain, much of it had been laid waste by overgrazing, drought, erosion, and locust invasions, "swept bare in many places to the solid rock," according to one visitor who reported seeing "acre after acre of dead and wilted maize."[1]

Today, the region has a new aspect. Instead of fields of dead and wilted maize, a common sight just a few decades ago, the thousands of small plots of farmed land in Machakos sport healthy stands of sorghum and cassava, beans and millet, banana and pawpaw trees. As for maize, production has doubled and tripled, even

61

as the population of Machakos's drier zones has been swelled by migrants from the moister but overcrowded highlands.

Like much of the remaining potentially cultivable land in Kenya, the Machakos district is classified as mainly semi-arid. Until recently, few Kenyan planners envisioned a role for the region in meeting the country's future food needs. But that was before Rose Maweu and Danson Ingala began transforming the face of Machakos. Along with thousands of other small farmers in the region, they have suddenly become central to the issue of whether Kenya can provide for a population that is growing by nearly one million each year.

Since they were married a decade ago, Maweu and Ingala have farmed a small hillside plot, about one hectare or 2.5 acres in size. Until recently, the fruits of their intensive labors to make it bloom have been meager: no more than about five bags (200 pounds) each of maize, beans, and millet per year. This year Ingala expects to double that output. Eager to explain why, he leads a visitor down the hill to view a long five-foot deep trench he has just dug with the help of a neighborhood work crew. The idea behind it is simplicity itself and at least as old as the Assyrians, who invented the idea of "harvesting" scarce water resources nearly 5,000 years ago.

In the past, the hard semi-annual rains of November–December and April–May swept precious topsoil down the hillside, leaving it more barren than ever. But adopting an idea introduced into Kenya when it was still under British rule, Ingala began terracing the land to conserve water. Dirt piled to create ridges that follow the contours of the land now demarcates a series of fifteen-foot wide strips of cropland and keeps the water from running down the hillside. The trenches, meanwhile, provide a holding area for excess water during seasons of heavy rain and an ideal environment for planting banana trees, which Ingala intends to do next season.

In a region where labor is abundant and cheap and monetary resources scarce, terracing has provided a logical solution to an old problem: slowing runoff and increasing water infiltration.

"If you don't do it, you lose both the soil and the water," says Ingala. "The problem is that you need both."

But water conservation has solved only half of Ingala's problem. Back up the hill, Maweu, flashing one of Kenya's most contagious smiles, demonstrates a solution to the other half: supplying the nitrogen- and phosphorous-poor soil with needed nutrients.

Using a technique familiar to millions of farmers around the world, Maweu has placed straw, greens, and dung from the family's small congregation of cows, goats, and chickens into a two-foot deep hole. The compost, which takes two months to form, has become a substitute for chemical fertilizers, which were once used in the region but which are now priced beyond the budgets of smallhold farmers like Maweu and Ingala.

As Ingala notes, the loss of fertilizer proved to be a blessing in disguise: "We know now that fertilizer doesn't give anything to the soil except during one crop season. Compost enriches the soil longer, with no cost to us and no damage to the soil."

One other technique—this one new—has helped replenish the coarse, weathered soil that keeps famine at bay for the residents of Machakos. Three years ago Ingala began planting munka, banya, calliandra, and Australian silver oak trees right down the middle of his crop fields. The practice was once considered verboten, as fields were routinely cleared of trees and shrubs before planting. But farmers like Ingala have discovered that the leaves dropped by "alley-cropped" trees are a rich source of the nitrogen and phosphorus that will strengthen the leaves and roots of his food crops. With a regular diet of nutrients, Ingala's land no longer needs fallow periods to rejuvenate. For Ingala and Maweu, the ultimate payoff is the higher yields—up to 40 percent higher in some regions of Kenya—that now provide at least partial insurance against the ever-present threats of scarcity and famine.

Rose Maweu and Danson Ingala have written one of the thousands of small success stories that are to be found all across Africa. Their experience provides one hopeful answer to a question likely to preoccupy experts and government leaders for a half-century to come: Can food production keep pace with rapid global population growth?

Relying on a combination of hard work and ingenuity, they have found ways to coax substantially more food from dry land on a sustainable, environmentally sound basis. In a country where 80 percent of the land is arid or semi-arid and where deteriorating soil quality threatens productivity, such small successes have large implications. The question is, if the Akamba people of Machakos can sustain a population that has quadrupled since the 1950s, might not millions more like them across Africa help make it possible to feed a continent that half a century from now, according to the UN's "medium" projection, could have nearly a billion and a half more inhabitants?

"What you're seeing in Machakos is that there are innumerable small initiatives by people operating on their own without massive outside aid or support," says Donald Thomas, a long-time professor of agricultural engineering at the University of Nairobi. "It gives you a sense of what African farmers are capable of."[2] The Kenyan government sponsors agricultural research, credit, extension, and marketing programs, but most are inadequate and underfunded.

But there is another way of looking at Africa's food future that is far less hopeful. Beyond the individual success stories, beyond the isolated examples of governments that have framed policies that actually promote rather than retard agricultural self-sufficiency, is a continent that labors under extraordinary handicaps.

Africa's troubles are epitomized in at least two dozen of its fifty-four countries. One is Burkina Faso, which illustrates an ominous cycle that will have to be broken if Africa is to be spared widespread famine. Pressed by rapid population growth, Burkinabe farmers have been forced to reduce or abandon the practice of periodically taking land out of production, and thus they have impoverished good soil. Driven to cultivate new lands, they have expanded into semi-arid areas and into forests and woodlands, exposing fragile soils to rain and wind. Squeezed by the expansion of agriculture, meanwhile, livestock herds have been forced onto fragile rangelands, hastening desertification in the north.

Now capable of producing only 40 percent of its food needs, this Sahelian nation will have to provide for double its 10 million inhabitants in twenty years. But with exhausted soils, diminishing amounts of available cropland, paltry infusions of foreign aid, and almost no prospect of developing an industrial base to generate cash for fertilizers or food imports, the future looks bleak. Lacking food or work, one million people—a tenth of the country's population—have already migrated to urban areas or across the border to the Ivory Coast.[3]

"Africa's environmental crisis will deepen and perpetuate her food, poverty, and financial crises," writes British environmentalist Paul Harrison. "It threatens not just the hope of progress, but even the hope of survival."[4]

It is Africa's lot to be a repository of both high hopes and extreme despair. Both will bear on the food future of the continent with the world's highest population growth rates.

In his seminal *Essay on the Principle of Population*, published almost two centuries ago, Thomas Malthus warned that there was no way food supplies, which grow arithmetically, could keep pace with population growth, which grows exponentially.

"The power of population," Malthus wrote, "is indefinitely greater than the power in the earth to produce subsistence for man."[5]

Malthus has so far been proved wrong. Writing at the turn of the nineteenth century, he could scarcely have anticipated changes that have made it possible for food production to not only keep pace but actually to outpace the spiraling growth in human numbers. The amount of land under cultivation has more than doubled since Malthus's day, for example, while advanced farming techniques and technologies have quadrupled total output. As farmers in even some of the poorest regions of the world are demonstrating, food production can do more than increase arithmetically. But in the long run the outcome of the race between food production and population growth remains too hard to call. Despite impressive gains in output, few experts are prepared to say with confidence what the speed or limits of growth in agricultural productivity may be.

One variable will be the pace of technological change, which has already transformed the face of agriculture. Another will be the speed of the transition from high to low fertility in the developing world, which will determine whether, by the end of the next century, the world's farmers will have to feed 8 or 10 or 15 billion people. Other possible and more remote variables include global climate change, which, in the worst case, could force vast acreage out of production; and oil price hikes, which could disrupt the petroleum-based agriculture of the industrialized world that generates most of the world's existing surplus. The simple truth, as Canadian agriculture writer Peter Hendry suggests, is that until such questions are answered, no one can say for sure whether we will be obliged eventually "to acknowledge Malthus's foresight or permitted to celebrate his misjudgment."[6] Optimists point out that there is an abundance of good news.[7] Globally speaking, there is enough food to go around. The world is growing more food than it now eats, thanks to recent record-yield increases in food grains like wheat, rice, corn, and barley, and staple crops like beans and lentils. One consequence is that the proportion of the world's population suffering from malnutrition has actually declined in recent years, and average caloric intake has increased. Thanks to improved farming techniques and technologies, the same amount of land that supported 3 billion people in 1960 now feeds nearly twice that number, with resulting declines in real food prices in the world market. Possible breakthroughs in agricultural technology like crop strains that can resist pests and diseases, meanwhile, offer the prospect of vast new increases in agricultural output. Combined with the possible resurgence in farm output expected in Eastern Europe and the former Soviet Union, global excess capacity could remain high for years or decades to come.

"The world can take significant pride in the fact that we have been raising food production—without raising its real cost—faster than the population has been growing, and that we have done so at the height of the largest population expansion phase in world history," notes Dennis Avery, an agricultural economist who heads the Center for Global Food Issues at the Indianapolis-based Hudson Institute, a conservative think tank.[8]

But there are grounds for pessimism as well. Even though developing countries produce between three and four times as much food today as they did in 1950, food production has failed to keep pace with population growth in two-thirds of developing countries, including more than 80 percent of African countries. On a per capita basis, the global production of cereal grains peaked in 1984 and has declined since, while in Africa such declines began in 1967, exacerbating a growing problem of malnutrition.[9] Many poor countries, meanwhile, are unable to afford the food imports needed to bridge the gap between supply and demand, a circumstance made worse by the long, slow decline of international food aid as a proportion of foreign aid.

"The current food crisis in Africa portends a disastrous food shortage that could hit other parts of the developing world by the end of the decade if governments do not act to prevent it," notes Per Pinstrup-Andersen, director-general of the International Food Policy Research Institute in Washington.[10] Despite impressive global gains in farm output, the food future of individual developing nations is mortaged by demography, a diminishing resource base, and distracted, unresponsive national leadership. Technologies that rescued large regions of the developing world from famine starting in the 1970s have reached a point of diminishing returns, while replacement technologies remain for the most part on the drawing boards. Meanwhile, despite lower rates of birth, relentless increases in actual numbers now cause Africa's population to double every twenty-four years. Africa's population will grow by more than 3 percent between now and the end of the century, while food production during the same period is projected to grow only 2 percent. The result: The food gap in Africa, which was self-sufficient in food in 1950, could be twenty times wider in the year 2000 than it was a mere decade before, according to the World Bank.[11] Looking further into the future, Africa may have to support four times its present population in sixty years and eight times its present population in ninety years. It is a fact that prompts all but the most optimistic experts to worry that the limits of the continent's carrying capacity will eventually be reached and exceeded.

Says the IFPRI's Stephen Vosti: "Africa is a Malthusian train crash waiting to happen."[12]

In the face of sharply divergent assessments, there is at least one thing most optimists and pessimists can agree on: More can be done than is now being done to enhance global food production—enough even, in theory at least, to keep up with birthrates that could triple the population of Africa alone by the middle of the twenty-first century. They continue to disagree over whether, given the high political and institutional barriers to change, and the high cost of training, agricultural infrastructure, and "inputs" like seed, fertilizer, and pesticides, that the possible can be translated into the actual in time to rescue poor nations from hunger.

So far history has favored the optimists, who point to two dramatic instances in which sheer ingenuity has redeemed humankind from the Malthusian curse. The first was the beginning of the end of the periodic European famines that contributed to Malthus's pessimism, when seventeenth-century farmers in the Belgian lands of Flanders and Brabant demonstrated that manuring and crop rotation eliminated the need to let land lie fallow. This seminal idea eventually spread to other European farmers, who also learned the advantages of periodically rotating cereal crops (like wheat and corn) with root crops (like turnips and cassava) and forage crops (like clover) to restore nitrogen to the soil.[13]

The other ingredient of the first modern agricultural revolution was the industrial revolution. Iron became cheaper, so strong but inexpensive tools like the iron plow became available to common farmers for the first time. New inventions like the steam plow, threshing machine, and reaper led to significant farm workforce reductions. Thus, even as food production and nutrition levels soared in Europe, farm labor decreased, dropping in France, for example, by nearly 20 percent during the second quarter of the nineteenth century alone.[14]

If the first modern agricultural revolution redeemed Europe from famine, the second—the so-called "green revolution" of the 1960s and '70s—rescued vast stretches of the developing world from the same fate. The green revolution harnessed the two scientific breakthroughs that have underpinned modern agriculture, producing the most dramatic increases in food production in human history. One was the advent of chemical inputs, including improved pesticides, now in use in half the world's agricultural production, and fertilizers, the use of which has increased ninefold in the three decades since 1954. The other was advanced cross-breeding techniques that have produced crops—especially corn, rice, and wheat—with earlier and higher yields and far greater resistance to disease and pests.[15]

The results are seen in an array of dazzling statistics that, for the moment at least, have dispelled Malthusian gloom throughout much of the developing world. In Asia, high-yielding seeds of rice, the daily staple for 1.5 billion people, doubled harvests between 1950 and 1980, with only a 17 percent increase in land use.[16]

World grain output, meanwhile, expanded nearly 3 percent per year between 1950 and 1984, nearly twice as fast as the average population growth rate. In Mexico, wheat production quadrupled

during the same period, while globally it grew 2.6 times. By less
dramatic leaps, production of root crops, vegetables, meat, and
milk have also increased. The result: Famines, once endemic in
parts of Asia and Africa, have largely ceased to occur except in
cases of war and civil strife.[17]

The hopeful expectation was that the green revolution would
provide a respite from food shortages, giving poor countries a
chance to lay the groundwork for a better future by reducing poverty and cutting birthrates. But despite impressive gains in food
output globally, per capita food production remains low in many
developing nations. And despite significant fertility reductions in
Latin America and East Asia, most of Africa and parts of South
Asia are still at the beginning of the transition to low fertility.
Meanwhile, recent years have seen a worrisome development: The
green revolution is faltering at the very moment that annual increments in global population growth have reached an all-time high.

"Twenty years after the green revolution we're in a situation
where the new technologies have run their course and we still
don't have the brakes on population growth," says Lester Brown,
founder and president of the Worldwatch Institute in Washington.[18]

Corn yields have not increased since 1985 in the United States;
wheat yields have not increased since 1984 in the United Kingdom; rice yields have not increased in Japan since 1984. If Japan
cannot increase rice yields, says Brown, the prospect that less developed nations can do so appears remote.[19]

Despite scientific advances in food production that saved millions from starvation in the 1960s and '70s, echoes the IFPRI, the
combination of population growth and slowing food production
once again threatens global food security.[20] The problem is epitomized by India. In the mid-1960s, the Asian giant was in such dire
straits that it had to import one-fifth of the entire U.S. wheat crop.
But within a decade, green revolution technologies doubled wheat

production, saving millions from famine, creating exportable surpluses, and making India agriculturally self-sufficient.

But the gains of India's green revolution have been offset by environmental damage to cropland and by population increases of 19
million per year, leaving it with no real margin of safety. Per capita
food consumption was sustained but not increased. Despite significantly increased aggregate food production, output on a per capita
basis is actually well below what it was in the early decades of the
century.[21] In 1992 India was forced to resume wheat imports,
marking the end of a brief era of self-sufficiency.

"At the time we knew what needed to be done in countries like
India," says Brown. "We had to change pricing policy and get fertilizer there and new rice and wheat seeds that we knew would
work because they were tested. All the ingredients were there. But
now that India and other developing countries have made these
changes, we don't know what to do for an encore."[22]

The problem is illustrated again in neighboring Bangladesh,
which is a test case for the possibilities but also the limits of what
can be achieved in the face of rapid population growth. In the
early 1960s Bengali agriculture consisted mainly of subsistence
farming. Low agricultural output, exacerbated by the country's
war for independence in 1971, produced one of the worst famines
in the region in 1974. But within a decade huge amounts of foreign aid, the introduction of high-yield strains of rice, improved
farming techniques, imported fertilizer, and irrigation projects
transformed Bangladesh into one of the success stories of the
green revolution. Rice production doubled on the same amount of
cultivated land, turning the "basket case" of Asia into a net ex-
porter.

Yet even as Bangladesh celebrates its success, some experts
caution that the country is nearing the limits of its agricultural
miracle, threatening a resumption of food shortages if population
growth is not significantly slowed and if farming techniques are

not developed that are based on locally available, not imported, re-sources.[23]

Paradoxically, one reason for Bangladesh's cloudy food future may be the side-effects of the green revolution itself. The switch to intensive agriculture prompted many Bangladeshi farmers to plant three rice crops per year instead of two, forcing them to rely on chemical fertilizers rather than the natural annual inundations of the flood season to replenish the soil. Dikes erected to channel floodwaters to the sea have diverted rich nutrients, leaving the country hostage to the higher import bills and long-term environmental consequences that stem from dependence on manmade fertilizers. Long-term sustainability is also jeopardized by shrinking farm holdings and diminishing water supplies, as Helmut Hess, a Stuttgart-based agricultural consultant who has done extensive fieldwork in Africa and Asia, explains.

To sustain the high yields, says Hess, Bangladesh will need increasing amounts of water. The problem is that despite its reputation for monsoons and floods, Bangladesh is becoming increasingly dry. The aquifers that feed the groundwater irrigation are being depleted, in some localized areas at a rapid rate, intensifying yearly drought periods. Therefore the big increase in production that has doubled rice output over the past ten years is on the verge of falling back, not surging ahead with population growth.[24]

Bangladesh can maintain and even increase food production. But here, as in many developing nations, a more secure food future may depend less on the technologies of the green revolution and more on expanded conservation and water harvesting measures, crop diversification, and improved irrigation management.

Agronomists say increases from the package of green revolution technologies that transformed agriculture in Asia and Latin America may be likely for another decade or more. Since the benefits of the green revolution have often failed to trickle down to farmers with plots of less than fifty acres, the major residual market exists among small farmers who were bypassed. Other gains are likely to come from making use of technologies that have already been developed.

"Agricultural growth over the next twenty years will have to come from small- and medium-sized resource-poor farmers that have not completely adapted or efficiently used existing technology," says the IFPRI's Stephen Vosti. "More uniform application of all the green revolution technologies will get better yields with what's already on the shelf."[25]

How much extra food can be provided once recently developed technology becomes widely available is a matter of some disagreement.

Optimists, led by Dennis Avery at the Hudson Institute's Center for Global Food Issues, say that new cropping systems, pest control methods, land management systems, and hybrids created without genetic tinkering can produce an abundance of additional food.[26]

Redesigned rice strains, for example, the forebears of second-generation "miracle rice" varieties now being tested at the International Rice Research Institute (IRRI) in the Philippines, can channel more of the plant's energy into grain heads, creating the potential for significantly increased yields over the next two decades. The IRRI has also found that it can use temperature sensitivity to achieve sterility in male rice strains, thus enabling the mass production of new hybrids. Another example can be found along the Persian Gulf coast, where Saudi agronomists are experimenting with salicornia, a ubiquitous saltwater reed that could provide a protein-rich diet for livestock. If their hopes are realized vast acreage along desert sea coasts around the world could be harvested with saltwater, freeing up better land for food crops.[27]

These are not isolated examples but elements of a trend that Avery contends can be replicated in every crop and every region. If he is correct, and if they can be matched by genetic breakthroughs that would produce higher resistance to salt in basic food crops—or, better yet, by affordable technologies to desalinate sea water—they could have a significant effect on global food production.

"If we could pull either of those off, then we would have a lot more time to get the brakes on population growth," says Lester Brown. "If you could reduce water desalinization costs dramatically, to the point of affordability, then you could farm large areas of the desert that are adjacent to the ocean."[28]

Even though a substantial amount of agricultural research is devoted to maintaining the gains of the green revolution, many other experts believe the era of dramatic yield increases based on the package of green revolution technologies is about over. One reason is that in many irrigated areas, especially in Southeast Asia, plants have reached the limits of their capacity to absorb the nutrients in fertilizer. That means a point of diminishing returns has been reached, at which increases in fertilizer no longer convert into the high yields achieved during the peak years of the green revolution.

The main reason the green revolution has reached the end of its spectacular run is that the basic genetic trick of turning plant matter into grains has been played and may not be repeated.

"There are simply biological limits to the yields crops can have," says Robert Chandler, whose strains of dwarf rice developed at the IRRI spread the green revolution to Asia. "You can't go much farther. We've had our big jump."[29]

Proceeding from here involves difficult choices. If the intensive agriculture of the green revolution cannot be sustained, more farming will have to spill over onto valuable forest lands. If it is sustained, the environmental damage inflicted by chemical fertilizers and pesticides could outweigh the additional gains in output that could be realized.

"If we do things right, we can keep the green revolution going one more decade, but that will be it," concludes Stephen Vosti. "Then totally new technologies will be needed to sustain per capita food availability."[30]

In the midst of the uncertainty that attends the future, three things are clear.

One is that providing for the food needs of 100 million new people every year will require country-specific strategies. Rosy statistics on aggregate food production offer small comfort to nations that cannot afford a seat at the banquet. The inability to be self-sufficient is not a problem in Singapore, which can pay for all the food it needs, nor in Saudi Arabia, which can afford to pay five times the world price for wheat for the luxury of growing its own with nonrenewable groundwater. "You don't have to be producing as long as you have purchasing power," says the IFPRI's Eileen Kennedy.[31] But it can spell disaster for poor nations like tiny land-locked Rwanda, where the cost of fertilizer is six times higher than in Rotterdam. Global surpluses can likewise be meaningless to the dozens of poor nations that have overwhelming demands placed on slim foreign exchange reserves. Such reserves are needed not only to pay for food imports but for critically needed infrastructure, imported energy, and development projects. Even local surpluses, like a recent bumper crop produced in Malawi, may be insufficient if the poor have no access to them. "Despite the currency of phrases like 'world hunger' and 'global famine,' those conditions don't exist and probably never will," notes Scott Pendleton, writing in the *Christian Science Monitor*. "Starvation is local."[32]

The fact that few poor nations have the money to pay for food imports means that they will have to rely on their own agricultural capabilities to meet their food demands for years to come. But with foreign assistance to developing world agriculture in decline, that will be harder. Aid for agricultural development has dropped from $14 to $12 billion in recent years, while resources from commercial banks have been cut in half, from $2 to $1 billion.[33]

"What this means is less irrigation, less access to technology, limited funds for trade financing, and, even worse, undermining long-term public activities like research, training, and education," says the IFPRI's Joachim Von Braun. "In the end that could mean reduced global agricultural output, increased prices, and the failure to create the food supplies critically needed in hard-pressed regions like Africa."[34]

Local self-sufficiency is further hindered by widespread environmental damage. In Nepal, for example, widespread deforestation has forced farmers to burn agricultural residues that would have been used as fertilizer for fuel and to invest more time away from the farm gathering fuelwood. Deforestation is thus one reason for a gradual, decade-long decline in agricultural output in Nepal.[35]

The second certainty—affirmed in conversations with dozens of officials and private experts around the developing world—is that efforts to expand food production by themselves will be insufficient to ensure long-term food security.

"You have to emphasize family planning measures as well as production in agriculture," notes a senior economist in Kenya's planning ministry. "They go hand in hand because the momentum of population growth is so great. The major resources being diverted to changing attitudes toward family planning reflect the recognition that there's no other way to avoid a bleak food future."[36]

Keeping food production up with existing rates of population growth will put a nearly intolerable burden on African agriculture and on African treasuries, since 60 percent of the continent's food will have to be imported by 2025 if birthrates remain high and agricultural inputs remain low. Conversely, as Paul Harrison calculates, a reduction of only 20 percent in African birthrates would cut in half the effort required to produce or import food.[37]

To get to food self-sufficiency by 2020, food production must be doubled, outside investment and aid increased, and fertility sharply reduced, according to the World Bank.[38] Failure to significantly reduce current high birthrates within two decades will render useless all other efforts to feed Africa, relieve its poverty, and save its land and forests, adds the IFPRI.[39]

Population works in more indirect ways to retard food self-sufficiency and adequate nutrition. At least 25 percent of malnutrition in the developing world is the result of illness, mostly diarrhea. One of the conditions for food security, therefore, is clean drinking water, to which 1.2 billion people had no access in 1990.[40] Population growth can also preclude the kinds of investment in infrastructure needed to get crops to market in a timely fashion, leading to high spoilage rates.[41]

The third certainty is that huge obstacles block the path to agricultural self-sufficiency in many third world nations where that goal is appropriate and at least theoretically attainable. These obstacles range from the shrinkage of agricultural land due to urbanization and other competing uses, to endemic water shortages, to the reduction of forest land and other habitats that provide the raw material for producing improved strains of food crops. Even if these obstacles can be surmounted, they are likely to slow the process of achieving food self-sufficiency.

One of the most serious problems is also one of the oldest. Twenty-three hundred years ago it was described by Plato, who surveyed a stretch of Greek countryside and lamented that "what now remains compared with what existed is like the skeleton of a sick man, all the fat and soft earth having wasted away."[42]

Soil degradation caused by overgrazing, destructive farming practices, and excessive cutting of fuelwood have left 22 million acres nearly dead biologically, according to the World Resources Institute. Another 740 million acres—an area five times the size of France—requires restoration that is beyond the capacity of most developing nations.[43]

Since 1945, 11 percent of the earth's vegetated surface—an area the size of China and India *combined*—has become degraded through human intervention to the point that biological productivity is impaired. Two-thirds of seriously eroded land is in Asia and Africa, where most of the world's poor live and where food needs are most acute. Erosion has been a major contributor to declining per capita food production in eighty nations, according to the WRI.

When he received a Nobel prize in 1970 for his research leading to the green revolution, Norman Borlaug warned that the new technology would buy only a limited amount of breathing room—thirty years at most—for governments to implement effective policies to slow population growth.[44] But population growth has not declined fast enough, nor have investments in human resources—the medical care, education, and nutrition needed to keep farmers healthy and productive—risen fast enough during the 1970s and '80s, to provide a cushion against food shortages in dozens of third world nations.

"Those two things have come too slowly. That's why we're still in a mess," says Joachim Von Braun, who notes that within a decade countries like Kenya and Rwanda could have two and a half times as many mouths to feed as in 1980.[45]

One possible answer to the problem of continuing localized food shortages is to do what farmers have historically done to increase output: expand the total acreage under cultivation. Right now about 11 percent of the earth's land surface is under cultivation. That translates into about 2,800 square meters of arable land for each person on earth. Without expanding the amount of land under the plow, population growth will reduce the per capita average to 1,700 square meters by 2025, placing far more pressure on farmers to increase yields on existing lands.

Just how much new land is available for cultivation is difficult to calculate. At one extreme are the estimates of the Hudson Institute's Dennis Avery. Avery calculates that the development of acid-tolerant seeds now makes it possible to convert up to one billion acres of acidic savannah land into high-yield acreage that could also support large cattle herds. Avery points to another half billion acres of inland wetlands in Africa that could be fitted with dams and dikes to produce high-yielding wet rice.

"If we brought back the 60 million acres of diverted cropland in the U.S. and cultivated the Pampas at their full potential, 1.5 billion more people could be fed," says Avery.[46]

At the other extreme are the estimates of the Worldwatch Institute, which says that most of the potentially cultivable land is now being farmed and warns of the environmental consequences of exploiting the kind of marginal lands—including Africa's wetlands—that remain.[47]

The most widely cited estimates have been issued by the Food and Agriculture Organization, which in 1988 calculated the world's potential arable land to be just over 2 billion hectares, a 40 percent increase over today's usage. With significant drainage and irrigation, farmland could double worldwide, according to the UN agency.[48]

If the FAO's calculations are correct, the expansion of cropland alone—in theory, at least—could keep food production rising as fast as the UN's medium population projections through the mid-twenty-first century. In fact, the estimates may be somewhat misleading, partly because of the added costs that would be required to bring marginal land under cultivation. As a result, only a small part of the surplus cultivable land in developing countries is likely to be tapped by the end of the decade, the UN agency estimates.

Most of the surplus land lies in regions of irregular rainfall. Costly irrigation projects would therefore be required to bring two-thirds of the FAO's estimated surplus area under cultivation, at a time when the number of irrigated acres per capita is declining precisely because of the high costs involved and because of the growth in human numbers. Countries that need the surplus land the most, moreover, would be least able to afford the costly inputs like fertilizers and pesticides that would also be needed to make the more marginal surplus land productive. The new land would thus cost more to cultivate and earn less when harvested.

Predicting how much more land can be brought under cultivation is complicated by two other factors. One is the speed with which land is losing agricultural value due to erosion. The FAO calculates that a fertile area the size of the island of Ireland is being lost to erosion each year, the length of time it takes to add 100 million to the world population.[49]

The other factor is the value of alternative uses. In theory, Kenya, for example, could turn game parks into cropland. But the income produced by tourism, the country's largest source of revenue, far outweighs the potential benefits of increased food production. Other governments have to calculate the consequences of felling valuable tropical and hardwood forests to create farmland that, while helping alleviate poverty in the short term, may be only marginally productive over the long term.

Even if most of the potentially cultivable land were not too wet or too dry, too saline or too acidic to be brought under cultivation cheaply, the problem of maldistribution remains. Vast surpluses exist in countries like Brazil and in Argentina, where up to 80 million acres of the Pampas await cultivation. But countries in which population pressures are greatest are not so favored. In 1988, 95 percent of potentially cultivable acres in Asia, including nations with high birthrates like India, Pakistan, and Bangladesh, were already under cultivation, according to the FAO. In the Near East and North Africa, virtually all suitable and partly suitable land is under cultivation.[50]

The situation is better in sub-Saharan Africa, where only eighteen of thirty-seven countries will be using more than half their farmable land by the end of the century. But even here usable land is irregularly distributed. Zaire and Zambia, for example, have large reserves. Rwanda, for one, has none, which means that however much new land is brought under the plow worldwide, only higher food import bills await at home. The crucial consideration, therefore, is whether the distribution of land resources coincides with the distribution of people. In most countries it does not, which is one reason why new land alone may not be a major factor in expanding agricultural production. Another reason is that water supplies don't always exist where the available land exists. What's left once the unlikely is subtracted from the possible in terms of added land use is difficult for experts to say. Some gains are clearly possible but not without high investments, accelerated deforestation, and land degradation. Even at such cost, new land alone is not likely to be the key to long-term global food security.

As University of Minnesota agronomist Vernon Ruttan notes, the world is at the end of an era of horizontal expansion.

"We are, during the closing decades of the twentieth century, approaching the end of one of the most remarkable transitions in the history of agriculture. Prior to the beginning of this century almost all increases in agricultural production occurred as a result of increases in the area cultivated. . . . By the end of the century there will be no significant areas where agricultural production can be expanded simply by adding more land to production."[51]

The most promising—some say the most worrisome—possibility for expanding food production emerged in 1973, when two California scientists, geneticist Stanley N. Cohen of Stanford University and biochemist Herbert W. Boyer of the University of California, San Francisco, announced the discovery of a new technology called recombinant DNA.

Using molecular "scissors" known as restriction enzymes, the two took genes from the chromosomes of a toad cell and inserted them into a plasmid, a tiny packet of DNA that could introduce genetic information into foreign bacteria. When the bacteria reproduced, it reproduced the toad genes as well, creating a new type of bacteria. The experiment a success, evolution suddenly lost its monopoly over the power to produce new species.

American consumers got their first taste of the incipient bio-technology revolution in the spring of 1994, when the first genetically altered food item—the Flavr Savr tomato—hit the market after two decades of research.[52]

Traditionally grown tomatoes are picked green off the vine to prevent premature softening, then refrigerated to further retard rotting. They usually taste bland because they are picked before the plant has the chance to add important sugars and aromas. Refrigeration hardens the tomato and saps away much of the remaining taste. In a quest to build the better tomato, scientists at Calgene, the Davis, California, company that "designed" the Flavr Savr, honed in on the enzyme that causes softening, known as PG, and deactivated it by inserting a copy of the gene made in reverse. This gives the tomato an extra week on the vine and eliminates the need to pick it green, giving it more taste. Just as important, it gives the tomato a four-week shelf-life.[53]

Other breakthroughs from splicing and transferring genes from one species to another are imminent: leaner, high-litter hogs; cereals that resist insects, diseases, and herbicides; field crops engineered to retard the formation of ice during frosts; raspberries that last longer before going bad; potatoes with less starch to improve frying; other food crops resistant to salt and drought. The list of possibilities appears endless.[54]

The gestation period of biotechnology ended in May 1992 when, after long deliberation, the U.S. Food and Drug Administration ruled that gene engineering per se was not hazardous, that it would not require labeling on genetically altered food, and that it would leave the responsibility for food safety in the hands of producers. In short, the agency deemed, foreign DNA would not be considered an additive, though it said labeling could be required in specific cases where genetic engineering depleted nutrients, increased natural toxins, introduced allergy-producing substances, or posed environmental threats. The FDA's ruling has energized research, which has absorbed $10 billion in the last decade alone.[55]

Even skeptics are dazzled by the possibility that biotechnology could solve Africa's food crisis by making possible both the intensification and extensification of agricultural production. For example, genetically altered cassava and other food crops that could resist pests, diseases, and weeds could make possible huge additional harvests on existing land. Crops that could grow in brackish soil, meanwhile, could expand onto millions of acres of unused land.[56]

"If you could develop strains of crops that are much more tolerant to salt, then you could really potentially break open the ballgame," acknowledges the Worldwatch Institute's Lester Brown. "That would make an enormous difference."[57]

Biotechnology could also rescue farming from its own environmental consequences by reducing or even eliminating the need for the pesticides and chemical fertilizers that were the key agents of the green revolution and that have been overused by farmers the world over. By transferring a gene that is lethal to a certain insect, for example, geneticists could create a plant with its own insecticide built right in.

Whether the "gene revolution" can produce the quantum leaps in food output achieved by the green revolution has become a matter of intense debate. Optimists say the advent of biotechnology marks the beginning of the end of a prolonged period of declining per capita food production in Africa. They envision a day when sophisticated genetic, satellite, and computer technologies will be combined to make it possible for experts to respond to crop failures anywhere in the world by quickly engineering resistant strains, mass-producing seeds, and rushing them to the afflicted region in time for the next planting.

But the potential of biotechnology, like that of the green revolution, is assessed in different ways by different people. Some say it will save millions from starvation. Others say it will merely expand the use of pesticides, lead to greater food import bills, and hasten the decline of subsistence farming. The two views are not entirely incompatible.

Agronomists say the most promising applications of biotechnology in food-strapped regions of the third world would be the development of protein-rich strains of rice, sorghum, wheat, maize, and cassava that could resist disease and drought. Once developed, they could be delivered to farmers without expensive improvements in infrastructure or the costly inputs—machinery, fertilizers, and chemicals—that were the catalysts of the green revolution. But the path from idea to implementation is strewn with obstacles that make it likely that for years to come biotechnology will lag behind advances achieved by traditional plant breeding.

One major problem is that only a fraction of the money spent on biotechnology research in the past decade has been applicable to third world agriculture. The lion's share of available funds is devoted to biomedical research. Of the mere billion dollars or so spent annually on agricultural research, most is devoted to what some call the "gee-whiz" discoveries like the Flavr-Savr tomato, not to improving the subsistence crops that make up a major portion of the diets of third world poor.

It could be a decade or more before the potential advantages of biotechnology trickle down to the less developed nations. With little profit to be made, little research is likely to be undertaken in the areas where it's needed most—at least not without prodding and money from private foundations or public sector donors.[58] One promising example of public-private sector cooperation that could benefit the developing world is a project jointly funded by Monsanto and U.S. AID to develop sweet potatoes resistant to viruses that can kill up to 75 percent of annual crops in Africa.[59]

Even if developing countries could afford it, biotechnology will be of marginal value without the technical expertise to adapt it to local conditions. Some companies like Monsanto, Britain's Imperial Chemical Industries, and the New Jersey–based DNA Plant Technology have begun programs, funded in part by international agencies, to train scientists from developing countries, but so far only a handful of developing countries, including Egypt, China, and Ecuador, have significant biotechnology programs of their own.[60]

Even where biotechnology research has progressed in developing nations, it is sometimes at the expense of the rural poor. Much of the research is devoted to cash crops, which are normally controlled by large estate owners, while the production of staple foods is left to stagnate. In Brazil, which has invested more in biotechnology research than any other Latin American country, one research group recently developed an improved strain of Rhizobia, used to increase legume yields. Yet 99 percent of the technology has been used to improve soybean harvests, a cash crop mainly used for export, instead of local staple crops like the black bean. In a country where 10 percent of the landowners control 80 percent of the land, biotechnology threatens to widen the gap between rich and poor.[61]

Biotechnology may also need to transcend religious and cultural barriers.

"One of the problems we're going to have to face in the third world is having people understand that when we transfer a gene from a pig to a plant we're not transferring the essence of the pig and therefore not violating religious precepts," says the USDA's Alvin Young, alluding to dietary restrictions prescribed by Islam and Judaism.[62]

In one paradoxical respect biotechnology may be an actual threat to third world agriculture, since scientists can now make vanilla, cocoa, and coffee—three of the developing world's most valuable export commodities—*in vitro*, that is, in the laboratory. Wholly apart from problems of implementation are concerns raised by environmentalists, scientists, and even ethicists who warn that the "miracle" of biotechnology could turn out to be a curse. The most extreme worry is that genetic tinkering could have unpredictable results that could make a mockery of the high hopes that now attend biotechnology research.

"It's very dangerous to play God, to think we can find substitutes in the laboratory for things that have taken millennia to evolve, without unintended consequences, some of which could be catastrophic," says Andrew Kimbrell, an attorney who is policy director of the Foundation on Economic Trends, the nation's leading antibiotechnology lobby.[63]

"Far from feeding the world, using viruses as vectors to get genes into a plant could pose massive dangers to the food supply," says Kimbrell, whose book, *The Human Body Shop*, is critical of what he calls "the engineering and marketing of life."

For the most part the case against biotechnology stems from more mundane concerns, concerns that have helped galvanize opposition that could retard the pace of biotechnology research to the possible detriment of agricultural productivity around the world. For example, critics have invoked an anticorporate argument, charging that chemical companies are engineering plant strains that are dependent on the pesticides and herbicides they manufacture.[64]

"The fact that the same companies that are making herbicides are now creating plants that are resistant to larger and larger amounts of herbicides is far from comforting," says Kimbrell.[65]

There is also the danger, skeptics believe, that the use of bioengineered crops will threaten the diversity of plant and animal species—the very genetic material that will be required for future biotechnology research. Several centers, like the International Board for Plant Genetic Resources in Rome, have begun collecting germplasm from around the world in an effort to preserve biodiversity. But even if it is maintained in the laboratory, losing it in nature could prove catastrophic. If insects learned to adapt to genetically engineered plants, the result could be widespread crop failure and famine, critics warn.[66] A worrisome precedent is the potato famine that decimated Ireland in the nineteenth century and which has been traced to the narrow genetic base of potatoes that were then being cultivated.[67]

"It's a poor argument," responds the USDA's Young of the contention that every farmer in the world is going to plant the same strain of bioengineered wheat or maize. "We learned a lesson from the corn crisis of 1972, when disease wiped out so much of the crop in the American Midwest because everyone was growing the same kind of corn."[68]

If farmers are not able to increase yields with new technology, they will have to do it by expanding onto new land, which in many countries will mean cutting down forests. With biotechnology, says Young, it will be possible to double and triple production on land already under cultivation.

By some estimates, without high-yield farming it would have been necessary by now to put another 10 million square miles of wildlife habitat under the plow—habitat that therefore remains as an important source of the wild genes needed for new biotechnology research. If crop yields can be doubled or tripled again, the practical benefits of biodiversity could prove the savior of the forest land environmentalists are seeking to protect.

"We have fundamentally altered the likelihood of wild forest intrusion," says Dennis Avery of the Hudson Institute. "So where are the cheers from the natural scientists? Where are the plaudits from the environmentalists?"[69]

At the most basic level, the debate between defenders and critics of biotechnology reduces to the propriety of changing rather than adapting to nature, of opting for human selection over natural selection. One battleground in the debate is the issue of whether biotechnology threatens sustainable agriculture. Critics worry that if researchers develop in wheat or corn crops the nitrogen-fixing properties of legumes, farmers might delete legumes from their repertoire of crops, eliminating nature's own mechanism for restoring nitrogen to plants. A more extreme worry is that biotechnology could eliminate traditional farming altogether, as biotech companies seek to expand control over all phases of production, from the manufacture of seeds to harvesting.

"Modern agricultural technology—to the extent that it takes

away autonomy from individual farmers—creates a situation in which valuable custodians of natural and social resources are displaced and no one takes their place," says Clifton Anderson, an agriculture writer at the University of Idaho. "We need the individual farmer who has a stake in his farm and his community to protect the environment."[70]

If there is any consensus on this controversial issue it is that biotechnology has the potential—eventually—to make a significant contribution to increased agricultural output, first by enhancing the survivability of crops and only later by increasing crop yields by the more complex process of multiple gene transfers. But among most mainstream experts, hopes are tinged with doubt.

"It's possible that biotechnology could pull our chestnuts out of the fire," says Anderson. "But the whole history of the agricultural revolution suggests that the problems we deal with are never solved for all time. We are dealing with a dynamic and changing universe and with an environment that adjusts to our changes. Our efforts in agricultural science are thus, at best, temporary expedients. We don't deal in final solutions. There's no assurance that the interventions we make will hold the field for us. Given this, you have to wonder about placing too much hope in biotechnology."[71]

Biotechnology is not likely to be a panacea. But as one part of a multiple strategy, it could play an important role in helping keep food production apace with population growth.

Paradoxically, the other key to global food security lies at the opposite end of the technology scale. It is to encourage the very kind of low-technology, small-scale agriculture practiced by Danson Ingala and Rose Maweu, especially in Africa.

Africa has the potential to be a productive continent. Its farmers are inventive and adaptable. It has 20 percent of the world's cultivable land but only 9 percent of its people, which translates into a third fewer people per acre than the developing world as a whole.[72]

But in most African countries food production is not keeping up with population growth, a circumstance that has bred considerable pessimism about the future of a continent that, by 2025, could have almost five times its 1985 population.

Not all the reasons why can be helped. Much of Africa has poor soil and erratic rainfall. Most of its best agricultural land is already overcrowded. Good land that remains uncultivated is largely concentrated in two countries, Zaire and Zambia. Thanks partly to its colonial legacy, much of its best land is devoted to cash crops that in many cases fetch only paltry prices on the world market and contribute little or nothing to food self-sufficiency at home. A few countries, like Zimbabwe, have managed to grow enough food to satisfy local needs even while exporting staples for profit that can be used to import more food, but they remain the exception.

But not all of Africa's problems are imposed by nature and foreign trade. One of the most serious handicaps to African agriculture has been the home-grown policies of dozens of African governments that have placed the welfare of urban dwellers over that of small farmers. The result has not only been low output. Bad policies have also perpetuated old patterns of slash-and-burn agriculture that have led to widespread ecological damage in Africa.

The urban bias has been expressed in various pricing and exchange-rate policies designed to keep food prices low but that have had the secondary effect of depressing farm production. Research in twenty-two developing countries conducted between 1960 and 1984 and supervised by the World Bank's Alberto Valdes indicated that on average agriculture was taxed at 27.9 percent to subsidize the manufacturing sector.[73] "Such policies have pervaded sub-Saharan Africa for decades and have exacted the inevitable penalties: an erosion of productivity, pragmatism, and entrepreneurial energy," comments former World Bank president Robert McNamara.[74]

Self-sufficiency has also been at cross-purposes with the agenda of international financial institutions like the World Bank itself, which have urged production for export as a means of generating needed foreign exchange.

Most experts agree that the basic problem is that African governments neglect agriculture shamefully. It is a circumstance reinforced by the political impotence of small African farmers and rooted in what one U.S. AID official, R. Stephen Brent, has described as the "fundamental conflict between the economic imperative of empowering the countryside and the antirural bias of African governments and skilled workers."[75]

Only a few developing nations have ever achieved sustainable agricultural growth at a pace that exceeds Africa's current population growth rate of nearly 3 percent. Those that have, including Mexico, the Philippines, and Thailand, have done so under far more favorable conditions than now pertain in most of Africa.

Creating more favorable conditions in Africa begins with establishing an enabling environment based on a long-term interest in the land. One model is China, where only tiny amounts of arable land exist per capita, but where the introduction of free market incentives has boosted output fast enough to keep up with growing demand. Where such policies have been implemented in Africa, the consequences have been similarly impressive. During the 1970s, production of cereals in Malawi soared, thanks primarily to agricultural research, rural road construction, extension services that benefited small farmers, and trade and exchange policies that favored large food producers and exporters. Sustained high agricultural growth has resulted in other countries—Cameroon, China, Indonesia, and Thailand, to name four—where the constraints on small-scale agriculture have been removed.[76]

One needed measure is to provide security of land tenure, without which few farmers are likely to make the long-term investments, such as planting hedges and trees, that are needed to arrest soil erosion. Another needed measure is investment in rural infrastructure, including water and irrigation systems, bus and truck transportation, agricultural extension services, and rural credit.

The beneficial affects of such investments were demonstrated recently in Tanzania. A 1989 study showed that every $1 invested in transportation in this African nation yielded $1.50 in increased income, in part because new roads gave farmers confidence that their goods could get to market.[77]

A third reform needed to spur small-scale agriculture in Africa is an adjustment of policies that favor large commercial farms at the expense of smallholders. To choose one example, Zimbabwe produces most of the fertilizer it uses, but most goes to commercial farmers, not the small subsistence farmers who could make a far larger contribution to the country's food security. Preferential interest rates also favor commercial over subsistence farming in many countries.

African nations also need to do more to assist women, who may be the key to Africa's food future. Eighty-five percent of rural women produce 80 percent of Africa's food, but because of laws and policies that discriminate against women, less than 10 percent of them own land or resources.[78] Disproportionate workloads make the burden on African women heavier. Jomo Kenyatta University researcher Mbaari Kinya describes a scene in Kenya's Embu district that is replicated throughout the continent and elsewhere in the developing world: "In general, women were observed working on the farms while men sat around the markets and shops. Where men were found helping on the farms the number was quite small, the ratio being one man to four women."[79]

Women head nearly half of rural African households, which means having responsibility not only for childbearing but for gathering water and fuelwood and growing the food needed to support the family. But most women have no access to the credit, training, or tools that would enable them to increase their output.

One World Bank study of Kenya indicates that, if given the same resources now available to men, women would be producing 10 to 15 percent more food and giving more of it to their families.[80] "Although these ideas are not new, they are not widely applied," notes another World Bank report, on African agriculture. "Controlled prices and restrictive marketing, disorganized research and weak extension services, poor rural roads and few effective farmers' associations, insecure land and poor environmental practices, are still the rule rather than the exception."[81]

For various reasons—its small population, abundant land, and scarce water resources—Africa has been slow to adopt intensive agriculture. But as Lester Brown notes, the green revolution has provided at least one lesson applicable to Africa: "It has demonstrated that rapid change is possible in traditional societies if there is an incentive for it. Reforms may not help dry countries where the problem is not price but soil, but in others, along the Nile Valley and in the East African plateau, they could make a big difference."[82]

Idriss Jazairy is the former president of the International Fund for Agricultural Development (IFAD), a small UN agency that deals with rural poverty. He says the key to Africa's food future is the very small farmer so long ignored by African governments and outside donors.

"The failure of past development strategies is that they have been based on a trickle-down, social safety net approach that emphasizes the consumption needs of the poor and identifies the poor as a burden on the growth process. Instead, we need to focus on their producing possibilities. We need to see that development is something that happens because of the poor, not in spite of the poor."[83]

"There's little doubt that Africa can feed itself," says Paul Harrison, voicing a widely held view. "It's just a question of whether it will."[84] Somewhere between the "can" and the "will," the food future of Africa and other developing regions will be determined.

There are limits to what technology can achieve in the absence of sustained, high-level government interest in agricultural policy.

One concern voiced repeatedly by farmers and food experts in Africa is that despite imminent or existing food shortages, many government leaders still ignore agriculture and particularly small-scale agriculture.

"It's astonishing, but nobody seems to see this as a major problem that needs to be addressed," says one African government official, speaking anonymously, who attributes the problem to corruption, inefficient bureaucracies, and unexperienced leadership.

One example of this lack of interest is that thousands of small farmers like Maweu and Ingala have had to operate without the technical support needed to rapidly disseminate new farming techniques and technologies.

"I've never seen an agricultural extensionist," says Ingala, who learned the techniques of water harvesting and alley cropping from agronomists from a nongovernmental organization based in Kenya. "You just use your common sense, and if you don't have any you're in trouble."

Another example is the gap that exists in many African nations between the community of agricultural experts and the government officials charged with implementing agricultural policy.

Gideon Mutiso is an American-educated development consultant who for five years was deputy managing editor of the *Daily Nation*, the largest circulating daily in black Africa. He recalls that following a massive crop failure in Kenya in 1981, the United States offered to provide satellite photos that would help the government estimate yields, predict future food shortfalls, and budget the agricultural sector more rationally. But because it instantly became the object of a bitter jurisdictional dispute within the government, the Landsat data have never been used.

"It's not that we don't have people in this country who know how to use Landsat," says Mutiso. "It's that at the political-organizational level we are disorganized. The politicians don't know these things are available. They don't encourage intellectual work. They feel terribly threatened by scientific work because it doesn't fit their biases."[85]

"The technical part is largely known," adds the University of Nairobi's Donald Thomas. "What we need is a political environment based on an active and long-term interest in the land that will facilitate change."[86]

Many experts believe that making Africa self-sufficient in food will require the kind of massive investment usually reserved for wartime to pay for roads and education, irrigation and infrastructure. But given the skewed distribution of political power in many African nations, such a commitment seems unlikely. Notes Stephen Brent of U.S. AID: "Political power is inversely correlated with economic productivity. Urban elites are economically parasitic but politically dominant. Farmers are the backbone of the country but politically impotent."[87]

"The tragic thing," says the Kenyan official, "is that over the next ten or twenty years I don't see the state putting very much money into agriculture."[88]

In the end the future will be decided not only by what is technically possible but also by what is practically possible and in Africa, especially, the two are not always the same. The hunger equation involves economics and politics as much as it does science. In Africa, politics weighs heavily on the future.

"Technically, it's possible to increase agricultural production fast enough to keep up with population growth. Technically it's possible to have a perfectly functioning democracy. But the possibility of that happening in the areas where it needs to happen most seems pretty remote," says the IFPRI's Stephen Vosti.[89]

"Ethiopia could feed itself tomorrow if it got things right. But that means getting new rice strains, irrigation, political empowerment for farmers, and training farmers to be efficient managers of new resources. It will take a generation or two for all that to happen, and by then Ethiopia could have two or three times as many people to feed. While the technical potential exists, there are lots of socioeconomic, historical, and political factors that could keep it from happening."

Given such factors, the potential for Africa remains highly uncertain. It can be realized only if policymakers understand that efforts to reduce fertility have to be part of any strategy to increase agricultural production.

"For most developing countries in East Asia and Latin America, I am moderately optimistic on the assumption that the governments there will pull their socks up," says the FAO's Robert Brinkman. "But for Africa I am seriously worried. For twenty years the world has poured billions into Africa. During those twenty years the situation for the average African has become worse. The implications of being left behind are ominous. We are talking about famines, aggravated by the collapse of civil order."[90]

The broad range of solutions proposed by experts across the ideological spectrum all represent constructive contributions to the debate over whether food production can be made to keep pace with population growth. Economists typically regard high technology as a panacea, while many biologists and environmentalists hold up the standard of "sustainability" in advancing their own less grandiose solutions. But such approaches are not necessarily incompatible. Used prudently, advanced hybrid or bio-engineered crop strains could make a potentially significant contribution to third world agriculture. Channeling resources to small-hold African farmers like Rose Maweu and Danson Ingala could only brighten Africa's food future. Unleashing the productive potential of women could not but make a decisive contribution to solving the endemic problem of food shortage that exists in many developing nations. Who can doubt that, if and when such shortages become a thing of history, that all three strategies and others besides will have played a useful role?

Whether shortages *do* become a thing of history will be determined only partly by what *can* be done; it will also be determined by what is *likely* to be done. In a continent where governments have been disrupted by civil unrest (over 200 coups and coup attempts since the 1960s) and displaced populations (60 million during the 1980s alone), what is likely to be done—in the immediate future, at least—should not be overestimated. Under the circumstances avoiding widespread hunger in Africa seems a fifty-fifty proposition at best.

THREE

"The Limits to Growth":
Environmental Degradation
and the Multitudes

Guatemala

Few questions vex population specialists more than this one: To what extent is rapid population growth to blame for environmental degradation and resource depletion? A brief history of Reinberto Lopez Alala suggests that it is not a question with a simple answer.

Like his father before him, the forty-two-year-old father of six made a passable living cultivating a plot of land he rented from the owner of one of the large coffee plantations located along Guatemala's southern coastal plain, where the soil is rich and the land expensive.

When his rent was raised in 1970, he was forced to make a fateful decision. With no resources to fall back on, he cut his links with the south and moved his family north, into the relatively uninhabited region of the Guatemalan Petén. There, with twenty-two other families driven from the south by rent hikes, he joined a government-sponsored cooperative called Bethel, located in the scenic lowlands that rise up from the Usumasinta River about ninety miles west of the regional capital of Flores.

Two decades later Lopez has become a success story of sorts. He earns a comfortable living growing beans, corn, rice, and squash on land he has hacked out of the dense forest that three decades ago covered 80 percent of the Petén. His children now grown, he is free to supplement his income by working from time to time as a *launchero*, transporting residents and tourists in his own boat from Flores to the villages that dot the shore of Guatemala's third-largest lake, Petén Itza.

Lopez is successful in one other respect. After working with the representative of a local nongovernmental organization he learned the value of conserving forest land. He now clears just what he needs to support crops and a few head of cattle. The rest he leaves for fuelwood and for future generations.

"The reason we conserved the forest is that when the children grow up they can benefit from its richness," he explains. "If they don't have another way of making a living, the forest will be there for them to clear."

But if Lopez is the rare conservationist among the settlers who have colonized the Petén, he is also, inescapably, one of the reasons Guatemala's lowland tropical forest is disappearing at a worrisome rate. He is a textbook example of how complicated it is to assign blame.

Lopez was pushed out of his ancestral home in the south by a skewed pattern of landholding inherited from colonial times that has left less than 3 percent of the country's farmers in control of 65 percent of its best farmland. The rest are left to rent or work as plantation labor in the south, to cultivate the steep, overcrowded slopes of the central highlands, or, like Lopez, to turn Guatemala's last forest into crop- and pastureland.

Simultaneously, Lopez was pulled to the Petén by Guatemala's decision to open the region to settlement and exploitation starting in the early 1970s. Unwilling to redistribute land and unable to provide enough jobs in Guatemala City, the government chose to treat the Petén as a short-term safety valve rather than a long-term economic resource.

A third factor that has made Lopez an accomplice to the defilement of the Petén is the need for energy. With no access to gas or electricity, rural Guatemalans like Lopez have turned to the only source available: firewood from the forest. According to one Guatemalan study, 63 percent of trees felled in Guatemala are used for fuelwood, while only 29 percent are felled to clear crop- and pastureland.

One final factor adds to the pressure on Guatemala's remaining forest land: the vast growth of population occurring in the Petén. Swelled by migration from the south and high birthrates, the region's population has jumped from 22,000 to 350,000 since 1960. At 9 percent, its growth rate is three times that of Guatemala as a whole, which itself has one of the highest in the world. This fact underscores a point that is central to any discussion of how population growth impinges on the natural environment. Population growth was once merely one of several reasons for the deforestation of the Petén. It is now the first among equals.

Lopez's experience, duplicated with minor variations in forested nations all over the world, is the best illustration: The twenty-three families that formed the nucleus of the Bethel cooperative two decades ago have spawned 175 offspring. If Lopez is correct in predicting that his own children will have as many children as he had, the third generation of Bethel pioneers will soar to over 1,000. With marriages occurring early in the region, a Petén with three quarters of a million inhabitants could be no more than twenty-five years away. The almost certain result, say many environmentalists, will be further soil degradation, destruction of the Petén watershed, and the loss of most of the region's remaining forest land, along with its valuable biodiversity.

Unless population growth rates are reduced further and economic and land tenure policies in countries like Guatemala reformed faster, population will become the dominant factor contributing to deforestation, as successive generations engulf what remains of the world's virgin forests.

"What's worrisome is guys like Lopez," says Norman Schwartz, a University of Delaware anthropologist who has been doing fieldwork in Guatemala since the early 1960s. "In many ways he's a success, but he doesn't have long-range plans. His kids will have six kids and eventually the population will be too heavy to bear in the Petén. They pose a real threat within a generation."[1]

"Population is not the only factor at work in the Petén. But it will be difficult to keep the forests if population continues to grow at the present rate," concurs Alfredo Mendez, a research professor at Guatemala City's Universidad del Valle.[2]

The word *Guatemala*, which comes from the Mayan, means "land of forests." But Guatemala has not always lived up to its name. New interpretations of texts chiseled onto pillars found near the ancient Mayan capital of Tikal, located in the heart of the Petén, hint that massive deforestation in Guatemala has occurred before.[3] Then, as now, the Guatemalan hillsides were cleared to gather fuelwood and to plant crops to support a fast-expanding population. Then, as now, population pressures pushed cultivation into ever-steeper and more marginal growing regions. In the downward cycle that followed, soils were depleted, erosion intensified, crop yields diminished, and conflict intensified as Mayan cities competed for diminishing resources.

Centuries later, many environmentalists worry that history is repeating itself. Between 1960 and 1990 nearly half of Guatemala's 1950 forested area was lost, and deforestation is occurring at an accelerating rate. If current trends continue, all natural forest land with significant commercial value will be gone within a generation.[4]

Is that outcome inevitable? Is population the main culprit? The questions get to the heart of a debate that is nearly as old as history and that today sharply divides the growing global community of scientists, demographers, and economists concerned with the pace of population growth and its implications for the global environment. The debate bears centrally on the extent to which foundations, giant international lending institutions, and scores of national governments around the world will craft policy and commit resources to slow population growth—and whether they will do so in time to keep the world's population from exceeding the UN's medium projection of 10 billion by the middle of the twenty-first century.

Unlikely as it may seem in a world of nearly 6 billion people, population was a concern in a world one-twentieth that size. The reason is not so surprising: Long before human numbers began to have an impact on the global environment they had an impact on the local environment.[5] The specter of widespread deforestation and soil erosion in ancient Greece, for instance, occasioned mostly by overgrazing, convinced Plato and Herodotus that the city-states of Attica had to balance population growth with available resources. Moderation in population size, as in all other matters, was desirable, the Greek philosopher and historian reasoned. Aristotle, the intellectual godfather of the pessimistic persuasion of many modern-day demographers, anticipated other problems that would attend rapid population growth. It is necessary that the state "take care that the increase of the people should not exceed a certain number," he cautioned, adding that the failure to do so "is to bring certain poverty on the citizens." It is evident, Aristotle warned, that "if the people increased there must many of them [sic] be very poor."[6]

Across the Mediterranean, in the capital of the great empire of antiquity, Cicero believed that the more Romans the better.[7] But a neighbor of later times was unconvinced. When "every province of the world so teems with inhabitants that they can neither subsist where they are or remove elsewhere . . . it must come about that the world will purge itself through floods, plagues, or famines," warned the Florentine statesman Machiavelli in the sixteenth century.[8]

To a list that included environmental degradation and poverty, Sir Walter Raleigh, a century later, added another danger of rapid population growth: imperialism. "When any country is overlaid by the multitude which live upon it, there is a natural necessity compelling it to disburden itself and lay the load upon others, by right or wrong," wrote the explorer, who had reason to know.[9]

Plato and Aristotle, Machiavelli and Raleigh provided one answer—a resounding *yes*—to the central demographic question of the ages: Is there such a thing as too many people? The seminal affirmative response to the question was issued nearly two hundred years after Raleigh and not far from the Tower of London, where he was executed in 1618 for breaking with the Crown.

In 1798 an unassuming professor of economics sat down and penned a brooding essay that conveyed the simple point that high rates of population growth were destined to hold the future in thrall. Titled *Essay on the Principle of Population,*[10] the name of its author, Thomas Malthus, has become virtually synonymous with the gloomy outlook embodied in every tract written since to advance the notion that the world is facing a population "crisis."

The Malthusian thesis was a repudiation of the optimism of the mercantilist writers of the sixteenth and seventeenth centuries, who saw in larger populations only greater possibilities for enlarged wealth and military power for the nation-states just beginning to make their appearance on the world stage. Their case was made by the Netherlands, densely populated but nonetheless powerful and prosperous. Their optimism was buttressed by utopian writers like the Frenchman Condorcet, who penned convincing assurances that man's technology and ingenuity would combine to create the economic opportunities needed to accommodate expanding populations. But by Malthus's time such opportunities seemed remote. Industrialization had created great wealth but also great poverty in Britain, which reeled from a series of economic crises and bad harvests.

The man at the center of the great demographic debate was an immensely popular figure in London, a tall and handsome scholar, "in appearance and conduct a perfect gentleman," according to one contemporary magazine.[11] Malthus looked out from Britain's cauldron of troubles and concluded that progress would be stymied because economic growth and food production would be unable to keep pace with population growth. Peering into the future, he predicted that population would expand to the limits of sustainability and be held there in perpetuity by famine, disease, and war. Any efforts to raise the income of the poor would make matters worse, Malthus predicted, since higher incomes would only prompt the poor to have more children and thus perpetuate the population-poverty cycle. The only hope lay in "prudential restraint" or celibacy and later marriages that would ensure smaller families.

"Whenever population is not kept down by the prudence either of individuals or of the state, it is kept down by starvation or disease," concurred another of the *classical* economists, John Stuart Mill, elaborating Malthus's view.[12]

Malthus's 1798 essay, which was later revised and toned down, turned out to be one of the most influential economic treatises ever written; it set the terms of a demographic debate that has lasted to the present day. The essayist William Godwin, whose optimism Malthus had set out to repudiate in the essay, was nevertheless impressed by it and called Malthus "the most daring and gigantic of all innovators."[13] Thomas Carlyle was depressed by it and dubbed Malthus's new discipline the "dismal science."[14] Decades later Karl Marx was simply angered by it, and he vilified the essay as "nothing more than a schoolboyish, superficial plagiary [that] does not contain a single sentence thought out by [Malthus] himself."[15] More vociferous than Marx was Friedrich Engels, coauthor of *Das Kapital*, who thundered against "this vile and infamous doctrine, this repulsive blasphemy against man and nature. Here, brought before us at last," Engels roared, "is the immorality of the economists in its highest form."[16]

Part of Malthus's pessimism stemmed from the conviction that when population increased the price of labor would drop. In short, too many people would mean lower wages and more poverty. Marx and Engels rejoined that low wages were not a function of population but of class exploitation, which resulted from the concentration of wealth in the hands of a few. Factor out the inequities of capitalism, they argued, and population growth would pose no problem.

The other main criticism of Malthus, echoed by Marx but anticipated nearly a century earlier by the French utopians, was that technology would offset the diminishing price of labor, rescuing mankind from a future of population-induced food shortages.

"New instruments, machines, and looms can add to man's strength and improve at once the quality and accuracy of his productions, and can diminish the time and labor that has to be expended on them. The obstacles still in the way of this progress will disappear," Condorcet predicted in an essay published in 1795, a year after his death. "A very small amount of ground will be able to produce a great quantity of supplies."[17]

Malthus was burdened by a fatalism induced by fears of population growth and resource shortages. His critics were buoyed by an optimism induced by faith in market forces and the power of technology. Together, they defined the poles of a debate that, under far different circumstances, continues today. Once confined to economists, it is now largely waged between economists, on the one hand, and biologists and environmentalists on the other. Once focused on conditions in the industrialized nations, it now centers on the implications of rapid population growth in less developed countries where the lion's share of growth is now occurring. Once limited to issues like industrial wages and food supplies, it now extends to the viability of the very ecological support systems on which human life depends. Only the question remains the same— though with numbers that Malthus, who lived in a world of less than one billion inhabitants, would have trouble comprehending:

Can the planet, regions of which are already sagging under the weight of its 5.5 billion passengers, sustain 5 or 10 billion more?

The modern demographic debate has been set in the context of unprecedented population growth rates that took off in Malthus's day and peaked during the late 1960s. Surveying the developing world, modern Malthusians, which for the first three decades after World War II included the vast majority of population experts, were sure that population growth was largely responsible for the famines, economic slumps, and political unrest that were endemic in the postcolonial era. To this scene of disarray they brought a bold policy prescription unknown to Malthus: family planning. The use of modern contraceptives, they argued, would reduce fertility and speed economic and political development.

One school of modern Malthusian thought held that population growth retards economic development. Too many people, the reasoning went, led inevitably to poverty and unemployment. It was a view that deeply influenced American policymakers during the Cold War, who worried that the negative equation between population and development was an open door to communism in the third world. They responded by adding a family planning component to U.S. aid programs starting in the 1960s.

Another more pessimistic version of modern Malthusianism dealt less with economics and more with the ecological limits to growth. Because supplies of life-supporting resources like land, water, and minerals are finite, pessimists argued, high rates of population growth could endanger the survival of humanity.[18]

This argument was given enormous credibility by a publishing event in 1972 that, demographer Kingsley Davis notes, seemed at the time to settle the debate in favor of the alarmists.[19] In that year a group of scholars associated with the Massachusetts Institute of Technology fed data on land use, food supplies, pollution, and patterns of industrialization and resource use into a computer and watched in awe as it cranked out projections of a bleak future for mankind. They concluded that the world's population would grow so fast, that pollution would reach such high levels, and that resources would be drawn down so far and so fast that the inevitable result would be "overshoot" and "collapse." They called their study *The Limits to Growth*.[20] As Donella Meadows, a Dartmouth biophysicist and one of its principal authors, later put it, "The world is racing ahead like a speeding car heading for an accident."[21] The only way to avoid such an accident, *Limits* argued, would be to slow industrial and population growth.

But even as *The Limits to Growth* succeeded in galvanizing public concern that a population crisis was at hand, the aura of crisis it helped to create unexpectedly dissipated almost as fast as it gathered. By the mid-1970s fears of famine began to diminish because of the green revolution in Asia and Latin America, the latest manifestation of a two-century advance in agricultural productivity that has continued to the present day. In many developing nations, meanwhile, birthrates began to drop from the historic highs attained in the late 1960s, presaging eventual population stabilization. Elsewhere in the developing world, economic growth rates started to rise, notably in the densely populated nations of East Asia. Suddenly the correlation between population and underdevelopment was in doubt.

Such doubts energized the smaller community of demographic revisionists, who emerged to do battle with their Malthusian brethren. The most vocal among them were New Right conservatives and libertarians who unexpectedly resurrected the old Marxist critique of Malthus, arguing that faulty economics, not rapid population growth, was the cause of scarcity.[22] Unlike Marx, they looked to an unfettered market economy, not socialism, to create opportunities for the earth's masses.

Harbingers of this revisionist view had appeared in the 1930s, when a few writers ventured the opinion that, in the industrialized nations, at least, population growth could stimulate economic growth. In the mid-1930s Harvard economist Alvin Hansen[23] argued that the underemployment and underinvestment of the

Great Depression were the result of insufficient population growth, a view elaborated by the influential British economist John Maynard Keynes.[24] After World War II, conservative economists reaffirmed the link between population growth and business expansion. "The importance of family growth on business activity is beginning to be realized by business planners," *U.S. News and World Report* noted in 1950. "They are revising upward their estimates of future markets."[25]

The notion that population growth is a neutral or even positive phenomenon gained wider acceptance in the 1970s in response to the failure of apocalyptic forecasts of many doomsayers to materialize. Contrary to such forecasts, nearly all the indices of human progress have improved since the dawn of the industrial age. Aggregate statistics on life expectancy, literacy rates, global economic output, and per capita income are higher than ever before, despite rapid population growth. Infant mortality rates, mineral prices, and food prices, meanwhile, have fallen to record low levels.

"The data shows that Malthus had it backwards," says David Osterfeld, a political science professor whose book *Prosperity and Planning* was published just before his death in 1992. "The population explosion didn't limit production. It was made possible by the explosion of production, of resources, food, scientific information, and medical advances. Thus, if anything, the limits to growth are receding rather than growing nearer and the world is therefore growing relatively less populated."[26]

Predictions of catastrophe have been wrong on two counts, according to revisionists. The first is that economic models, like the one used for *Limits to Growth*, project far into the future using the technology and know-how available today and thus vastly underestimate the potential achievements of future generations. The other, related mistake is the persistent tendency of Malthusians to underestimate human ingenuity. If population growth creates problems, they say, then history has proved time and again that it also calls forth the innovation needed to solve them. One case in

point is the green revolution, which catapulted growth in agricultural output above population growth rates in some of the most
densely packed nations on earth. "The basic problem," concludes
Osterfeld, "is that Malthus underestimated everybody's intelli-
gence but his own."[27]

Optimists find cheer not only in history but in current events, as
Ben Wattenberg, an economist at the American Enterprise Institute in Washington, notes. "Defense budgets are coming down,
market economies are taking root, and democracy is spreading.
That's an enormous boon to economic development and that's the
key to lowering fertility rates."[28]

"Why should we worry?" Wattenberg shrugs. "We've gone
from one to 5 billion while living standards have gone up
exponentially. There's no evidence that population growth dimin-
ishes or dilutes development."

Like David and Goliath, two combatants have stood out from the
academic armies engaged in the great demographic debate. Like
Davids, both prefer to think of themselves as virtuous underdogs.
Like Goliaths, both are armed to the teeth with graphs, charts, and
computer models designed to penetrate the other's intellectual de-
fenses. The rivalry pits what the *New York Times Magazine* called
"the Cassandra and the Dr. Pangloss of our era." According to
script, one is an environmentalist—Paul Ehrlich of Stanford—and
the other is an economist—Julian Simon of the University of
Maryland.[29]

Paul Ehrlich first came to notice when, as a young biologist, he
penned the book that carried the population issue from the realms
of academe to a mass popular audience. *The Population Bomb*, published in 1968, extrapolated out from a simple mathematical calculation: finite natural resources divided by a rapidly expanding
population. The nearly inevitable result, Ehrlich wrote, was mass
starvation and ecological overload.[30] "The birthrate must be

brought into balance with the deathrate or mankind will breed it-self into oblivion," Ehrlich warned. "We can no longer afford merely to treat the symptoms of the cancer of population growth; the cancer itself must be cut out. Population control is the only an-swer."[31]

The Population Bomb sold 3 million copies and made Ehrlich the leading Jeremiah of his age. Thirty books, dozens of articles, and innumerable media appearances later, he is still the most sought-after expert on the population issue. Unlike Cassandra, the myth-ical figure whose dark predictions were always right but usually ignored, Ehrlich has commanded and held a large popular follow-ing.

His biggest media triumph was an appearance on the Johnny Carson Show in 1970, earned by the overwhelming success of *The Population Bomb*. A scheduled ten-minute interview turned into a forty-five minute media event that produced the biggest response in the show's history, generating 5,000 letters to Carson in the weeks that followed. The reaction to the show, the first of twenty-five appearances, was "absolutely astonishing," Ehrlich remembers nearly a quarter of a century later. "It taught us that if you want to get the word out you have to go on big national TV."[32]

Admirers and critics alike attribute Ehrlich's success to a glib speaking style and a gift for analogy, talents he has harnessed to the task of purveying to popular audiences a compelling image of im-minent disaster.

"It's an image that grabs a lot of people," grumbles one skeptic. "It's much easier to convey than the image of a world in which hu-man beings create institutions and ways of producing goods that mitigate against most of the adverse effects of population growth."[33]

But fame has brought criticism as well as praise. Ehrlich is re-peatedly reminded that some of the dark prophesies contained in *The Population Bomb* have failed to materialize. Hardest to live down has been a projection of massive famine within a decade of the book's publication. "In the 1970s the world will undergo famines—hundreds of millions are going to starve to death in spite of any crash programs embarked upon now," Ehrlich had warned.[34] He acknowledges the error but insists that developments in the quarter-century since the book was published—like global warming, for example—have proved that, if anything, it was not pessimistic enough. And Ehrlich insists that on balance ecologists have been better forecasters than economists, like the one in the 1950s who, he says, predicted that India would be one of the strongest nations on earth by the end of the century precisely because of its large population.

"It's true that we didn't foresee the great success of the green revolution," Ehrlich says. "But it's also true that we missed a lot of other things: depletion of the ozone layer, acid rain, the accelerating destruction of tropical forests, playing Russian roulette with the atmosphere—all of which are at least partly due to population growth. It makes you wonder what else is going on out there that we don't know about yet. We did miss a lot of stuff. But the fact remains that we were too optimistic."

Ehrlich chafes at the complaint that he blames environmental degradation entirely on population growth, particularly in poor nations, where it is occurring at the fastest rates. "We've published more pounds of paper than anyone else trying to explain that the real problem is overconsumption in the United States," he says, referring to various academic colleagues (including his wife, Anne, a biologist at Stanford) with whom he has collaborated in print. "Seventy percent of global environmental damage is because of the rich countries. The problem is not just the poor."

But rapid population growth ranks a close second in Ehrlich's hierarchy of concerns. Some economists say that declining population growth rates have defused the population bomb. Ehrlich disagrees. With China factored out, fertility in less developed countries remains high, he says. Even in countries with successful family planning programs, like Indonesia and Mexico, fertility declines have stalled well above replacement level. Not to worry about birthrates and not to promote family planning aggressively under such circumstances, Ehrlich says, is folly.

"It's like designing an airplane where you worry more about how many you can get on board than how many you can fly with," Ehrlich says. "The attitude of let's just hope something comes along, that technology will save us, is fine if you want to play dice with the future of your children and grandchildren."

Ask Ehrlich about his opposite number, Julian Simon, and he responds with the acerbic wit that is one of his trademarks. He warms up with a blanket indictment of economists who pass judgment about the natural sciences. "Getting economists to understand ecology," Ehrlich says, "is like trying to explain a tax form to a cranberry."

"It's as if Julian Simon were saying that we have a geocentric universe at the same time NASA is saying the earth rotates around the sun. There's no reconciling these views," says Ehrlich. "When you launch a space shuttle you don't trot out the flat-earthers to be commentators. They're outside the bounds of what ought to be discourse in the media. In the field of ecology, Simon is the absolute equivalent of the flat-earthers."

The two old adversaries, now both in their early sixties, have never met in person. But in a letter in 1980 they arranged the twentieth-century equivalent of a duel to determine whose view of the future was more accurate. Ehrlich and two colleagues accepted a longstanding Simon bet that the prices of five minerals—tin, copper, tungsten, chrome, and nickel were agreed upon—would be lower in ten years. The stakes were $1,000 but also much more than money.

"We knew if we bet on metals there would be a fair chance we'd lose," Ehrlich says now. "But we knew at the very least that if we took him on we could keep him quiet for a decade. But the bet was trivial: We could have bet on the state of the atmosphere or on biodiversity loss, but it would be too hard to determine who won. With metals it's unambiguous."

As it happened, the price behavior of metals—and what it says about future scarcity—turned out to be the trump card in Simon's hand.

It was Dr. Pangloss in Voltaire's *Candide* who advanced the sunny notion that "all is for the best in this best of all possible worlds." For Julian Simon, there has been much to be cheerful about lately. Fifteen years ago he was on the sidelines of the great demographic debate, a man of unorthodox views and—as a professor of business administration—atypical qualifications. An intense and prolific advocate like Ehrlich, he has since elbowed his way into the debate and nearly single-handedly shifted the mainstream in his direction. Though he has not won the popular acclaim of his Stanford nemesis, even some critics grudgingly acknowledge that there is some merit to his optimism.

Simon was not always sanguine about the population issue. When he was younger, he says, he "enlisted in the great war to reduce population growth."[35] He set out to learn the theory and data of demography. In the process he came across the statistical correlations between population growth and economic growth, developed by demographer-economists Simon Kuznets and Richard Easterlin, that challenged the conventional wisdom. "I realized the data did not square with the theory that population growth causes resource depletion and environmental degradation. So I decided I'd better follow the path of the data, not the theory." It was a path that led to the conclusion that the population growth that is a curse to Malthusians is really a blessing in disguise.

One reason, he says, is that by stimulating larger demand for goods and services, population growth increases markets, leading to economic growth. Another reason is that population is the necessity that is the mother of invention—in particular the invention of the technologies that Simon is convinced will "liberate production from the land, find substitute materials, and overcome damage to the ecological base." It was the massive growth of population in southern Asia, he points out, that set agronomists to work on the package of technologies that created the green revolution. "Again and again, temporary scarcities induced by the growth of population and income have induced the search for solutions which, when found, left us better off than if the scarcities had never arisen," Simon says.

But Simon does not merely make a virtue of necessity. He says population growth is a positive good in the long run because the more children that are born the more likely it is that the world will produce more Mozarts and Einsteins. "It's not just Mozarts and Einsteins but the myriad unknown others who contribute their talents and energies toward the progress of humankind," Simon elaborates.

Simon's views burst forth upon on an increasingly divided population community in 1980 in an article in the prestigious journal *Science*. There, he argued that government should not interfere with high fertility since "more people not only means the use of more resources but more units of creativity and productivity. More people compete creatively for ways to develop or find substitutes. Thus the world's resources are not finite."[36]

If Ehrlich's *Population Bomb* was "a gloomy book for a gloomy age," as Jonathan Mann writes in the *Atlantic Monthly*, Simon's seminal and highly controversial article was a cheerful rebuttal for an era determined not to be pessimistic about much of anything.[37] The article and Simon's later writings found a receptive audience with conservatives and the editors of the *Wall Street Journal*, making the Maryland economist an influential figure in the administration of two presidents, Reagan and Bush.

Though rarely the dominant view, the notion that population growth can confer benefits on society has had a long history and distinguished expositors going back at least as far as Condorcet. Simon's contribution was to make the populationist argument so aggressively that it commanded attention, even as it made him the archenemy of the environmental movement. "A lot of what Simon said had been said earlier but ignored," says Fairfield University sociologist Dennis Hodgson, who has written widely on the demographic debate. "What Simon did was to marshal the arguments and put them forth in a form that was difficult to ignore and he did it at a time when people were more receptive to them."[38]

On at least one issue Simon was right, and the cost to Ehrlich and his friends was $1,000, paid without comment and on time in 1990. When it comes to so-called nonrenewable resources, the economist had insisted, the whole concept of "finiteness" was meaningless because reserves of any mineral are merely a function of price and demand. Natural resources "will progressively become less scarce and less costly, and will constitute a smaller portion of our expenses in future years," Simon says.

Sure enough, despite a population increase of nearly one billion during the decade, the price of each of the five metals dropped. And despite massive increases in the demand for metals since the start of the industrial age, supplies of most minerals have not shrunk but expanded. Rising prices have made deeper extraction financially rewarding. Improved methods of locating minerals have been discovered. Businesses and consumers are more conservation-minded. The use of alternatives has increased. The result: Reserves of copper, to choose but one example, grew from 91 million tons in 1950 to 555 million tons in the early 1980s, according to UN statistics.

If price is any indication of scarcity, food and minerals have never been more abundant, confirms the Cato Institute's Stephen Moore. "Measured in terms of how long a person must work to purchase them, natural resources were 20 percent cheaper on average in 1990 than in 1980, half as costly as in 1950, and five times less costly than in 1900."[39]

Ehrlich concedes that over the short term prices have fallen. But even if Simon has been right so far with respect to sone nonrenewable resources, he says, the combination of continued population growth and increased worldwide consumption is catapulting the world toward a point of diminishing returns. More to the point, it is not minerals but the depletion of renewable resources like air, water, and soil that pose the real risks to the future of mankind. Despite the still-prevalent impression that the future is secure, he says, appearances can be deceiving.

He uses the familiar analogy of a pond to illustrate the deceptive speed with which the process of life-threatening environmental degradation is occurring. "You have a pond and put a weed in it. The area it covers doubles every day and in thirty days the whole pond is covered. How much of the pond is covered on the twenty-ninth day? Only half. That's the position we're in now. We're somewhere around the twenty-ninth day but it doesn't look like it because only half the pond is covered."

"Societies show an amazing capacity to turn around," adds Ehrlich. "We're not yet beyond the threshold of recovery. But we're playing right at the threshold. I don't have the slightest doubt that we're living on borrowed time."

"Ehrlich says we're at a perilous moment, but the history of his demographic predictions gives us reason to be humble," responds Simon. "Today we're at a less perilous moment than in the past, and the future is likely to be decreasingly perilous because our power to manage our environment has been increasing throughout human history.

"If we just lift our gaze from the frightening predictions and look at the data, we'll see that economic life in the world has been getting better rather than worse. And there's no persuasive reason to believe these trends will not continue indefinitely. Everything—rising income, life expectancy, declining pollution and disease, human ingenuity—points to a brighter future ahead."

When *The Population Bomb* was written, the earth had 3.4 billion inhabitants. The addition of over 2 billion since then has done lit-

tle to diminish the intensity of the great demographic debate, nor
to break the stalemate that has existed since the battle was joined
by the revisionists during the 1970s. It is a debate that, to the consternation of a confused public and frustrated policymakers, has
generated more heat than light. It is a debate that has failed to establish with any degree of certainty whether there are limits to
growth and, if there are, when they might be reached.

That the debate has been so inconclusive has several explanations, not the least important of which is the extent to which the
parties to it have been talking past each other. Economists think in
terms of labor, capital, and production; ecologists think in terms of
finite supplies of land and water and natural habitat. Economists
say the ecosystem is basically healthy; ecologists worry it may be
on the verge of being irreparably damaged. Economists celebrate
the prosperity of densely packed countries like Japan; ecologists
fret that Japan is merely exporting the environmental costs of such
crowding by exploiting the forests and mineral resources of other
countries. Economists accent aggregate trends and exalt that, on
average, the world's citizens are better fed, housed, educated, and
cared for medically than ever before; ecologists accent the maldistribution of such gains and fret that aggregate statistics provide
cold comfort to the hundreds of millions of people in individual
countries who have not benefited by them and who live on the
hard edge of want and starvation.

It is as if the two sides, which have access to the very same data,
are talking about different subjects, and in a sense they are. Nathan
Keyfitz, a professor emeritus of sociology and population at Harvard University, has spent considerable time analyzing the debate.
It is stuck on dead center, he concludes, because the parties to it
live in "largely noncommunicating worlds."[40]

One problem, says Keyfitz, is that many of the participants in
the debate have drawn conclusions that extend far beyond their
specific areas of professional expertise. Within their own disci-

plines, he says, individual scholars are held to a high standard of scholarship: "There's enough internal discipline that if there's a flaw in their logic or a contradictory argument, they won't be able to get away with it." But when economists and ecologists range beyond their disciplines—as when economists talk about biodiversity loss or ecologists about the price behavior of minerals—they venture into a realm that has fewer checks and balances, permitting predictions, generalizations, and conclusions that under normal circumstances might not pass muster. The result has been a gap between levels of analysis that, in turn, has led to irreconcilable conclusions, as a point-counterpoint between Ehrlich and Simon on the subject of biodiversity illustrates.

Simon insists that there is no scientific proof that species are becoming extinct at any significant rate and that until there is, scientists should operate on the assumption that losses are minimal. For his part, Ehrlich cites frightening statistics on deforestation—the direct cause of species loss—which give a misleading impression of quantitative certainty. There are, in fact, large data gaps. Rates of deforestation and reforestation in China, for example, are largely unknown to Western scientists. Many scientists nevertheless believe that forests in general and rain forests in particular, where most species are found, are disappearing at an alarming rate. Bruce Wilcox of the Institute for Sustainable Development squares the circle: "There's no question that a loss of rain forest is occurring at a catastrophic rate, but there's no way we can produce statistics to prove it with more than plus or minus 50 percent confidence."[41]

The problem is that the very frameworks the two sides have built up make them mutually incomprehensible, writes Nathan Keyfitz. "Because of the overlap of interests, those preoccupied with months are at the moment engaged in a lively controversy with those preoccupied by millennia. . . . When biologists and economists try to talk to one another the biologists speak concretely about the fragile character of rain forests and the economists more broadly about the power of substitution impelled by the price system. There is plenty of goodwill but effectively no dialogue."[42]

Keyfitz uses world fisheries to illustrate the problem of communication.[43] The economist's goal is to optimize the catch. He judges success based on how the equipment on the boat is operating, by the efficiency of boat and crew, by how many fish are caught. His frame of reference is only one part of the commodity cycle: If the maximum number of fish are caught, providing the greatest array of choices at the lowest possible prices to consumers, the operation is a success. He thinks in the relatively short term and with a focus on human needs.

The biologist is willing to reduce efficiency in the interest of sustaining the catch. He judges success by how effectively human needs are reconciled with the needs of the ecosystem. His frame of reference is the entire commodity cycle, and he worries that the economist's objective is consistent with the destruction of the habitat. He thinks in the longer term and with a focus on balancing the needs of man with other species that share his habitat. The differences reduce to a question of values: Is saving fish or meeting consumer needs at the lowest cost the higher good?

"There's one basic question you have to ask, and depending on how you answer it the rest becomes clear: Are we concerned with the well-being of humans alone?" explains University of Pennsylvania demographer Samuel Preston.[44]

Economists assign value to resources based on their relative value in the production process, Preston says. And since the cost of resources is minor compared with the cost of labor and capital, they place a low value on resources. As to the matter of valuing other species relative to human beings, the issue is beyond the economists' ken. "The concept of stewardship is foreign to economists," says Preston. "If you're concerned with ethical and religious considerations regarding the well-being of the natural world, then you're into an entirely different ballgame and it becomes very hard to know how to proceed. Those are choices that have to be made through the political process."

The failure of the dialogue to clarify the effects of population growth on ecosystems and mineral supplies has other causes. One study conducted in 1980 examined seven economic-demographic models constructed to project the future of food and resource supplies and pollution levels.[45] Though each was serious and academically rigorous, the results were dramatically different, ranging from the doomsday scenarios projected in *The Limits to Growth* to the far more benign projections of study groups based in Argentina and Japan. The problem, as Keyfitz notes, is that "no one of them proves anything" because each one of them reflects the assumptions factored into them.[46]

The problem of bias is not confined to econometric and biometric models. It runs deep in disciplines nominally dedicated to the search for truth and in which analysis is so essential to answering the questions that relate most directly to the future of mankind. As noted by Michael Teitelbaum and Jay Winter, co-authors of one informative essay on the demographic debate, the adversaries in it have been curiously united by a tendency to marginalize or exclude information or frames of reference incompatible with their own.[47] The selective use of evidence, in turn, has had the effect of oversimplifying an immensely complex subject, driving wedges between disciplines that need to cooperate.

As Teitelbaum notes, such selective use of evidence is a problem deeply rooted in human nature: "People with strong views tend to be enthusiastic about evidence that's consistent with those views and unenthusiastic about evidence that isn't," he says.[48] University of California at Berkeley philosopher of science Paul Karl Feyerabend has a more pessimistic view. He says the compulsion of scientists to find the absolute truth can lead to a kind of intellectual tyranny.[49] Whatever the explanation, the tendency to filter out opposing views subverts the process of academic inquiry that, ideally, should produce the unbiased conclusions policymakers need to make intelligent choices. The filtering process is reinforced when scientists or economists become popularizers and thus partisans and simplifiers. Journalists do little to help when they accent environmental scare stories, which has aided the Malthusians, or magnify the influence of minority views, which has abetted the revisionists.

"Unfortunately, academic research is not always about telling the truth. Sometimes it's about drawing conclusions and making the data fit them," says Bruce Wilcox.[50] The tendency is reinforced by the way research grants are awarded. To facilitate grant-making, science is compartmentalized into narrow subdisciplines by megafunders like the National Science Foundation and the National Institutes of Health. The process has retarded the kind of interdisciplinary research required by complex environmental and population issues.

Perhaps in the end, as the American Enterprise Institute's Nick Eberstadt suggests, it is no more reasonable to expect that demographers can come up with comprehensive "laws of population" than for historians to create a unified theory of history. "For all the mathematical rigor of some of its investigations," writes Eberstadt in the *Wilson Quarterly*, "population studies is a field of social inquiry. . . . Researchers may uncover relationships between population change and prosperity, poverty, or war in particular places at particular times, but none of these findings can be generalized to cover the world at large."[51]

Even so, the debate that has raged over these very issues has been bad for all the disciplines involved. Worse, it has sent a signal to policymakers and public alike that, in the absence of a consensus on what its implications are, population growth can safely be ignored. "Policymakers conclude that since there's no certainty about anything, you don't have to pay attention to the issue," Teitelbaum says.[52]

"And what is the public to do?" Keyfitz asks. "They don't know who's right. It's hard to overstate the damage this does."[53]

A quarter-century after books like *The Population Bomb* and *The Limits to Growth* reignited and popularized the debate over the consequences of population growth, important tactical gains have been won by those who challenge these apocalyptic views of the future. Economists like Julian Simon and the American Enterprise Institute's Ben Wattenberg have made it impossible to ignore the huge contributions science has made to human welfare, even in the face of the most rapid population growth in history, or to discount the argument that further advances could diminish the impact of projected future increases. In the presence of decades of declining prices, meanwhile, the case for limiting population growth is now rarely argued on the basis that supplies of nonrenewable resources are likely to be jeopardized in the near term by rapid population growth. Many mainstream Malthusians are more guarded about using the word *crisis* to describe the implications of population growth. Their willingness to at least gesture to the arguments made by their opposite numbers, the cornucopian economists, has become an unexpected new form of political correctness. Still, while the global community of population experts is generally less skeptical of their thesis, a nagging worry persists among many— probably most—that, as Rockefeller University demographer Joel Cohen notes, even if Malthus has been wrong for the past two centuries he may not be wrong for the next two.[54]

Their hesitance about the future is based on a concern that the stunning technological advances that have so far mitigated the worst effects of rapid population growth may have merely postponed, not necessarily precluded, an ultimate day of reckoning. While most experts acknowledge that technologies like those of the green revolution have rescued mankind from hunger and want, some point out that such advances occurred when global consumption rates and real annual increases in population growth were smaller than they may be in the near- to medium-term future. Within the next half-century, the UN projects, twice as many people will be seeking three times the food and fiber and four times the energy and engaging in five to ten times the level of economic activity.[55] That means dramatically higher energy use, more resource consumption, more wastes, and more environmental degradation associated with mining and refining nonrenewable natural resources. Moreover, while the point has been proved that rapid economic and population growth can occur simultaneously, such growth has not been taking place in an infinite world but within the confines of a closed biosphere, which is now exhibiting unmistakable signs of overburden.

"You can't ignore the forces that have worked in the past: technological innovation and market adjustments. In the future, these could take different forms and operate even more rapidly than before," acknowledges the World Resources Institute's Robert Repetto. "But when you think about the expansion in the scale of the population and the scale of economic activity, especially in the third world, there's every reason to believe that renewable resources are going to be altered drastically, probably irreversibly: forests, coral reefs, wetlands, wildlife habitat, soils."[56]

In general, population experts appear to be less confident that "skilled, spirited, hopeful people," to quote Julian Simon,[57] can make social and economic contributions significant enough to compensate for their absolute numbers, especially under the conditions of poverty and overcrowding that hold so many in the grip of ignorance, joblessness, and ill health.[58] They are also less sanguine about the long-term implications of what British ecologist Paul Harrison describes as the "enigma" of the simultaneous depletion and expansion of nonrenewable resources. Economists have made much of the paradox that even as demand has increased for many nonrenewable resources, supplies have expanded and prices have dropped. Harrison voices what may be the more prevalent view that, under the impact of rising consumption rates and population growth, a point of diminishing returns may eventually be reached: "The magic porridge pot that has spewed forth riches in the past may work for us for a few decades more. But it would be imprudent to rely on it forever. A world of 10 to 16 billion people cannot continue to consume resources at current Western levels. Something has to give."[59]

Studies to establish undisputed cause-and-effect relationships between population growth and environmental degradation have been too few, too country-specific, or, like one conducted recently by the International Union for the Conservation of Nature and reported by the UN Population Fund, too circumstantial to be definitive. After surveying habitat loss in fifty African and Asian nations, the IUCN concluded that the 20 percent of countries that lost the most habitat (averaging 85 percent) had 1,900 people per square kilometer on average, while the 20 percent that had the least loss of habitat (averaging 41 percent) had only 300 people per square kilometer on average.[60]

While highly suggestive, such studies have not always met the test of scientific proof. But for most policymakers enough such suggestive studies have been conducted to justify measures to limit population growth. As one World Bank official notes, inferences have often had to substitute for conclusive data to justify investments by national governments and international lending institutions in population programs. No airtight case has been made, for example, that population retards economic development, he says. "But we do know that too many births too closely spaced strongly correlate with infant mortality, and that large families diminish the productivity of women and increase national health costs. Those are the arguments we use at the Bank [to secure money for population programs]. We're coming in the side door but it's honest and it works."[61]

The growing body of solid and circumstantial evidence linking rapid population growth with environmental degradation is so worrisome that even the scientists some economists have been banking on to rescue the future have been gripped by a belated failure of confidence. In one widely noted warning issued jointly in 1992, the U.S. National Academy of Sciences and the Royal Academy of London predicted that if current population and consumption trends continue, "science and technology may not be able to prevent either irreversible degradation of the environment or continued poverty for much of the world. . . . Some of the environmental changes may produce irreversible damage to the earth's capacity to sustain life."[62]

Another warning, dispatched the same year and signed by 1,700 scientists, including over a hundred Nobel laureates, cautioned that "pressure resulting from unrestrained population growth puts demands on the natural world that can overwhelm any efforts to achieve a sustainable future. Not more than one or two decades remain before the chance to avert the threat we now confront will be lost and the prospect for humanity (and nature) immeasurably diminished."[63] Yet another report, this one issued by fifty-six national academies of science in October 1993, cautioned that "it is not prudent to rely on science and technology alone to solve problems created by rapid population growth, wasteful resource consumption, and poverty."[64]

Buttressing that view are growing indications suggesting that environmental change may be occurring on a scale unprecedented since the advent of the glacial ages one million years ago, and that population growth is one contributing factor. Such indications have been accumulating quickly in a world of just 5 billion people who have been indulging, on average, in fairly moderate levels of consumption. Permanent damage to fragile local ecosystems has already resulted, and many demographers and scientists worry that the added pressures that are likely to be imposed by simultaneous increases in population and living standards could catapult threatening global trends across critical environmental thresholds. Meanwhile, as Repetto notes, even though the world's renewable resources—water, soils, and living organisms—have yielded up increasing production, it has been at the cost of sacrificing current and future productivity, which could undermine the capacity of many countries to provide for the much larger populations expected in the near future.[65]

The problem is epitomized in the forests of Guatemala, where settlers like Reinberto Lopez Alala have hacked out the only living available to them, halving the country's last remaining forested area in less than two decades. Haiti, which has one of the highest population densities in the world, is a worse case. Once heavily wooded, only 2 percent of the country is still forested, and the trees that remain are at the mercy of over 6 million people starved for fuelwood. Thirty years from now, 12 million Haitians will compete for what's left. Population is not the only reason for Haiti's deforestation. But as one population expert notes, if impoverished Haitians turn the country's last trees into firewood, irreversible damage may be done to the country's watershed and eventually to the country's arable land and freshwater—results paralleled in other countries, including India, where deforestation has caused flooding during the rainy season and water shortages during the dry season.[66]

Deforestation has also led to the loss of one of the most important habitats for animal and plant species, along with wetlands and coral reefs. As already noted, scientists have been unable to estimate reliably either the number of species in nature or the speed of their loss. But their presumptive reasoning has not led to encouraging conclusions. Most species live in tropical rain forests. But the rain forests are now disappearing in Washington state–sized chunks each year, according to the UN Food and Agriculture Organization.[67] In the handful of nations where the world's remaining tropical forest land is concentrated, population doubling times are as low as twenty-two years. With most of the wood harvested in developing countries used for fuel, a drastic shrinkage of forests and species seems all but certain.[68]

But the problem is not just forests. At stake is the extent to which all the earth's renewable resources and its ability to absorb

wastes are being taxed by a combination of bad government policies, inappropriate technology, high levels of consumption, and
rapidly growing populations. However much scientists and economists may differ on the scope and implications of such global
changes, the fact is that most developing nations now operate on
the assumption—correct or incorrect—that rapid population
growth is a serious problem that needs to be addressed quickly and
decisively. Accordingly, nearly all have adopted ambitious programs to lower birthrates, sometimes adopting coercive measures
at which even staunch Malthusians have winced.

Government leaders have been galvanized not only by the conviction that rapid population growth will mortgage economic development, but also by a lengthening inventory of small and large
environmental calamities to which population pressures have contributed. All across the developing world, for example, population
pressures, livestock, and wasteful agricultural practices are putting
pressure on soils, contributing to the process of desertification that
has led to a steady exodus from the land.[69] And desertification is
only the most extreme result of the relentless pressure that is being
placed on land to feed swelling populations. As much as half the
world's wetlands have been drained to provide farmland since the
turn of the century.[70] Meanwhile, the world fish catch, which provides the main source of protein for the populations of forty countries, has leveled off and may have reached a point of diminishing
returns because of overharvesting and the destruction of spawning
habitats, according to the Worldwatch Institute.[71]

Freshwater, the resource most likely to impinge on human development, is also under pressure, in substantial part because of
population growth. In 1990, a third of a billion people lived in
countries defined as water-stressed or water-scarce, according to
Population Action International (PAI).[72] Without a breakthrough
in desalination technologies, the number could increase to 3 billion, or one in every three people, by 2025, mostly in Africa and
Asia. Compounding scarcity is the growing problem of water deg-

radation caused by saltwater intrusions, chemical pollutants, and human sewage.

The effect of population growth on finite water supplies is illustrated by comparing Iran and Great Britain. In 1990, the two countries had the same number of inhabitants—just under 60 million—and access to equivalent amounts of renewable freshwater. Assuming supplies remain stable, by 2025 Iran would have only half the amount of water per capita that it has now because its population, according to the UN's medium projection, will double. In Britain, where population is expected to grow by only 5 percent during the same period, per capita availability would stay about the same.[73]

As PAI reports, there is no more freshwater on the planet today than there was 2,000 years ago. Yet the earth's population today is more than 20 times greater, which is one reason why chronic freshwater shortages are expected soon in Africa and the Middle East, northern China, parts of India and Mexico, the western United States, northeastern Brazil, and several former Soviet republics.[74] More troubling, some of the highest population growth rates are occurring in some of the most arid regions. "Within a decade," PAI reports, "water could overshadow oil as a scarce and precious commodity at the center of conflict and peacemaking."[75]

Water is a natural renewable resource. But like land and ambient air, it can also be a repository for waste, which is yet another reason many demographers and scientists view the future with misgivings. Human activity has severely taxed the planet's absorptive capacity. Vast flows of toxic, chemical, and human wastes now pollute the earth's rivers, streams, and oceans, damaging aquatic life and posing health hazards to humans. Air pollution from factory emissions, motor vehicles, and utilities has brought disease to European forests and to crops in Africa, damage to the ozone layer, and loaded the atmosphere with greenhouse gases. The estimated global emissions of carbon from fossil fuels alone have tripled since 1950.[76]

As in the case of global warming, global environmental degradation has mostly to do with profligate energy use in the first world. Japan, Western Europe, and the former Soviet republics account for about 35 percent of the carbon emitted into the atmosphere.[77] The United States, with 5 percent of the world's population, accounts for another 25 percent. Per capita fossil fuel consumption is actually declining in the United States, but the decline has been more than offset by an annual population growth of 2.6 million, so the U.S. contribution of carbon to the atmosphere continues to rise.

But the balance between developed and developing countries is beginning to shift as living standards, and thus energy and resource use, gradually rise in developing countries. Such improvements hint at what many environmentalists see as a potentially tragic paradox: that human progress could push environmental degradation to a point that could produce human suffering. Given the persistently high rates of population growth in many developing countries, the environmental effects of even small increases in per capita consumption could be magnified, shifting more of the blame for global environmental degradation to poor countries. The third world share of the global consumption of aluminum and copper alone rose from 10 percent in 1977 to 18 percent in 1987, according to one study.[78] If incomes in less developed countries continue to grow at about 3 percent annually, forty years from now "these countries will produce more than half the global waste loadings (though still less per capita than the rich nations), and the world economy will be five times as large as it is today," according to Mark Sagoff of the University of Maryland's Institute for Philosophy and Public Policy.[79]

The dark threat posed by the combination of simultaneous population and consumption increases in the developing world is suggested in projections issued by the Futures Group, a Washington, D.C., strategic planning firm, based on a study conducted in the Philippine capital of Manila. Manila's population of 8 million will soar to 12 million within twenty years under a low-growth scenario, and to 16 million under a high-growth projection. Concurrently, the number of motor vehicles in Manila is projected to double, from one for every ten people to one for every five. At 17,000 tons per year, the level of air pollution from particulate matter in Manila is already three times the maximum level deemed safe by the U.S. Environmental Protection Agency. With the projected population and consumption increases, the volume will grow to between 25,000 and 33,000 tons, or nearly six times maximum safe levels.[80] Such dry statistics translate into human tragedy, which, for monetary and bureaucratic reasons, is unlikely to be mitigated by effective pollution-control efforts.

"In the absence of legal, regulatory, and incentive programs, there's no chance of tight emission controls," says the Futures Group's John Freymann. "What the figures demonstrate to policymakers is that lowering population growth is a fundamental part of any environmental strategy."[81]

In the end, the concern exhibited by large numbers of population experts is mostly inferential, an educated hunch about global trends backed up largely by evidence drawn from local trends that the order of population growth projected for the future will pose challenges of unprecedented magnitude. But it is a hunch that has generated a degree of passion even among natural scientists.

The other two factors besides population that determine the impact human beings have on the planet—technology and consumption—are more malleable. Technology can be changed, abandoned, or made efficient enough to partially relieve the impact of population growth. Consumption patterns, meanwhile, can be altered under stress of circumstances, as events like the Great Depression and the 1970s' OPEC oil embargo have demonstrated for brief periods, albeit on far different scales. Population patterns, on the other hand, are largely nonnegotiable, except over the course of generations. It is the overriding consequence of this fact that worries so many scientists and demographers: As world population proceeds toward a doubling (considered likely) or a tripling (considered possible), it will be more and more difficult for individuals and nations to implement environmentally sound policies on the scale necessary to avoid overloading the assimilative capacity of nature. In a world of 8 or 10 or 12 billion it will be harder to escape the unintended consequences of government decisions, technological innovations, or even economic prosperity, which, although something to cheer about in every other respect, can be the greatest magnifier of all. All of which has led experts like former World Bank president Robert McNamara to the conclusion that there can be no solution to the global environmental problems scientists are just beginning to understand that does not include action to slow projected population growth rates.[82]

Economists, demographers, and ecologists have managed to agree on at least one thing: that population growth is only one factor contributing to environmental degradation. The consensus view is that poverty and inappropriate government policies are the main problems—so far. In many developing nations, sluggish economic performance has led directly or indirectly to measures that have had a lethal impact on forest lands. Unable to keep up with massive foreign debts incurred in the 1960s and 1970s, for example, they have been pressured by international lending institutions to accept austerity measures that have led to deep cuts in government services. The result has been the dislocation of the poorest and dispossessed, some of whom have spilled into virgin forests in countries like Guatemala. Countries like Brazil, which have been pressured to generate more foreign exchange, have exploited the forests for minerals and timber for export, often with devastating ecological results.[83]

Governments have frequently made matters worse by granting concessions to cattle ranchers on terms that have created incentives for reckless exploitation. Or by granting squatters' rights to settlers who "improve" the land by clearing it. In the notable case of Costa Rica, squatters who clear forest land are entitled to sell it to parties who are allowed to take immediate title. As a study of Costa Rica released by the World Resources Institute concludes, "many enterprising poor and landless could make a business of simply clearing marginal public and private lands, selling them to eager cattle ranchers or other speculators, and moving on to repeat the process."[84]

Even without population pressures, such policies could have placed pressure on forest lands. But with rapid population growth, all the negative effects of poverty and ill-conceived government policies are magnified. Another example of the lethal synergy at work between bad policies and rapid population growth is the concessions many governments have given to logging interests. The logging industry accounts for only one percent of trees that have been cut in the Petén, according to a Guatemalan expert.[85] But the statistic is misleading because, under conditions of high population growth, the roads that loggers construct become highways for rapid and extensive exploitation by settlers. "To get the wood out you have to build the roads in, and when the roads go in the farmers go in," says one Guatemalan official. "After they plant a few crops the land is abandoned and the settlers move further into the rain forest."[86]

The classic example of synergy between population and bad government policies, and an underlying cause of much of the deforestation in Latin America, is the inequitable landholding patterns that have long existed in many Latin American nations. Under conditions of low population growth, they have had minimal impact on forest land. But where the growth in real numbers occurs rapidly—which is to say, in nearly every developing nation—such patterns have pushed poor farmers like Reinberto Lopez Alala into the only areas remaining for exploitation. Land redistribution could sharply reduce the impact of population growth on forest land, but it has occurred in only a handful of nations.

"It's not out of ignorance that the squatters are cutting the trees; it's out of a very normal human reaction that you want to survive," comments Helmut Hess, an agronomist who works for Bread for the World in Stuttgart, Germany. "If good farmland is not available elsewhere, then they climb the hills, cutting the most beautiful forests. The big plantations at the foot of the hill leave them nowhere else to go."[87]

Richard Bilsborrow is a demographer at the Carolina Population Center in Chapel Hill who has studied the process of deforestation in Guatemala for nearly two decades. He shares the view that population growth is an indirect but highly important agent of deforestation. "Population growth leads to fragmentation of the land and forces people to migrate to other parts of the country, where they continue the process of deforestation," he says. "The exact amount of deforestation is directly related to the size of the families that engage in it."[88]

In theory, one means to retard deforestation would be to create jobs in regions like the Petén to discourage farmers from expanding into cattle ranching, which is far more lucrative but also more destructive to soils and forests. One means to do that would be for the government to invest in low-impact eco-tourist facilities that would create the demand for service jobs like cooks and drivers and tour guides. The problem is that even prosperity could redound to the detriment of the Petén's remaining forests.

"The NGOs [nongovernmental organizations] all assume that if the farmers make a good living from tourism they won't go into or expand cattle ranching, but there's always the possibility that they might," says the anthropologist Norman Schwartz. "If they make more money from tourism they might expand the size of their ranches because they'll have extra income to invest. In that case, the forests won't be helped but hurt. The long-term implication is that if we—the Guatemalan government and the NGOs—can't demonstrate that there are alternative ways of making a living, the forests will go. It's a race against time."[89]

The good news is that where economic or tenurial policies that have encouraged land clearing have been changed—as in Costa Rica and Brazil, for example—deforestation rates have slowed.[90] The bad news is that such changes are rare and are unlikely to be enacted and implemented in other countries in time to save more than a fraction of the vast forests that once covered countries like Guatemala. The reasons are largely political. Unlike logging interests and large landowners, forests as a rule have no constituency, although a green movement, reinforced by the presence of a rapidly expanding number of NGOs, is beginning to take shape in the forested nations of Central and South America.

In the last analysis, the case of Guatemala may best explain why the future looks so uncertain to so many population experts. It is not that the future *has* to be so, but that it is *likely* to be so given the factors that countervail against mankind's indisputable ingenuity and innovative technology. One such factor is economic: Poor nations are simply unable to afford environmentally sound consumption and production practices.[91] Another factor is political: In the face of widespread poverty, diverting resources to environmental protection is largely out of the question, as Norman Schwartz explains.

"Given the problems that Guatemala faces, who could give conservation first priority? You're facing a hungry population, increasing land shortages in the mountains, ethnic problems, urban unemployment, antigovernment guerrillas, a powerful oligarchy that says land distribution is a communist plot. Then you say, but far away in the north there are trees and forests that we have to conserve. As important as conservation is, there are other things that, no matter what you believe, are just going to get first priority."[92]

Even if governments were not so constrained, they would have limited ability, for example, to enforce revised property laws designed to prevent squatters from despoiling forest lands. As for reducing poverty, perhaps the principal cause of deforestation, it is a task that is likely to take more time than the forests have available at current rates of destruction. It is precisely such limitations that cause environmentalists to worry. If poverty remains pervasive, if the regulatory arm of government remains weak, or if governments continue to make bad policies, the doubling or tripling of populations that is likely before population stabilization occurs seems certain to become the most important factor in the process of deforestation, placing much of the world's remaining forest land in jeopardy.

Environmental writer Clive Ponting observes that human history is one long record of mankind's attempt to circumvent the limitations imposed by nature. The biggest departure from these limitations has been the growth in human numbers that, Ponting says, has far exceeded a level supportable by natural ecosystems. The departure was made possible first by advances in agriculture, then by the use of fossil fuel energy, which opened the door to the quantum increases in the production of goods required to support a growing population.[93]

As viewed by some, the escape from nature's constraints has been a triumph of human ingenuity, a testament to the promise of technology. As viewed by a large number of natural scientists, it has been something else, rather more of a borrowing against time than a permanent escape from ecological limits. If bad policy, social inequities, and simple incompetence were the only factors contributing to environmental degradation, the debate between them would be academic. But increasingly, there are signs that there is something more involved. As Population Action International's Robert Engelman points out, bad policy is nothing new. Social inequities are ancient. Land has always been badly distributed. Why is it, then, that only in the past three decades has deforestation suddenly begun occurring at such a rapid rate all over the tropics? Why is it that peasant farmers like Rienberto Lopez Alala have suddenly become such lethal, if unwitting, agents of forest destruction? Many scientists now believe that the answer may have something to do with the synergy between bad policy and population growth that appears to be tending toward a dangerous critical mass.[94]

When population growth was slow and other frontiers remained to be conquered, the latitude for bad judgment and bad policy was broad. With population high, the latitude is shrinking. In the past, the planet forgave mankind's mistakes, except in local settings. With over 5 billion people on the earth, it is considerably less forgiving. It is likely to be still less so as the world presses on toward its next 5 billion.

FOUR

"Fewer Is Better": A Model of Family Planning

Thailand

Other than the shattering roar of "long-tail" boats, there is almost no reminder of the twentieth century on the short trip up the Ghor canal from the village of Nong Chok to the four hamlets of Pai Dam (Black Bamboo).

For over a century, the hundred-kilometer waterway was the only link to Bangkok. Even in an era of macadamized roads that radiate from the capital, the canal and dozens of small tributaries are the only highways into the tiny communities that dot the canal's upper reaches.

The long-tails offer speed but at a high price: Their exposed, unmuffled outboard motors violate the tranquillity that is an artifact of a disappearing Thailand. The canal slices through stretches of banyan and tamerind trees, past houses and storefronts perched atop stilts along the riverbank. Peasant farmers paddle by in quieter flat barges, while workers hand-load large bags of newly harvested rice onto a larger double-decked barge bound for a local processing plant.

About four miles upstream, on the right bank, three small huts are clustered in a grove of mango and jak-fruit trees. They are made of bamboo, their sides partially open to the weather, but with enough corrugated roofing to drain off the frequent warm tropical rains. Along the riverbank a broken-down "spirit house" the size of a large birdhouse provides a habitat for spirits who live on the property. Scattered about, a few large, forlorn sunflowers make a game attempt to brighten a scene of dismal rural poverty.

Twenty-seven-year-old Mariam and her husband, Sam Ruang, thirty-six, have lived here since they were married twelve years ago. Their first child, San Wa Luck, now nine, was born in a car on the way to the hospital. Their second child, a daughter named Mali Wan, was born two years ago. Miriam hopes she will be their last.

Not that they don't like children. Mariam was the third of six. Sam Ruang was one of eight who survived in a family of twelve. He remembers the dim view his grandfather had of family planning.

"Granddad always said if there had been contraceptives in his day I wouldn't be here," he says with just a hint of a smile. He is shirtless. A large tattoo of a mythical bird, affixed when he was in the army, adorns a biceps enlarged by work on construction crews and as a day laborer in nearby rice fields.

Sam Ruang would like to have one more child, but he understands that that is beyond his means. For her part, Mariam will have none of it. Since the birth of Mali Wan she has been impatient to get back to work, also as a day laborer. The extra income is not the only reason. Like millions of other women around the world, she has learned that work outside the home has expanded her horizons.

Like clockwork, she goes to the local health clinic every third month for three new cycles of free birth control pills. If she couldn't get the pills there, she says, she would buy them in town, where they sell commercially for about ten Baht (forty cents) per cycle. "If they cost a hundred Baht per cycle," she says emphatically, "then I would get sterilized."

"People say you forget to take the pill, but I don't. I take it with me everywhere I go because I'm afraid I'll get pregnant. If it weren't for the family planning program we'd be having children by the dozens and we'd keep having them till we were fifty."

Sam Ruang, who listens quietly, says decisions on matters like family size belong to Mariam. But later he discloses that it was he who bought Mariam her first cycle of pills, after the birth of their second child, and it was he who taught her how to use them.

As Mariam and Sam Ruang talk to visitors, half a dozen scruffy children, including their own, are glued to a television. Apart from the long-tails, it, and the tin roof above, are the only signs of modernity that have reached the primitive world of Mariam and San Ruang. Mariam says that by increasing the costs of raising children, TV is one reason many Thai couples are choosing to have smaller families.

"TV increases what they want," says Mariam. "We go to the market and they say buy this and buy that."

Perhaps fittingly, television has also helped Mariam and Sam Ruang keep their family small. Every day they hear government-sponsored messages pitched to Thailand's rural poor, who are literate but rarely schooled beyond the primary level. Sometimes they are in the form of announcements. Sometimes they are plotlines woven into soap operas. In Thailand and dozens of other countries, such messages—the long, electronic arm of government and private family planning programs—are reaching into the remotest regions of the globe. Repeated day after day, they bear the same message: Many children make families poor.

The message reaches home in other ways. Every Tuesday a loudspeaker on a tower at the Buddhist monastery across the canal broadcasts information about family planning services available at the local government-run health clinic. When Mariam goes to the clinic, which is frequently, she gets the word again.

"When you get sick you go to the health center, and that's when you see the posters and the pamphlets. They all say that big families are bad," she says.

One way to gauge how effectively the message is getting

through is to look at the numbers. Statistics compiled by the government and various international agencies testify to a dramatic drop in Thailand's birthrate. A simpler gauge is Mariam, who needs no statistics to confirm what she and the other women in the village know full well: "A lot of people are using family planning, so it's easy to know. Nowadays, very few people would not use contraceptives."

In Thailand and across most of the developing world, a quiet revolution is taking place that marks the beginning of the end of an era of unprecedented population growth. Using new technologies and innovative advertising campaigns, governments like Thailand and hundreds of private family planning organizations around the world have begun tapping into a sizable latent desire for small families. The result, a sharp increase in the use of contraceptives and a corresponding decrease in the size of the average family, has far surpassed the expectations of population experts. A dramatic success story, it is perhaps the single most significant development in post–World War II history.

An era of declining birthrates began during the 1960s and 1970s, when leaders of many less developed nations first grasped the implications of rapid population growth on economic development and living standards. Armed with two revolutionary new contraceptives, the birth control pill and the IUD, dozens of fledgling public and private family planning agencies sallied forth with an equally revolutionary message: that family size is a matter of choice, not fate. In response, fertility—that is, the average number of children per family—has dropped in developing nations from 6.1 to 3.7, halfway to "replacement" level or to the 2.1 children a couple needs to replace itself. With China factored out, fertility in less developed countries is 4.4. Fertility in the vast majority of industrialized nations has now dipped to below replacement level. The wider significance is that a new balance of low birth- and deathrates is in the process of replacing an earlier balance of high fertility and mortality, with huge long-term implications on population growth rates.

The revolution in contraceptive practice has reached into nearly every corner of the globe, slicing across continental lines and transcending religious and cultural barriers. Fertility declines have been sharpest in East Asia, where a combination of strong, voluntary family planning programs and rapid economic growth has lowered the average family size in South Korea, Taiwan, Singapore, and Thailand to near or below replacement level. China has matched that accomplishment largely through aggressive, sometimes coercive measures to limit family size. Significant fertility declines have also been posted in Latin America, where Cuba has led the way, as the Population Reference Bureau president Peter Donaldson notes, by taking the "sting from leftist charges that family planning was Western imperialism in disguise."[1]

Largely excluded from the trend toward lower fertility has been sub-Saharan Africa, where women still bear an average of more than six children and where, in most countries, fewer than 10 percent of married women are using modern contraceptives. Africa exemplifies the unforgiving catch-22 that operates in many poor countries, where a cultural preference for large families begets high fertility, which, in turn, contributes to deepening poverty. Family planning in Africa has been the victim of tribal conflicts, a history of colonial rule that has retarded the development of strong national leadership, and inadequate infrastructure that has foreshortened the reach of government services of all kinds, including family planning. "Getting Africa on the right track is *the* challenge for the 1990s and early twenty-first century," says Population Action International vice-president Shanti Conli.[2]

But even in Africa there are heartening exceptions. In Botswana and Zimbabwe, where national leaders have taken an active interest in limiting population growth, the use of contraceptives has increased significantly over the past fifteen years. Under different

social and cultural conditions, nations in North Africa have performed even better. In Morocco, for example, where mobile teams
of nurses and midwives bring contraceptives to every doorstep,
women now average 4.5 children, down from 6.9 in 1980.[3] Even
Kenya, once known for the world's highest birthrate, has experienced one of the more rapid fertility declines on record. Where
women were giving birth to an average of eight children in the
1970s, fertility is now down to 5.4 children, according to the 1993
Kenya Demographic and Health Survey. Contraceptive use, meanwhile, has jumped from 6 to 33 percent just since 1989.[4]

As Population Action International summarized in a 1990 report, such cases "debunk the myth that population growth is an
intractable problem against which world leaders are powerless or
that fertility declines must await major social and economic transitions in the third world."[5] The point has been strongly reinforced
by other national fertility surveys, which indicate surprisingly high
levels of unwanted fertility even in sub-Saharan Africa.

By 1990, nearly a hundred developing countries were providing
direct support for family planing and another fourteen were providing indirect support, according to the UN.[6] These countries
contain 95 percent of the population of the developing world,
where 95 percent of all future population growth will occur. Only
six countries, including Iraq and Saudi Arabia, are still dedicated to
pronatalist policies that keep birthrates high and contraceptive use
low. But these six are merely exceptions to a trend that, as the Population Institute's Werner Fornos suggests, has achieved a kind of
critical mass worldwide.

"The transformation of perceptions about family planning . . .
is all but complete," says Fornos. "Experience, circumstances, and
time have established a developing world consensus that population must be brought into balance with resources and the environment. The consensus marks perhaps the first major milestone in
the struggle toward population stabilization."[7]

India was the first developing country to embrace an official policy to slow population growth by promoting family planning. That was in 1951. By the mid-1960s Pakistan, Korea, China, Fiji, Egypt, Singapore, Sri Lanka, and Turkey had followed suit.[8] At that time the use rate of contraceptives in the developing world (mostly "traditional" methods) hovered around 10 percent, as compared with use rates in the industrialized world (mostly modern methods) of 70 percent. Fertility averaged over six children per couple, as compared with 2.7 in the industrialized world. In the years since, developing nations have closed the gap with remarkable speed. It took the United States fifty-eight years (from 1842 until 1900) to lower average family size from 6.0 to 3.5 children. It took Sri Lanka and Indonesia only twenty-seven years, Colombia and South Korea only twelve, and China a mere seven. In the race from high to replacement fertility, Bangladesh has made it 40 percent of the way in twenty years, India halfway, Indonesia 60 percent of the way, and China virtually all the way.[9]

Other factors besides family planning account for such rapid declines. Modernization and industrialization have contributed to later marriages, for example, as have improvements in educational and employment opportunities for women. Declines in infant mortality may have contributed indirectly to declining fertility, though evidence on the matter is inconclusive. But the most important factor in most countries is the one that was not present to speed the transition to low fertility in Europe and North America: the availability of family planning services and advanced contraceptives.[10] Starting in the 1960s, the pill and IUD, and later new methods of female sterilization and improved early abortion procedures, all helped make fertility control simpler, safer, less expensive, and more accessible. New, long-acting implants and injectables show promise of having as much impact during the 1990s and beyond.

Among the large global community of population experts, satisfaction is tempered by the recognition that the quality of family planning services is still poor in many countries. Scarce resources have often translated into inadequate counseling services and limited choices of modern contraceptives—1.9 methods on average across the developing world, well below what is needed to meet the contraceptive needs of women through their reproductive years.[11] Some programs, meanwhile, have been marred by abuses, occasionally as a result of government policy, as in the case of India's forced sterilization policy during the late 1970s, but more often as a result of overzealous implementation by local officials. Satisfaction is also tempered by the fact that, for now, lower fertility translates only into lower rates of growth, not an actual stabilization of world population, which is not expected for another century or more. Indeed, several decades of the fastest growth in human numbers lie ahead.

"Things aren't as bad as they would have been, but they're still getting worse," says Philander Claxton, a former State Department adviser who was the first special assistant to the secretary of state on population issues.[12]

But while the quality of services is still uneven, the World Health Organization says fully 60 percent of people in developing countries now have "easy" access to at least one modern method of contraception, the measure of ease being investments of less than one percent of annual wages and less than two hours of time to obtain contraceptive services.[13] Where family planning programs exist, there is evidence to show that they have made a significant and direct contribution to improving child and maternal health, protecting the environment, preserving finite natural resources, and enhancing economic opportunities for users.[14] Moreover, as the Rockefeller Foundation's Steven Sinding notes, the contraceptive revolution has been "as impressive as agriculture's green revolution and perhaps equally important in averting widespread famine in many developing countries."[15]

Research conducted by the Population Council's John Bongaarts indicates that public and private sector family planning programs have been responsible for fully half of the fertility decline that took place between the mid-1960s and the late 1980s. It is a remarkable achievement given the relatively low cost: Family planning programs usually account for no more than one percent of national budgets in developing countries and only one percent of overseas development assistance worldwide. In 1991 Bongaarts estimated that the population of the world was 412 million less than it would have been without the organized family planning programs that were launched three decades ago. Looking to the future, the implications appear even more dramatic. Without the reduction in fertility rates produced by family planning programs since the 1960s, the world a century from now would contain 4.6 billion people more, an additional number equal to the world population in the early 1980s. Twenty-two million births have been averted in China alone.[16]

Perhaps the best way to understand the contraceptive revolution globally is to examine the factors that produced it locally. One of the best examples of a family planning success story is Thailand, where the transition from high to stable population growth has been attained in just over two decades.

A number of auspicious factors have played a role in Thailand's success. Distributing contraceptives to remote rural areas has been relatively easy in Thailand because it is a flat country with a good road system, much of it constructed by the United States during the Vietnam war. Communicating the family planning message has been relatively easy because nearly everyone in Thailand speaks the same language and adheres to the same religious faith, Buddhism.[17] Buddhism itself has abetted the fertility transition. Although Buddhist injunctions against taking life have contributed to continuing legal restrictions on abortion in Thailand, its emphasis on individual responsibility and the autonomy of women has opened the door to the widespread practice of family planning.

"Thailand is an amazingly adaptable society," says John Knodel, a leading expert on Thailand who conducts research at Chulalongkorn University in Bangkok and teaches at the University of Michigan. "There are no hangups on sexuality, no bans on contraception, and very few barriers to changing behavior. If family planning is going to succeed anywhere it's going to succeed here."[18]

Thailand's reproductive revolution has resulted from the nearly identical reasoning process that, in the years following World War II, led the Thai government and vast numbers of individual Thais to similar conclusions about the desirability of smaller families. For its part, the government concluded that lowering the population growth rate would enhance the prosperity of the nation. For their part, individual Thais concluded that having fewer children would enhance the prosperity of the family. The government's reasoning prompted it to begin providing contraceptive services. The reasoning of millions of Thai couples prompted them to accept such services with alacrity. When supply and demand came together, starting in the mid-1970s, fertility in Thailand plummeted.[19]

Like many countries touched by World War II, Thailand emerged from the conflict worried about its population losses. Convinced that a large population was necessary for trade and development, government leaders began urging women to have more children and even held contests to reward fecundity. As recently as 1956 the government was offering bonuses for large families.[20]

The first of two turning points that put Thailand on the road to lower birthrates occurred in 1957, when a World Bank study warned that high population growth would produce high unemployment. The second turning point came when the results of a 1960 census were published. Government leaders were shocked to discover that the country's population was 3 million more than they had estimated. The figures were a measure of the explosive postwar population growth that has tripled Thailand's population between 1950 and 1988, from 19 million to 56 million.[21]

The government's first response to the problem, embodied in Thailand's first five-year economic plan in 1961, was to attempt to raise living standards by investing more in the infrastructure needed to expand the country's agricultural and service sectors. In addition to job creation, the plan envisioned improving the quality of the labor force through education and training programs. The objective of the policy, as one UN study of Thailand notes, was to create new jobs without taking measures to reduce the number of people who would eventually be seeking them. In short, development was seen as the solution to the population problem.[22]

By the time of the third five-year plan in 1971, the premises were reversed, as rapid population growth continued to skew the country's age structure, swell the ranks of the younger, working-age population, and produce high unemployment and underemployment. Recognizing belatedly that development alone would not be enough to prop up per capita incomes, the government began factoring into its plans the projected consequences of future population growth. Policies were recommended to slow population growth to levels that made desired development goals attainable. Since 1971 development plans have included specific population targets.

By tending to economic growth and family planning simultaneously, Thailand has enjoyed the fruits of both. The country's gross national product tripled between 1966 and 1986. Despite the existence of pockets of relatively high fertility, contraceptive prevalence overall jumped between 1970 and 1987 from 15 to 67 percent of couples, while the average number of children per family fell from 6.1 to just over two. Virtually 100 percent of Thai women now know of at least one modern method of contraception.[23]

"The family planning situation in Thailand is solved," concludes John Baker, an American who works at the Population and Community Development Association in Bangkok. "It's like teaching people to tie their shoes. Once they learn, they know how to do it forever. The Thai people are now practicing family planning in very high numbers."[24]

For individual Thais, the reasoning process that led to acceptance of family planning was a roughly similar shift in the cost-benefit assessment of having large families.

Half a mile upstream from Mariam and Sam Ruang are two houses owned by their most important neighbor, Durian, known to the community as Uncle Rian. His comparative wealth, accrued from rice harvested on the two dozen acres of land he owns across the canal, have earned him the title of village "headman." Less formally he is known as "Mr. Flashlight" because of his nightly trips along the dark path that connects the houses where his two wives reside. He speaks as a man who recognizes change when he sees it.

"It costs so much more money to have children today," he responds when asked why the younger couples in the neighborhood like Mariam and Sam Ruang are having smaller families. Like most of the villagers, he singles out the growing expense of education in a country where the cost of school supplies can seem as daunting as college tuition does to a middle-class American.

"Every day you have to spend something on education. You have to buy books and pencils and uniforms. In my time a lot of people shared from one book. It would be handed down from one sibling to the next. By the last sibling it would be in shreds. Now you can't do that. Before, you had one book for several grades. Now you have one book for every grade. Before, the curriculum was always the same. Now it changes all the time."

Sung is Uncle Rian's next-door neighbor and a frequent visitor. She is an animated sixty-five-year-old who makes no secret of her displeasure that Thailand's contraceptive revolution came too late to spare her seventy-two months of pregnancy. "In the past you could go to the market with a few Baht and get many things," she says. "Today you can go with many Baht and get only a few things.

The problem is that the young want more. They want to buy different things."

"Before, we used herbal medicine," Sung continues. "Now everyone has to go to the hospital. Before, we had babies at home. Now everybody has to have a baby at the hospital. Before, if a neighbor had a TV set, we went to their house to watch. Now everyone thinks: You have it, now I have to have it. They see things on TV and want them. We didn't splurge then like you do now."

As well as any trained economist could, Uncle Rian and Sung convey the essence of the economic and social changes that have come with modernization and that have transformed attitudes toward childbearing around much of the developing world.

That millions of Thais suddenly want smaller families is explained by two sweeping and simultaneous developments. One is the spread of the cash economy as the market has penetrated into rural Thailand. The result has been the "monetization" of daily life.[25] Villagers like Miriam and Sam Ruang have come to rely more on durable goods and specialized food items produced outside the home and advertised on the radios found in almost every rural hut. As John Knodel notes, most Thais are probably healthier, better fed, better educated, and better clothed now than ever before. But dependence on the market has created a sense, reflected in the observations of people like Uncle Rian and Sung, that, financially at least, life is more precarious and children more burdensome.[26]

The other development is the extent to which population growth has shrunk per capita holdings of farmland in rural Thailand. With diminishing land for succeeding generations to inherit, parents have begun preparing their children for the salaried jobs in factories and cities that will provide higher incomes—enough higher that children will be able to support their parents in their old age. And that has meant education—where possible all the way through secondary school.

Under traditional agricultural systems, the net flow of resources was from children to parents, who profited from their labor in the fields. Now, with education a necessity, education costs high, and children unable to perform farmwork and household chores because of time spent in school, the flow has been reversed. It has become a net expense to raise a child where there was once a net profit to be made. The whole calculus of childbearing for millions of individual Thais has thus been completely transformed.[27] As Knodel and two co-authors of a definitive study, *Thailand's Reproductive Revolution*, summarize: "Increased costs have resulted in an almost universal perception among Thai couples that large families are not affordable under present social and economic conditions. To adjust to these conditions, Thai couples have turned en masse to the limitation of family size through deliberate means of birth control."[28]

The inverse relationship between living costs and childbearing is found throughout the developing world. Another example is Kenya, where an austerity program imposed by outside donors has led to the elimination of government subsidies for education. Faced with the need to shoulder the costs of education alone, many parents have responded by embracing family planning and having fewer children.

Peter Donaldson summarizes the reasons for the relatively sudden desire for smaller families: "There's a different sense now of what constitutes a proper family. People have a new understanding of what they are, who their children are supposed to be, and that their families ought to have the 'good life.' There's an image that a child should finish secondary school, that he should be able to leave the village and farm and find a factory job. And there's a conviction that this is not going to disadvantage me; a sense that a well-educated son and daughter-in-law will offer the most help when I am old."[29]

The case of Thailand illustrates the short explanation for why family planning programs have been so successful in many countries:

Researchers have found sizable amounts of "latent demand" for family planning services even in remote rural areas. The extent of latent demand was demonstrated, in one of literally hundreds of such examples found around the developing world, at a hospital in Bangkok that began providing IUD services in the mid-1960s. After hearing about it from friends, thousands of women from all over Thailand made the long trip to the city to get fitted, even though the hospital made no promotional effort whatever.[30]

The same phenomenon was encountered by one U.S. diplomat who, as a young Peace Corps volunteer during the 1960s, served in an isolated region of Thailand near the Laotian border. "As soon as the women in the village found out where I was from they said, 'You're an American. How can we stop having more children? Our husbands want to have five kids and we want to have two and we're tired of it. Tell us what to do.' "[31]

"I was twenty-four at the time," the diplomat says with a laugh. "Unfortunately, this is something they didn't teach me about."

Peter Donaldson explains the huge response that is usually evoked when people show up in rural villages who *do* know how to provide family planning services: "Take the poorest village. Routine every day grinding poverty. Life on the margin. Show up with a nurse with a pressed white uniform and a full range of family planning methods and she says, Sister, here's an opportunity. You don't have to be pregnant. How would you like not to get pregnant again until your baby is three? Common sense tells you that you're going to get a lot of women to go along."[32]

Thus, before family planning programs were even begun, large numbers of people in countries like Thailand had already become aware of the incompatibility of large families and aspirations for a better life.[33] That awareness meant that family planning programs could make considerable gains just by tapping into the demand that already existed, even among the poorest rural women.

The longer explanation for why family planning programs have been successful has to do with the various strategies they have employed to turn such latent demand into active demand—that is, how family planning programs have helped translate new attitudes about family size into the concrete behavior reflected in the dramatic worldwide increase in contraceptive use.

Most of the world's hundred-odd family planning programs were launched from the top, as in Thailand, where services have since been decentralized. In a number of countries the critical impetus has come from the bottom, often from physicians who have been forced to deal with the health effects to mothers and children of pregnancies spaced too closely. Colombia is an example of a country where the government first articulated a population policy, then left the task of organizing a nationwide network of family planning programs to the private sector.

However they are organized, family planning programs have found that there are several preconditions to successfully capitalizing on the conclusion that "fewer is better." Perhaps the most important common denominator has been the element of strong national support. As the Population Council's John Bongaarts encapsulates the point: "The main element of success is commitment from the top. Leaders have to be on TV saying repeatedly that overpopulation is bad for us."[34]

In Thailand such commitment was cemented when concern that high population growth rates would mortgage the country's future broadened, spreading from key health ministry officials and an influential group of U.S.-trained demographers, to the cabinet, and eventually to Thailand's powerful military, which is also an important force in the country's economy. The support for family planning that resulted has been so strong that it has survived frequent changes of government and guaranteed the uninterrupted financial and administrative backing needed to ensure a successful program.[35]

The point is illustrated in other countries where national leaders have not only been highly visible supporters of family planning themselves but have elevated family planning administrators to senior government status or appointed prominent personalities to positions of authority in family planning programs. In Zimbabwe, for example, President Robert Mugabe briefly placed his sister-in-law in charge of a program that is now recognized as one of Africa's best. Bangladesh, a surprise success story, has been helped by consistent bipartisan political support.

National leadership is most important in countries where the authority of the central government effectively extends down through the political hierarchy to the local level. In Kenya, for example, President Daniel Arap Moi not only legitimized the country's family planning program but also prodded district officials to give the strong support to government and private family planning agencies operating at the grass-roots level.[36] Such trickle-down support, translated into pressure to meet ambitious goals for contraceptive acceptance, has also energized Indonesia's family planning program. Conversely, the failure of national government leaders to work with community leaders has weakened programs in countries such as India.[37]

On the other hand, the extreme case of China, which has 22 percent of the world's population, demonstrates the hazards of overzealous national leadership. As late as 1974, the Beijing government, adhering to Karl Marx's notion that socialism could accommodate high fertility, pronounced population growth a "very good thing."[38] Within four years, however, government leaders reversed themselves. Responding to successive postwar baby booms and fears of massive starvation, they threw their weight behind family planning efforts begun in the 1960s, set rigid demographic targets, and in 1979 launched a campaign to limit Chinese couples to one child each.

The program has succeeded in changing attitudes toward family size and raising contraceptive prevalence to Western levels of 70-plus percent. A significant fertility decline has also been recorded, most of it attained before the enactment of the one-child policy. But success has come at the high price of human rights. In urban areas, at least, the one-child policy is effectively enforced, not merely encouraged. Critics allege that Chinese authorities forcibly insert IUDs, mandate periodic X-rays to ensure that they have not been removed, and impose sanctions on those who conceive "illegally."[39] Ironically, despite such measures, tens of millions of rural Chinese couples still do not have access to adequate family planning services, according to Population Action International. Because of the phenomenon of population momentum, or the growth that takes place because of the large proportion of people in their childbearing years, China is expected to grow by 25 percent during the next two decades.[40]

But strong national leadership is only one precondition to a successful family planning program. A quarter-century of experience around the world has pointed to others that, taken together, can have the effect of dramatically expanding the use of contraceptives and lowering fertility.

Miguel Trias, president of Profamilia, the highly successful IPPF affiliate in Colombia, defines six characteristics of successful programs. "Curiously enough," he says, "each quality starts with the letter *a*: availability (time-wise); accessibility (location-wise); acceptability (culture-wise); affordability (money-wise); agreeability (pleasure-wise); and appropriateness (health-wise)." In Thailand and other countries with successful programs, most of these requirements have been met through the provision of locally oriented family planning services that have been designed to reach people who are uneducated, immobile, and fearful or suspicious of using modern contraceptives.[41]

The idea of decentralizing family planning services was pioneered in Thailand by one of the movement's most innovative publicists, Mechai Viravaidya. As a young government bureaucrat traveling about rural Thailand during the 1960s, Mechai saw firsthand the retarding effect that families of six and seven children— the average in Thailand at the time—were having both on rural development and the environment. Convinced that the government's fledgling family planning program was not reaching rural Thais, he quit the government and launched a one-man crusade that helped convince the country's elites of both the need and the means to disseminate contraceptive services more effectively.[42]

The U.S. diplomat and former Peace Corp volunteer in Thailand compares Mechai to Hyman Rickover, the blunt-spoken American admiral whose single-minded determination led to the creation of the U.S. nuclear submarine program. "When he started out there wasn't a lot of support for family planning," says the official of Mechai. "But he had a goal. He didn't suffer fools lightly. He plowed straight ahead."[43]

As eventual founder of what is now known as the Population and Community Development Association, Mechai instituted a village-based distribution system that relied on nonphysicians to pass out pills and condoms, insert IUDs, and refer women to government clinics for sterilization. Mechai's worldwide fame grew from his talents as a publicist, discovered one day, as he described to the *Reader's Digest* fifteen years ago, when he held up a condom in front of 2,000 schoolteachers while lecturing on the importance of lowering Thailand's birthrate.

"Suddenly, I had an impulse to blow it up like a balloon," Mechai recalled. "It was like magic. One minute they were sitting there looking self-conscious and the next they were roaring with laughter. My helpers—mostly pretty girls—went around handing out samples, and I announced that people with dirty minds were not allowed to have any. Everybody took one."[44]

Condoms, known as "Mechais" to most Thais, have not played a major role in Thailand's contraceptive revolution. Mechai's own contribution to Thailand's success, meanwhile, has been overstated in dozens of flattering press accounts. As the source of over 80 percent of contraceptives, the Thai government is, by far, the major provider. "He gets more credit than anyone else because there's a gray bureaucracy and then there's this colorful charismatic character," says the U.S. diplomat.[45] But the idea of providing community-based services, which took root when local government health centers started making pills and other contraceptives available in the early 1970s, and which Mechai helped to publicize, is now axiomatic in family planning circles. The point behind it is that rural villagers are far more likely to use contraceptives if they can get them close to home and from people they know rather than from agents of a distant central government.

Persuaded that decentralizing services was the best approach, the Thai government in 1971 began expanding its distribution of oral contraceptives, from 350 doctor-operated government clinics to over 3,500 health stations, most supervised by nonphysicians, high school graduates with two years of training as auxiliary midwives.[46] Mobile teams were created to back up the village outreach system, providing sterilization and IUDs. Later, the delivery system was decentralized further, when the task of resupplying pills was turned over to village health volunteers. The result is that most Thais do not have to travel farther than 2.5 kilometers or longer than thirty minutes to obtain basic family services, parameters that researchers have discovered are essential to success. Big drop-offs in the use of contraceptives occur when women have to invest more time and traverse greater distances to get them.[47]

The open secret of Thailand's success is accounted for by yet other factors, common to other well-established family planning programs. One is providing a broad range of contraceptives. Contraceptive preference has varied over time in Thailand, as IUDs, the pill, and female sterilization have become available or accessible. The introduction of new methods, including the injectable contraceptive DMPA and the implant NORPLANT, has helped attract more women.[48] Choice of methods is important because women switch contraceptive methods frequently throughout their reproductive years, depending on whether they are trying to delay, space, or terminate pregnancies, or because they have adverse reactions to particular methods. First-time users switch most frequently.[49]

Most countries still average less than two methods at most service delivery points, short of the number needed to accommodate the method-switching that is essential to sustained use. One study in Indonesia compared those who obtained their preferred contraceptive method and those who did not. One quarter of the former but 85 percent of the latter had discontinued contraception eighteen months after initial use.[50] Adding one new method in an established family planning program increases the acceptance rate by as much as 12 percent and increases the chances of sustained contraceptive use. Those countries in which programs offer six or seven different methods have reached a much higher prevalence rate than those in which only three or four are offered, a UN study found.[51]

The reverse has been demonstrated in India, where nearly exclusive reliance on female sterilization has left the contraceptive prevalence rate stuck at 45 percent and at only 40 percent for modern contraceptives. A World Bank study shows that half of all women of childbearing age in India are not aware of even the simplest alternatives to sterilization, like birth control pills. Nor are regular outlets available for condoms and pills. Nor are all government family planning workers trained to insert IUDs. Of the 45 percent of married women using contraceptives, only 5 percent are using condoms, only two percent are using IUDs, and only one percent are using pills, according to the Bank.[52]

"The emphasis on sterilization has meant that a larger fraction of the program's potential audience—younger couples who might be interested in spacing—are more or less ignored," the Bank concludes. "India has demonstrated that it is possible to rely on sterilization to bring TFR [total fertility rate] down from six to four, but its target replacement level of 2.1 will not be possible without placing much more reliance on temporary methods."[53]

Ironically, just as many family planning users are gravitating toward the use of more effective, long-term contraceptives like implants and injectables, the need for condoms has been given new urgency by the AIDS epidemic and the spread of other sexually transmitted diseases. The irony is epitomized by Rwanda, which relies heavily on the injectable contraceptive Depo Provera even as AIDS cases mount rapidly. Thus condom use is low even as needle use is up, despite the need for protection against AIDS. The result is a marginal increase in the risk of infection.

Besides having a choice of methods, having a choice of sources is also an important way of boosting contraceptive prevalence. In Thailand, government family planning services have been sufficiently strong that 80 percent of women get their contraceptives from government sources. Despite such heavy reliance on government outlets in Thailand, studies show that in areas of the country with four or more different sources of family planning services—for example, local health centers, district hospitals, and private commercial outlets—there are significantly higher levels of use than in areas with only one source. Contraceptive use sometimes increases when family planning methods are provided side by side with the delivery of basic maternal and child health services, as in Malaysia. But in Tunisia and South Korea, among other countries, integrating contraceptive and health services has had the opposite effect.[54]

Family planning in Thailand has also prospered because the government has harnessed the broadcast media to make the case for having smaller families and to promote the use of contraceptives. The government's big media blitz began in the 1970s, by which time radio had permeated the countryside, reaching villagers like Mariam and Sam Ruang. What they heard, typically, were music and entertainment shows interspersed with family planning messages. Because radio is controlled by the state, the approach was not only effective but free to the government family planning program. By the 1980s, women in Thailand were reporting that radio was their main source of information on family planning.[55]

The use of media outlets in other countries confirms that radio and television can have a significant impact on reshaping values and creating demand for contraceptives. In Turkey, for example, awareness of family planning increased from 69 to 86 percent and contraceptive use rose from 39 to 42 percent as the result of one three-month mass media campaign.[56] In Kenya, researchers found that exposure to family planning messages broadcast on the mass media helped to create a desire for smaller families. A study in Ghana found that women with more exposure to media advertisements were much more likely to be using family planning.[57] Even the number of vasectomies has been increased by media ads. After one campaign that used TV, radio, and various print media in 1986, vasectomy prevalence in Sao Paulo, though still not widespread, soared to 12 times the rate in Rio de Janeiro, Brazil's second-largest city.[58]

One other key to the success of family planning programs is sensitivity to the needs of clients, like the one who told a researcher in Honduras: "There should be more understanding for us humble people, because we go [to family planning clinics] with fear."[59] Many family planning agencies have not done so well in this respect, as researchers in Nepal discovered when they recruited local residents to visit clinics around the country to request information and advice on the use of contraceptives. Much of the information they were given was inaccurate and incomplete, dispensed with condescension or worse, and biased in favor of educated middle-class clients. Extrapolating from the experience of these "simulated" clients, the researchers concluded that many clients are apt to leave a family planning clinic without sufficient information to make an appropriate decision on the best contraceptive to use, without an understanding of how to use the method they adopt, and unlikely to return for followup help.[60]

Sensitive to such shortcomings, family planning agencies in many developing nations have taken steps to make services more accessible. Some Muslim countries, for example, have learned that women living in seclusion cannot travel to a clinic. So they have perfected the technique of doorstep delivery, using women instead of men to provide the needed counseling. In societies where women are not secluded, services have been provided along routes regularly traveled by the women.[61] Sensitivity also means respecting the privacy of women by providing counseling and examinations in separate rooms and having the patience to talk through the fears and concerns many women have about using modern contraceptives. In addition, it means followup services and better training so that providers can help clients tailor contraceptive use to specific needs. "In areas where people are hesitant to practice contraception, the key to success is the warm and supportive attitude of the family planning workers more than the type of contraception delivered," writes Australian National University demographer John Caldwell.[62]

Sensitivity also extends to the realm of culture. In Africa, where large families have been a tradition, successful programs like Zimbabwe's have emphasized the need to space children to protect the health of the mother rather than limit family size. Latin American programs have made the same distinction to sidestep religious sensitivities.

One example of accommodating cultural sensitivities can be found in the Katibougou district of the West African country of Mali, where a strong pronatalist tradition reinforced by fixed sexual roles has kept birthrates high. At less than 5 percent, the country's contraceptive prevalance rate is one of the lowest in the world, and at 6.7 children per family its total fertility rate is one of the highest; desired family size, 7.1 children, is even higher.

In Katibougou, as elsewhere in Mali, workers in the government-run health care center had been offering family planning services for years but with virtually no takers. So in 1986, with advice from a private American family planning and development agency, they adopted a new approach. First they changed the rationale for family planning, emphasizing its contribution to the health and survival of children. In a region where infant mortality is high, the argument struck a responsive chord. Then they transformed the way family planning services were offered by launching a community-based delivery system and integrating basic health services into the program. Finally, they decentralized the management of the program so that more district residents would have a role to play. Assistant midwives and matrons were designated to deliver family planning services. Dozens of other people were given basic literacy and numeracy training and enlisted to record client data. Outreach workers were given bikes to increase mobility and to follow up with clients to make sure they were continuing to use contraceptives without harmful side effects.[63]

Project workers then targeted one other problem, chipping away at the resistance of men by explaining the economic benefits of family planning: fewer children, healthier children, and wives more able to make an economic contribution to the household. Men were eventually recruited for village health teams and given responsibility for delivering condoms and promoting family planning to other men. As one summarized the benefits: "Family planning has reduced the need for purchasing medicines; it has improved our income; there is less sickness and our village is cleaner. We have fewer worries."[64]

By 1992, 57.7 percent of married women of reproductive age in the project area told interviewers that they were using contraceptives, proving the point that if programs are well managed, cultural taboos can be surmounted.

"The project demonstrates that the demand for modern family planning methods can be generated in cultures with traditional fertility patterns if these methods are accessible, if they respond to the traditional values of child spacing, and if they appeal to the universal concern for improved maternal and child health," says Peggy Curlin, president of the Centre for Development and Population Activities (CEDPA) in Washington, which sponsored the project.[65]

Overall, the cost of providing family planning services is surprisingly low, especially if administered as part of an existing health care system. According to UNFPA figures, the average annual per user cost of family planning programs in the developing world currently ranges between ten and twenty-five dollars, though expanding method mix will increase future costs.[66] In India, where the program relies heavily on surgical sterilization, the amortized per capita cost is a mere four dollars. An expanding body of data suggests that this modest investment can pay big dividends.

A 1988 study in Mexico, for example, found that every peso spent by the Mexican Social Security System on family planning services in urban areas between 1972 and 1984 saved nine pesos in reduced maternal and child costs. The reason: fewer unwanted pregnancies and thus fewer incomplete abortions.[67] A similar study conducted in the United States by the Alan Guttmacher Institute showed that for every dollar of federal funds spent to provide contraceptives to women of all ages, $4.40 was saved that would otherwise have been needed for medical care, welfare, and nutritional programs.[68] Other U.S. researchers have projected that the $412 million the United States spent on family planning services in fiscal year 1987 saved over $1 billion in domestic services.[69]

Similar benefits have been realized in the private sector. Since the early 1960s, every one rupee spent on family planning services by India's largest industrial conglomerate, Tata Iron and Steel, for its 73,000 employees has saved 2.39 rupees in reduced maternity leave, maternity-related health care costs, and education and health care costs for dependents. Company officials also report indirect benefits including improved productivity and reduced absenteeism.[70]

On a macro-economic level, the UNFPA reports that of eighty-two developing countries it studied, the forty-one with slower population growth managed to increase incomes by an average of 2.25 percent per year. In the forty-one with faster population growth, incomes per person fell by an average of 1.25 percent per

year.[71] The UNFPA's conclusions are corroborated by a World
Bank study of thirty-seven countries that demonstrates a correlation between low fertility and high GNP.[72] One UNFPA official
acknowledges that other factors besides low fertility contribute to
strong economic performance. But, he says, "the coincidence between higher economic growth and lower population growth is no
coincidence."[73]

In a downtown Washington office building, computer-
generated images projected onto a slide screen convey compel-
lingly the meaning of such statistics.

"Take the case of Guatemala," says Charles Pill, a senior
research associate at the Futures Group, which for fifteen years
and with the financial backing of U.S. AID has been projecting alternative futures for developing countries based on high and low
population growth projections.[74]

"Right now, there are 1.3 million primary-school–age kids in
Guatemala. About 60 percent of them are actually in school," says
Pill. "But look what happens depending on population growth."

He punches an instruction into his computer and a green line,
starting at the 1.3 million mark, begins to wind a slow path up the
graph. It stops at 1.8 million, the number of primary-school–age
children Guatemala will have to educate in the year 2030 under
the low population growth projection. He commands the computer again and this time a red line turns upward sharply, resting
at the 5 million mark. That's the number of primary-school–age
children Guatemala will have to educate in 2030 if its current population growth rate is not reduced.

He then calls up the budget estimates, which are based on constant 1986 queizales, the Guatemalan currency. Rows of figures
cross-referenced in five-year increments suddenly fill the screen,
driving home the point.

"Under the low population growth projection, Guatemala
could educate virtually 100 percent of its primary-school–age population for about 233 million queizales," says Pill. "It would cost

nearly twice that much to educate only 60 percent of the primary-school–age population under the high growth projection. In short, the budget impact is significant for a small, poor nation like Guatemala."

Similar presentations have been made to presidents and cabinet ministers all over the world, projecting the effects of population growth on economic performance, health care, education, the urban environment, and natural resources. The effect is invariably the same, galvanizing governments to take a more active interest in family planning.

"It has a powerful impact," says Thomas Goliber, who heads the Futures Group Rapid IV Project and who has watched the reactions of government leaders in dozens of countries since the project was started fifteen years ago. "The presentation tells them that lowering population growth is central to economic development; that if you want better health, education, food, and living conditions you have to take population into account. And that the way to get fertility down is through family planning."[75]

"You can't wait for development to bring fertility down over the long run," Goliber adds. "It takes too long, and high birthrates themselves inhibit development. Besides, the record shows that vigorous family planning programs can have a strong, independent impact on fertility."

The point is corroborated by comparing Pakistan, which has one of the world's weakest family planning programs, with South Korea, which has one of the world's strongest. A World Bank report shows that if Pakistan's school-age population were the same size as Korea's relative to its total population, Pakistan would save enough money to decrease its education budget by 40 percent. The savings could be used to enroll more children or to improve the quality of education for the children already enrolled.[76] Comparing enrollment rates and rates of economic growth, the Bank concludes that if, in 1960, Pakistan had had a primary-school enrollment rate as low as Indonesia's, to choose another example, its per capita income would now be as much as 25 percent higher—a surplus that would have contributed to Pakistan's economic growth and development. Conversely, if the share of the school-age population in 1988 had been as large in Korea as in Kenya, to choose a third example, Korea would have had to spend 5.6 percent of its GNP on basic education instead of the 2.8 percent it actually spent.[77]

"This suggests that low fertility rates saved Korea 2.8 percent of GNP [or nearly $8 billion]," says the World Bank report.[78]

"A lot of governments are now in favor of family planning because they're looking at the issue from the standpoint of the obligations a country will acquire in the future by having high fertility: more schools, roads, hospitals, general services, and housing," says Martin Vaessen, who has directed national surveys of reproductive behavior in developing countries for the Columbia, Maryland, firm of Macro International.[79]

"People are slow to think through the implications of population growth until it translates into something they can understand, like traffic congestion or unemployment," concurs the former chief of U.S. AID's population program, Duff Gillespie. "Even if birthrates decline it will be necessary to generate millions more jobs, more schoolrooms, more acres of agriculture. This isn't rocket science, but it's something people are finally beginning to think about."[80]

Meanwhile, back in Thailand, researchers have assessed the benefits of effective family planning programs in far more personal ways, demonstrating the contribution family planning programs have made to national development goals by measuring their effect on the prosperity of individual families. The results have challenged what was long the conventional wisdom in the developing world: that bigger families are needed to ensure economic well-being.

One study concluded that reduced family size has a significant, positive effect on a couple's ability to accumulate wealth. Comparing couples who started in similar economic circumstances at the beginning of childbearing years, those who ended up having fewer children did better economically than those who had large families. After controlling for other factors that contribute to family wealth, the research found that small families had more consumer goods. Twice as many small families owned refrigerators as large families, for example. They also owned more television sets and stoves. The comparative economic well-being derived from having smaller families was also reflected in better housing, a greater accumulation of savings, and the mobility needed to secure better jobs.[81]

Smaller family size has another economic benefit: With fewer responsibilities at home, women are freer to participate in more lucrative nonfarm, modern-sector employment away from the home. Ninety-five percent of mothers in the smaller families told researchers that they would have worked less if they had borne four or five children. Ninety percent of women with large families said they would have been able to work more with a family of only two children.[82] Using the same comparison between families with one or two children and those with four or more children, researchers found that family size also affected educational attainment: Children from small families are more likely to continue their study beyond the compulsory primary level than are children from large families.[83]

What benefits individual families has also benefited Thailand as a whole. During the 1960s, before the country's family planning program was launched, fewer than 20 percent of children continued into lower secondary school and only 12 percent to upper secondary school. Partly as a result of declining fertility, about 50 percent now continue on to lower secondary school and at least 27 percent to upper secondary school. Reducing family size has thus more than doubled the number of Thai children continuing into secondary schools, reinforcing the economic development that, in turn, is hastening fertility decline in Thailand.[84]

Measured against all reasonable expectations, the achievements of the international family planning movement have been extraordinary. But progress has varied dramatically, as various demographic surveys clearly indicate.

According to research reported by the Population Council's W. Parker Mauldin and John Ross, over forty countries were just beginning the transition to lower fertility by 1988, most of them in Africa. In nearly all, economic growth is stagnant and GNP is low. Fertility rates are high, averaging nearly 6.5 children, while contraceptive prevalence averages less than 8 percent. As for mortality, which indirectly influences fertility, rates among infants and mothers are extremely high, while life expectancy is extremely low.[85]

At the other end of the scale are a handful of countries like Singapore and Taiwan that are suddenly worried that they may have carried a good idea too far. Here, government leaders are concerned that a "birth dearth" resulting from declining fertility could lead to labor shortages that could slow the region's meteoric economic growth. Singapore, for one, has responded by selectively reversing its family planning policy and providing various incentives to help its well-educated Chinese keep pace with its more prolific ethnic Muslims. Parents of large families now get priority housing and school registration and subsidized child care services. Substantial tax rebates kick in after the birth of the third and fourth children. "Life will be lonely without a family. Don't leave it [until] too late," admonishes one government-sponsored advertisement, which has been largely ignored in a country where couples are now accustomed to the advantages of having smaller families.[86]

More typical is Thailand, where a rapid drop in fertility to near replacement level has triggered an instructive debate over whether the country is about to become the victim of its own success. One group of Thai academics now warns that declining fertility will nudge the population bubble up the age scale, threatening eventual labor shortages. Between three and four hundred thousand illegal immigrants, mostly Burmese and Laotians, have already taken over menial jobs that better-educated Thais now shun, and even some technical jobs at the upper end of the scale have gone begging. Faced with such risks, these experts caution, Thailand should consider emulating Singapore by reversing its antinatalist policy or, at a minimum, finding some way to hold the country's population at zero-growth.[87]

Such warnings are rejected by a larger group of population specialists in Thailand, who point out that even with slower growth rates, the country's population will continue to climb, from 56 million in 1990 to an estimated 85 million by 2015, according to UN figures. When Thailand's population eventually does level off, they say, it is not likely to drop below replacement level fertility because the average desired family size in Thailand is still—and is likely to remain—just over two. In the end, they say, the problem of existing labor shortages has more to do with the country's sudden economic growth than with its equally sudden decline in fertility. Prosperity has shifted jobs away from agriculture toward the more sophisticated service sector, creating demands for skills that Thailand's education system has not been able to satisfy. The need is therefore not for more Thais but for better-educated Thais. "Thailand needs more skilled people who can write computer programs instead of more who can gut fish and tap rubber trees," says John Baker.[88]

John Knodel concurs. "The argument that you need more people doesn't hold water," he says. "The problem is not a function of demographics but of rapid development coupled with a lagging education system. We need engineers and skilled people. And lower fertility, not high fertility, will help the government and families provide them."[89]

The observation underlies a significant point that is often overlooked when discussing family planning success stories. Even in Thailand, which has set the standard for family planning performance among developing nations, population is still growing by 730,000 people per year. It is an increment of humanity that will add significantly to urban traffic snarls, arguably the world's worst already, and swell demands on the country's remaining forests, which are already under enormous pressure.

Between the family planning failures and success stories there is a third category of nations. Scattered mostly through Latin America and Asia, they have all made significant strides toward the goal of replacement fertility. But in most the pace of fertility decline has diminished since the early 1980s. In a few, including Indonesia and Tunisia, fertility actually stalled or plateaued for a time before resuming a gradual downward course.

One reason for the slowdown is that family planning programs have run out of the easiest targets: people who had a strong desire for contraceptive services to begin with, for example, or who lived near family planning clinics. As the programs have matured, it has been harder to sustain the kind of success they enjoyed early on. "They're at a point now where getting the last 20–25 percent will be harder," notes Ann Way, a senior analyst at Macro International, which conducts the demographic and health surveys (DHS). "It's like selling anything: Once you saturate the market, those who are less receptive are harder to reach."[90] The reverse is also true: A slowdown can also result if family planning agencies lack the contraceptive supplies they need to meet demand or the financial and managerial resources to provide family planning services effectively. The main culprits in this case can be religious opposition, civil conflict, government inefficiency, or, as the case of Brazil illustrates, a weak political commitment to family planning on the part of government leaders.

Whatever the reason for the slowdown, the question of how to speed up the process of fertility decline is a matter that has come to preoccupy demographers and family planning experts. Most of them share a solid conviction that what often appears to be a saturation of demand is nothing more than a failure to provide family planning services the right way. Give us the money, the political backing, and the range of contraceptives needed to provide the kind of family planning services people want and need, they say, and the result will be a resumption of increases in contraceptive use, with consequent declines in fertility. Among the most optimistic, who point to successful family planning experiments like the Matlab Project in Bangladesh, there is a firm belief that in some countries better services alone can close the gap to replacement fertility.

While most experts are less optimistic on this score, nearly all would agree that one major requirement for stabilizing the world's population will be to increase the proportion of couples using contraceptives to roughly 70 percent—which means increasing the actual number of users by nearly 300 million. Of that number there are an estimated 120 million women who have expressed a desire to delay pregnancy or to stop having children altogether but who are not using family planning services because of the lack of convenient, affordable access.[91]

If the immediate unmet need for family planning services could be satisfied, contraceptive prevalence in developing countries would rise to about 60 percent, a level that would lower average family size to just under three children per couple. But meeting the need will be a tall order. Only 60 percent of all women in the developing world even have access to family planning services. And even though the use of contraceptives in developing countries has soared since 1960, the total number of women not using any form of contraception—over 350 million—has declined only slightly because of the large increase in the numbers of women and men of reproductive age.[92] Projections to the year 2010, meanwhile, suggest that even with further rapid expansion of contraceptive use, the number of men and women not using contraceptives will continue to increase substantially. During the 1990s alone, 18 million couples of reproductive age will be added yearly to the world's population, not counting sexually active young people.[93]

Unless such demand is met, tens of millions of unwanted births will occur.

Meeting the demand for family planning services will require supplies: 44 billion condoms, 9 billion cycles of oral contraceptives, 150 million sterilizations, and 310 million IUDs or Norplant insertions, to be exact, according to the Population Resource Center.[94] It will also require money—and lots of it, since few couples can afford to pay the full cost of birth control methods and because the cost of new contraceptive implants and injectables is more than even national budgets can bear in many developing nations.

One obvious way for developing nations to get the money is for outside donors to give it to them. Right now foreign donors pick up less than a fourth of the almost $5 billion annual tab for family planning services, which amounts to about one percent of total overseas development assistance. Increasing the total to 4 percent of foreign aid, or about $5.5 billion per year by the end of the decade, would cover nearly half of the estimated $11 billion that will be required by then to meet the total projected demand for contraceptive services.[95] To attract that kind of added outside support, developing nations themselves will have to make family planning a higher budget priority, especially relative to military expenditures.

One other way to help pay the bill is for the governments of developing countries to transfer some of the cost of family planning services to the private sector, where perhaps 20 percent of couples now turn for contraceptives. A small percentage of upscale users around the world obtain contraceptives from the for-profit commercial sector. Even in poor countries, some upper middle-class women buy at regular commercial outlets because of the appeal of using the best imported products. Millions of other couples concentrated in about thirty countries purchase subsidized contraceptives that are offered at lower prices through so-called contraceptive social marketing programs, usually referred to by the acronym CSM. The objective of CSM programs is to sell contraceptives donated by countries like the United States and Canada and agencies like the UNFPA and the International Planned Parenthood Federation at below-market prices and to use the proceeds to recover as much of the cost of distribution as possible.[96]

CSM programs rely on extensive commercial advertising and thousands of private outlets, from kiosks and convenience stores in India, to hairdressers in the Dominican Republic who sell government-donated condoms for a small profit, to village peddlers in Africa who now include condoms with their normal offerings of beer and cigarettes. CSM programs, which are strong in countries like Colombia, Egypt, Pakistan, and India (which pioneered CSM in 1969), typically reach between 5 and 15 percent of reproductive-age couples, according to the World Bank. Apart from the cost benefits, putting contraceptives into the market stream has been a way of attracting users from both high and low social and economic groups who, for entirely different reasons, do not generally utilize public family planning clinics.

One of the largest social marketing programs is in Bangladesh, where sales of highly subsidized contraceptives through existing networks of wholesalers and retailers has greatly broadened access to reversible family planning methods, especially in urban areas. The program supplies more than 30 percent of all couples using reversible contraceptives. The U.S. firm of PSI, which advises the local social marketing project, has become the country's second-largest advertiser, behind the tobacco industry. Contraceptives are hawked through the print media and on billboards. The sails of thousands of small boats that ply the country's network of rivers and canals now bear condom ads. To reach the most remote areas, the company uses a fleet of seventeen vans equipped with movie projectors that carry a two-hour program combining entertainment with information on family planning and contraceptive use. After rural areas are primed with advance publicity, with the vans doubling as sound trucks, crowds of several thousand are frequently attracted. The mobile units reach between 5 and 10 million people annually and are one reason the country recently celebrated the sale of the one billionth Raja brand condom.[97]

In 1991, Bangladeshis paid the equivalent of a dollar or less for a year's supply of condoms or pills. But in three-fourths of developing countries, commercially available contraceptives still cost more than the one percent of annual income demographers say is the breakpoint for affordability. The price sensitivity of contraceptives was demonstrated recently in Bangladesh, when a two-third decrease in the price of birth control pills was followed by a several hundred percent increase in sales.[98]

The success of CSM in countries like Bangladesh is one way developing nations have sought to meet the large unmet need for contraceptive services. But bridging the gap to replacement fertility, the precondition to stabilizing the world's population, will also require another difficult step: increasing contraceptive prevalence among hard to reach constituencies. Some of the problems involved are illustrated in the case of Mexico, a nation that, despite its restrictive religious environment, has become one of Latin America's family planning success stories (see Chapter 6, "Go Forth and Multiply.")

Half a century ago, Mexico had a mere 20 million inhabitants. Its capital of 2 million, graced with smart shops and wide tree-lined boulevards, is remembered by one UN official who first visited in the mid-1960s as "the perfect city," which combined the beauty and accessibility of Paris and Buenos Aires.[99] Today, the 20 million people who jam Mexico City alone fight snarled traffic and breathe the world's most polluted air. Seemingly overnight, explosive growth has transformed Mexico from a demographic midget into a population giant. It is now the world's eleventh most populous nation.

A turning point for Mexico came in the early 1970s, when President Luis Echeverria-Alverez, once an apostle of the creed that "more is better,"[100] abandoned a pronatalist policy to keep "more" from overwhelming the bright future promised by major oil discoveries in the Mexican gulf.

"Our economic growth prospects were very promising," explains Manual Urbina, who heads Mexico's National Population Council, known as "Popcon." "We realized that population could dampen those prospects if we didn't set a limit."[101]

Determined to turn the tide, government leaders created Popcon, set a target of one percent population growth by the year 2000, and then harnessed government hospitals, clinics, and health centers to the task of achieving it. In 1975 Mexico became the second country in the world to enshrine family planning as a right in its constitution. In a remarkable turnabout, Mexico's contraceptive prevalence rate quadrupled from 13 to 58 percent by 1990, while the fertility rate, once one of the highest in the world at seven children per family in 1960, has plummeted to a much lower 3.8—a level that will still double Mexico's population in thirty years.

But as Mexico has recently discovered, covering the first half of the distance to replacement fertility has been the easy part, thanks to a large body of pentup demand for family planning services. The hard part lies ahead and will require supplementing a general strategy of blanketing Mexico with contraceptives by targeting specific constituencies that have remained largely untouched by Mexico's contraceptive revolution.

"People already wanted to change. We were successful because the demand was already waiting for us," says Urbina. "Now we have to create demand. We have big gaps in our coverage and we need a strategy oriented to the specific targets we need to reach."[102]

One target is adolescents, whose high level of sexual activity has increased the health risks associated with early pregnancy and retarded fertility reduction in many developing countries.

The statistics on adolescent sexual activity are striking. Between

one-fifth and one-half of all unmarried teenagers in developing
countries are sexually active, according to the Worldwatch Institute.[103] Of all fourteen-year-old girls alive today, 40 percent will be
pregnant by the time they are twenty.[104] In some Asian and African
countries, teenagers below eighteen account for half of all pregnancies, according to the UN.[105] Between those who are married
and those who are not, there are different problems to contend
with but one common denominator: Nearly all remain largely untouched by the global reach of family planning.

Of sexually active teenagers, most are married. According to the
UN, 30 percent of Latin American women, 40 percent of Asian
women, and half of African women are married by age eighteen.[106]
Though family planning services are theoretically available to
them, they are not even contemplated at such an early age.

As Sidney Ruth Schuler, who directs a woman's empowerment
program for a firm that deals with public health issues, explains:
"What can you expect of a thirteen-year-old? How can she think
of family planning? She's bewildered, forced into another home,
faced by a man ten years older. It's a traumatic experience. A new
bride is the least powerful person in the household. At thirteen or
fifteen she won't stand up for herself. By the time she is able to she
already has several children."[107]

For teenagers who are unmarried and sexually active, there are
other complications. Like their married sisters, they are often be-
nighted when it comes to understanding sex. "In Mexico people
start having sex very early and they don't have any information.
They think nothing happens the first time or that they need deep
intercourse to make a woman pregnant," explains Alfonso Lopez
Juárez, who heads Mexico's IPPF affiliate, Mexfam.[108]

Compounding ignorance has been the failure of family planning
agencies to factor the needs of unmarried adolescents into their
repertoire of services, leaving millions vulnerable to unintended
pregnancies or sexually transmitted diseases. The most extreme

cases of exclusion are the handful of countries like Nigeria, where unmarried teens are actually prohibited from patronizing government-run family planning clinics.[109] But for the most part, the problem is not legal but social. Adults are uncomfortable with the reality of adolescent sexuality and unsure how to deal with it. Many outside donors, meanwhile, are reluctant to press a political hot button by funding projects that teach teenagers how to use contraceptives. "In theory, there's no problem if adolescents are served in clinics that serve adults," says the CEDPA's Peggy Curlin. "In practice, the nurses think it's terrible to serve an unmarried girl."[110]

The implications of such reluctance extend beyond the teenage years. Because of the growing trends toward later marriages and earlier sexual activity, women are spending a growing percentage of their reproductive years outside of marriage. Even so, most family planning programs continue to focus their attention on couples.[111]

One program to deal with teenage pregnancy has been mounted by Mexfam, whose ten-hour sex education curriculum reaches some 300,000 Mexican students, workers, and even street gang members each year. Mexfam's Lopez explains the rationale behind the program: "Mexicans start their reproductive life at fifteen. They have a family at sixteen. These young people have children and their children are going to have children very young. That's the chain we need to break."[112]

In a low-slung, cinderblock middle school in Huixquilucan, one Mexfam sex educator, Marta Tapia, tries to break it by taking the case to a mixed group of teenagers. In a series of classes she talks about family relations, sexuality, and dating. Today she gets to the bottom line.

"Why do you think young people get pregnant?" she asks. She runs the class with a casual authority that comes from knowing how to reach rapt teenagers who are hungry for information about their most pressing concern.

"They don't take precautions," says one girl, tentatively, after a long silence.

"When a girl wants a guy so bad she gets pregnant to keep him," adds another, as if she knows the feeling.

"It's because of TV ads that arouse sexual interest," says a third.

"They think it only happens to the stupid ones," chimes in one of the boys to a chorus of laughter.

The students wear purple sweaters bearing an insignia that reads "Official Secondary School 32." They listen attentively as Marta talks. She tells a story, then shows a twenty-minute film that tells it again.

"A boy and girl skip school," she says. "They walk a long way, and then find a field where they're alone. They begin petting. They have sex. After a couple of weeks the girl begins to get worried. Three months later her stomach starts to grow. She doesn't have her period. So she talks to her boyfriend. She says, Remember the time we skipped school? I'm pregnant. He says congratulations. Who's the father? He denies he has anything to do with it. The guy leaves. She goes home. She has to tell her parents. Her father says, I'll kill this guy if he doesn't marry my daughter. So they get married. The baby is born. The marriage doesn't work and the boy leaves. The girl has a baby to take care of now so she has to stop studying. You have to have a job to support the baby. Later, the boy starts making time with a new girl and the pattern begins all over again. So who pays for the mistake? In the end it's the baby who pays the price."

Marta stops, waiting for reactions. The boy who drew laughs is more sober now. "They didn't do it for love. They were just curious," he says. "They didn't think anything would happen to them. Now they're in it together."

Half a world away, in Kenya, a project sponsored by a private U.S. organization has adopted a more holistic approach to dealing with adolescents that has now been emulated in several other countries. Concerned about the number of girls who were coming back pregnant from jobs in nearby cities, a group of women in the village of Kamuthunga came up with the idea of combining family planning with education and employment opportunities to rescue teenage girls from the risks of early pregnancy. They established a bakery that eventually employed several hundred village girls on a part-time basis while they finished school. Girls who were already in school were encouraged to stay in school, while those who had dropped out were provided with nonformal education. The program meanwhile offered basic health care and family planning services. Though there is no statistical proof, abundant anecdotal evidence suggests that the girls are using family planning services and practicing contraception more and changing their sexual behavior as a result of the program.[113]

"There's been a lot of emphasis on women twenty and over because of micro-enterprise development and the emphasis on women's economic roles. There has been a lot of emphasis on children and child survival. But the age group in the middle is a gray area that's been totally neglected," says Suzanne Kindervatter of the CEDPA, which sponsored the Kamuthunga project.[114]

"We've got good pilot programs for dealing with adolescent girls," adds the CEDPA's Peggy Curlin. "We're beginning to learn what works. The parents of the girls and the village elders are saying, Please come and help us. But there's just too much resistance on the part of too many governments."[115]

Another hard-to-reach constituency is men, what one prominent family planning advocate, Malcolm Potts, calls "the forgotten 50 percent of family planning."[116] Men have largely been neglected because, absent the development of a male counterpart to the birth control pill, female fertility is still easier to regulate. But new circumstances have drawn attention to the role of men in the global movement to lower birthrates. One is AIDS, which has led to the promotion of condoms around the world. Another is advances in women's rights in the developing world, which has prompted more discussion of family planning in the household. A third is the advent of the no-scalpel vasectomy, pioneered in China, which obviates the need for incisions and stitches and has thus made the procedure more acceptable to men.[117]

Substantial anecdotal evidence indicates that men have not always been cooperative partners when it comes to the matter of family planning. In some traditional societies, large families are taken as a measure of virility or as a symbol of a man's status in the community. Opposition to contraception is often reinforced by religious teachings and the fear that contraceptives will encourage wives to be unfaithful. Male resistance to contraception, where it exists, is also linked to the sensitive issue of authority within the household.[118]

But research suggests that in many or most countries, male attitudes are not a major barrier to family planning. In countries where they have been, like Mexico and Nigeria, there is evidence that resistance is diminishing.[119] Though many women in the developing world cite their husbands' opposition as the reason for not using birth control, a simple lack of communication may be part of the problem. Godwin Mzenge, the executive director of the Family Planning Association of Kenya, cites conflicting data gathered by the Demographic and Health Surveys. Ninety percent of men say they are not opposed to family planning. But over 50 percent of women who are not participating in family planning say they are not doing so because their husbands are opposed.[120] Fear that the use of contraceptives will provoke physical abuse is so strong in some regions that millions of women select methods that don't require the participation or knowledge of a male partner, like the pill or injectable hormones.[121]

"I can only conclude that the two are not talking," says Mzenge. "The wife assumes the husband is negative. The husband assumes that the wife is doing something about family planning. And nothing happens."[122]

"Men are almost as readily convinced as women by education programs that show the economic and health advantages of having smaller families," adds a U.S. AID development specialist. "Experts are now convinced that if people really make vasectomy or the condom available to men, then the men will come along and use them."[123]

In country after country, governments and private family planning organizations have begun doing just that, promoting male contraceptive methods and encouraging men to take a more active role in family planning. The effort has been constrained by the limited number and type of male contraceptives. The most successful advertising campaigns have targeted cultural stereotypes by associating contraception with virility. Advertisements run during recent World Cup competition in Mexico, for example, showed a condom dressed in a soccer uniform hoisting a trophy beneath the caption: "Protector: a unique contraceptive just for champions." In Ghana, the logo of an IPPF-sponsored "Daddy's Club" at one company is an illustration of two condoms spelling out the words "wear me." Another tactic has been adopted in Brazil, where magazine and TV ads billing vasectomy as "an act of love" have led to a substantial increase in male sterilizations performed in government family planning facilities.

Elsewhere, a media campaign in Zimbabwe has prompted hundreds of men to begin talking to their wives about family planning, while new laws in Nigeria and a few other less developed countries require paternal child support, a responsibility usually borne by the mother. "You can't get fertility decline unless both men and women have some disincentive to high fertility," says the Population Council's Judith Bruce. "Until men bear parallel costs, what incentive do they have to cut fertility?"[124]

In Mexico, meanwhile, the government has turned adversity to good account, communicating the message that because of the country's protracted economic crisis, more children mean less for everyone.[125] "Family planning agencies are conveying the message that it's less macho to have fifteen children with one pair of shoes between them than three children, each with shoes, clothes, and schoolbooks," notes a senior UN population official.[126]

Beyond meeting the unmet need for contraceptives and reaching hard to reach constituencies, bridging the gap to replacement fertility may require another, more controversial step: providing universal access to safe and inexpensive abortion services as a fallback in case of contraceptive failure. Safe abortion relates most directly to the issue of maternal health: Where abortion is unavailable, illegal, or prohibitively expensive, often unsafe abortions proliferate, leading to higher rates of maternal mortality. But the existence of legal (or at least widely available) and safe abortion services also has important demographic implications. Research compiled by the Population Council indicates that abortion has contributed to, without being indispensable to, fertility declines in every region. The proportion of averted births resulting from abortion (as opposed to contraception) is estimated at between one-fifth and one-fourth in East Asia and Latin America, lower in South and Southeast Asia, and indeterminate in Africa. The demographic effect of abortion has also been visible in Eastern Europe, where, following the legalization of abortion during the mid-1950s, fertility declines steepened, according to the Council.[127]

An estimated 25 to 50 million abortions are performed worldwide each year. Even if women use contraceptives reliably, it is likely that over 20 percent of them will face an unplanned pregnancy sometime during the course of their reproductive lives. Roughly a quarter of all pregnancies are deliberately terminated, according to Population Action International, meaning that 150,000 abortions are performed every day, more than a third of them illegally.[128] Abortion rates are highest among married women with children, though rates are growing among younger, ummarried women, including teenage girls. Ten countries with 40 percent of the world's population, including Canada, China, and Italy, permit early abortions on request. But in most countries abortion is permitted only to save a woman's life or for a limited number of other health-related reasons.

Legal restrictions do not necessarily reduce reliance on abortion to limit births. In countries where such restrictions exist and where family planning programs are weak—in Peru and Bolivia, for example—research in individual communities indicates that married women have had as many as six abortions.[129] But legal restrictions can significantly increase health risks as abortion services are driven underground. The treatment of septic and incomplete abortions—a frequent consequence of having the procedure performed by unskilled providers under unsanitary conditions—has placed a heavy monetary and manpower burden on health care systems throughout the developing world. Even with such care, at least 100,000 women, mostly in the developing world, die each year from the consequences of unsafe abortions.

Where abortions are outlawed, the results can be dramatic. When Romania banned abortion and contraceptives between 1966 and 1989, the number of maternal deaths doubled. A year after the ban was lifted, the number of maternal deaths fell by half.[130] Where abortion services are legal or permitted, they can be a critical part of a broad national strategy to protect maternal health and to ensure desired family size. Experts say that Thailand's success is partially attributable to the fact that authorities have been willing to turn a blind eye to abortions, which remain technically illegal except to save the life of the mother. With safe abortions now available at private clinics, thousands are performed every year and no one has been prosecuted under the country's existing anti-abortion statute.[131]

Research suggests that in the early stages of the shift from high to low fertility, both contraceptive use and the number of abortions increases. But after contraceptive prevalence increases, reliance on abortion usually declines. Short of legalizing abortion,

lives could be saved if doctors were better trained to deal with septic or incomplete abortions.[132] The risks of abortion may also be
reduced if and when the French "abortion pill" RU-486, now unavailable in all but a handful of countries, is made available.

"There will always be abortion," says PAI's Joseph Speidel.
"The question is whether it will be a substitute for or a backup for
family planning. If it's a substitute there will be a lot more of it because there will be a lot more unintended pregnancies."[133]

In the struggle to bring population growth all the way down to replacement level, governments have for the most part focused on
the "supply side" of providing family contraceptive services. Behind the measures to improve the quality of family planning services, behind efforts to market contraceptives more effectively,
even behind the provision of abortion services for family planning
purposes, is often this implicit assumption: If it is easy enough for
women not to have children, substantial strides can be made in the
direction of zero population growth.

These strategies are commonsensical and have made a large
dent in the fertility of many nations. But there is a growing recognition, even among family planning advocates, that the wider and
more efficient provision of family planning services will not do the
job alone. Handing a poor man a condom or a poor woman a pill
can prevent an unwanted child. But it will have no effect on
planned pregnancies, on the desired fertility that still exceeds two
children in most developing nations. It will not break the snow-
balling effect of population momentum created by the high proportion of young people that is typical in third world societies.
Thus any successful effort to lower family size to replacement level
will almost certainly have to address the "demand side" of the population equation as well by reshaping the very environment in
which fertility decisions are made. It will have to encourage parents to want smaller families, a task that is often difficult, since

having three or four children is still a rational choice in many less developed countries. In many poor countries infant mortality rates are still high, prompting parents to compensate by having more children, and because children remain the major source of status for women and of old age economic security for both of their parents.

The good news is that in many countries the definition of what constitutes ideal family size is already evolving downward. Part of the reason is broad social and economic forces like urbanization and modernization. But family size preferences can also be nudged downward by the day-to-day policy decisions governments make, like the decision to invest more money in education for girls or to create more economic opportunities for women. Expanding access to education alone could delay marriage and childbearing by years, breaking the back of population momentum, some experts believe. Thus the education and empowerment of women will be a necessary part of any widespread drop to replacement fertility.

FIVE

"A Woman's-Eye View": Redefining the Approach to Population

Bangladesh

For a country reputed only for its abject poverty, Bangladesh's striking rural scenery comes as something of a surprise. The bumpy road that leads south and west from the sprawling, low-slung capital of Dhaka slices through vast stretches of emerald-green rice fields that shimmer in the warm spring sun. Miniature boats rigged with burlap sails ply intricate networks of rivers and canals. Peasant farmers, stooped over rice paddies or driving teams of oxen through freshly plowed fields, tend to the arduous but picturesque labors of rural life.

Two hours from Dhaka, a dirt road branches off through the town of Boalia, then into a small village of the Manikganj district perched on a mud embankment above the Kaliganga River. The river is benign now but will turn into a threatening torrent when the monsoons begin in early summer.

On the edge of the village, an old woman gathers straw for cooking amid the lush stands of bamboo, coconut, and banana trees that seem to blunt the impact of rural poverty in much of Bangladesh. A hard dirt path leads into the village past a cluster of small bamboo huts. In one, a woman harvests silkworms from mulberry leaves in preparation for processing at a nearby mill. In another, thirty earnest, brightly dressed grade-schoolers work out math problems on tiny handheld blackboards. When a stranger looks in, they rise, as one, and issue a boisterous *"Salam alaikum,"* the traditional Arabic greeting that has worked its way into the Bengali language.

The path winds around another group of huts, past two massive—fortunately sleeping—brahmin bulls, and ends up near the house of Ayesha. A thirtyish mother of three, she is one of thousands of Bangladeshi women who have become symbols of a vast stirring in the developing world that promises to have a significant influence on efforts to stabilize world population growth.

Ayesha was born in Boalia. And like every other woman in the village, she seemed condemned by birth and tradition to poverty and to a lifetime of submissiveness in the male-dominated culture of Bangladesh. But that was before an unexpected visit one day five years ago from her cousin Jorimon.

"You have no money," Jorimon reminded her. "Come to a meeting with me next week in my village."

Over the protests of her family, she agreed to go. At the meeting she listened as three dozen women talked about everything from raising children to planning families, then recited pledges to keep their houses clean, their children educated, and their families small. They also talked about something else: the small business loans being given to impoverished rural women by the meeting organizers, the Bangladesh Rural Advancement Committee (BRAC).

After making inquiries, Ayesha secured a loan for 400 takas (about $16) and bought 200 baby chicks. After two months she sold them to her village neighbors and used the profits to buy more chicks and to build a chicken coop. Later she got a second loan, which she used to buy a rickshaw, which she rents out to the villagers. She used a third loan to improve her bamboo hut, adding the ultimate luxury and status symbol of a tin roof.

Ayesha's budding prosperity did not go unnoticed. Village men told her that a woman should not run a business. One burned the chicken coop to the ground. But she persisted, eventually adding four more chick-rearing cycles to the year and quintupling her annual profits. At the same time she opened up a savings account, a precondition to getting a BRAC loan, to which she adds two takas a week.

She pulls out a worn savings book and points to the bottom line: 2,712 takas—about $85, nearly half of Bangladesh's average annual per capita income—that tell the story of a life transformed.

"You see the changes here," says Ayesha, gesturing to the tiny compound that now consists of her bamboo house and two chicken coops and which is the source of evident pride. As she listens to visitors talk, she holds a baby son and chews on the edge of the beige sari that covers all but her face. When it is her time to speak, she suddenly assumes the air of authority that has derived from becoming the most prosperous woman in her village.

"Before, I had nothing. I had to beg in the street or go to the neighbors for help. I had no money."

She pauses to let the gravity of her once dire circumstances sink in.

"Now," she continues, "I have a rickshaw. I have chickens. I have this house. I have a tin roof instead of bamboo. I have some savings. Before I joined the village group, I was afraid of everything. I was afraid to go to the neighbor's house. Now I have no fear. I have confidence. I go everywhere I like. This is the big change in my life."

Prosperity has bought a degree of independence and mobility that would have been unimaginable to a Bangladeshi woman even a decade ago. But it has produced another significant change in Ayesha's life, with implications just as profound. Like all young brides she expected to acquire status, labor, and eventual economic security in the only way available to most poor rural women: by having many children. But despite the birth of a son nine weeks ago—"It was an accident," she insists twice—she now says she's determined to have no more children. Asked why, she points to the back of her savings book. On it are inscribed the seventeen "promises" she has memorized and which she recites in unison with her peer group at the start of each weekly BRAC meeting. Promise number twelve: "We shall plan to keep our families small." Pressed to elaborate, she acknowledges the costs and lost opportunities a large family would impose on a budding entrepreneur.

"I have economic security. I own a business. If I have more children it would hamper my business and my health, so that it would be impossible for me to work."

Pressed further, she gets to the heart of the matter: "I'm a skilled woman. I have the possibility of a better future. I guess what it comes down to is that I now have different choices."

Though she could hardly be aware of it, Ayesha and millions of women like her in the developing world have become the focus of an animated debate that has sharply divided the large global community of population experts. At issue is a deceptively simple question: Is it enough to provide a poor woman with family planning services?

For three decades the remarkable success of the international family planning movement has been based on the straightforward strategy of legitimizing the idea of small families and providing the wherewithal to reduce fertility.

But Ayesha's case illustrates why an increasing number of researchers, practitioners, feminists, and donor agencies believe that "parallel efforts" and "holistic approaches" to the problem of rapid population growth—that is, combining the delivery of family planning services with other programs that improve women's health and standing in society and that foster economic and social development generally—are critical to reducing birthrates to replacement level.

"It seems increasingly clear," says Sharon Camp, the former senior vice president of Population Action International, "that if you can do good family planning and secure improvements in the status of women—legal, economic, social, and political—those things interact so powerfully that you can get declines in birthrates at breathtaking speeds. That's probably the solution to the world's population problem."[1]

Historically, family planning agencies in some countries have been more concerned with the effects of population growth on economic development than with the health needs or status of the women they have been trying to reach. But a growing body of evidence demonstrates that improving the status of women is not only a prod to development but, like family planning itself, one key to reducing fertility. As one recent UN report notes, there is an important connection between a woman's productive role—the improved health, education, and economic opportunities that are the source of empowerment—and a woman's reproductive role.[2] It is a connection few women's groups would dispute. But the conviction that has melded them into a vocal network over the past decade is that quality reproductive health services and educational and economic opportunities for women are rights in and of themselves, no matter how they affect reproduction.

The argument on behalf of a more woman-centered approach to the population issue has particular salience today. With the pace of fertility decline diminishing even in countries with successful family planning programs, family planning agencies are more open to new ideas on how to bridge the gap between existing and replacement fertility. Says Kim Streatfield, the Population Council's representative in Bangladesh: "To find new [contraceptive] acceptors you can expand the range of contraceptives or provide better counseling. Or you can take a hard look at the feminist agenda. If you want to get above 50 percent CPR, you have to do something different."[3]

The coalition of women's groups seeking to bring a gender perspective to population issues has evolved over the past two decades from a fragmented group of country- and region-based networks. They had in common an outlook shaped by the shared experience of being caught in the crossfire between advocates of family planning, on the one hand, and pronatalist groups, including religious fundamentalists and right-to-life organizations, on the other.[4] The former, in some cases, imposed contraception and sterilization; the latter, in all cases, denied the right to abortion. "Neither takes the interests and rights of the individual woman as their starting point," writes one reproductive rights advocate. "Both . . . attempt to control women, instead of letting women control their bodies themselves."[5]

The incipient reproductive rights movement began taking shape after government agencies and august foundations started pumping money into research projects on women's issues starting in the late 1970s. It coalesced into a global movement at the 1985 UN Conference on Women in Nairobi. It reached critical mass at a UN conference on human rights in Vienna in 1993, where it attracted media attention and gained a degree of international recognition. Today thousands of reproductive rights and reproductive health advocates are scattered around the world, linked by a computer network that they have used to share information, coordinate strategy, and advocate a reframing of the debate over global population policy.[6]

One target of the movement has been the family planning programs that emerged from the forty-year, $40 billion quest to slow global population growth. Many of these programs have gone a long way toward meeting the existing demand for contraceptive services. But many women's groups say that the poor quality of many programs, characterized by a limited choice of contraceptive methods, poor counseling, and even outright abuses, has led millions of women to discontinue the use of contraceptives, even though their professed fertility aspirations are lower than their actual family size. Meanwhile, the emphasis on fertility control has led many family planning programs to overlook the broader reproductive health needs of women who, women's groups say, are frequently treated only as acceptors of contraceptives.

The criticism has drawn a strong response from family planners who insist that, however desirable, providing reproductive health care is beyond the financial and technical means of most poor nations. Women's groups dispute the point, responding that such services are affordable but ignored by governments that are exclusively concerned with the goal of reducing population growth. They say contraceptive services should be part of a broader program to meet women's reproductive health needs and not the other way around.

In Chicago, a Brazilian-American who runs the MacArthur Foundation's population program elaborates. In order to sell the "solution"—that is, family planning—says Carmen Barroso, family planners have sometimes misrepresented the "problem," adopting scare tactics to describe the effects of rapid population growth and setting aside complexities in describing the relationship between population and problems like environmental degradation.[7]

"This is not new," she says. "It's the same strategy that was popular in the 1960s when demographers were warning that population was the cause of underdevelopment. The problem is that it's an oversimplification. No one denies that we have to pay serious attention to the population issue. But what I fear is that exaggerating either the seriousness or the urgency of the problem may lead to justifications of a programmatic approach that in the end will be self-defeating."

Women's groups complain that overstating the consequences of rapid population growth has created a crisis atmosphere in some countries, which has led to human rights violations in the name of controlling fertility. The extreme case is China, where measures to implement an aggressive one-child policy have led to forcible insertion of IUDs, mandatory sterilizations, and forced abortions. But subtler forms of coercion reported in other countries—for example, a 1985 warning by Kenyan leader Daniel Arap Moi that having more than four children would trigger the loss of certain social benefits[8]—have nourished the perception that family planning agencies think only in quantitative terms, without regard to the welfare of women.

Particularly offensive to women's groups are financial incentives that reward doctors and family planning workers in over two dozen countries according to the number of acceptors they recruit. Payments of various kinds to mothers or parents also rankle. They range from countrywide programs, like one administered in South Korea that extends housing loan preferences and free medical care to children under five to two-child couples that have been sterilized, to the kind of localized schemes found in Indonesia that tie government grants for public works in individual villages to collective levels of contraceptive practice.[9] A form of coercion by default is noted in the failure of a few countries to provide a wide range of modern, temporary contraceptives. In India, for example, the result has been an overreliance on sterilization that ignores the birth control needs of younger women.[10]

Family planning advocates insist that programs to encourage contraceptive use are legitimate and point to the advantages that accrue to families and society from reduced population pressures. Feminist groups say incentive schemes place a higher value on reducing population growth than on enabling women to decide whether and when to have children. At the root of this disagreement is the matter of what constitutes an incentive. In Bangladesh, women who agree to get sterilized are provided with 180 takas and a sari. The Bangladeshi government says the money is merely to defray travel and food costs, while the sari is provided to ensure proper hygiene after the surgical procedure is completed. Not so, say feminists, who insist that under conditions of extreme poverty such offerings may be inducements, not merely compensation, for sterilization.

"For people who are desperately poor, there is no such thing as free choice. . . . Thus in practice incentives often have more to do with coercion than with choice," writes Betsy Hartmann in her book *Reproductive Rights and Wrongs.*"[11]

The other target of the feminist critique is third world governments that place the whole burden of reducing population growth on family planning. While family planning addresses the need for contraceptive services, it is less relevant to the other critical part of the population problem: the continuing demand for large families in many poor countries. For many women, the only path to status and economic security lies in having many children. Pervasive gender bias reinforced by custom, law, and government policies in dozens of nations has deprived women of the very resources, jobs, and educational opportunities—in short, the very means of empowerment—needed to reduce their dependence on children.[12]

Jodi Jacobson, who directs the Health and Development Policy Project in Washington, has spent a decade trying to convince policymakers to re-evaluate the cause-and-effect relationship between poverty and rapid population growth. She says by focusing on the "supply side" alone (that is, on providing contraceptives) without getting at the "demand side" (that is, at the root of problems like poverty that create the demand for large families in the first place), policymakers all but ensure failure at the outset.

"There's been too much emphasis on contraception as a solution to high fertility," says Jacobson. "People must have the option and the means to control their fertility. But the problem with this approach is that it ends up becoming an end in itself. It becomes the only measure of success and ignores the larger question of development goals, like improving health care and education and ending social inequities. Experience shows that quick fixes— programs aimed more at curtailing birthrates than at improving women's health and productivity—don't work precisely because they don't address fundamental development issues like gender bias."[13]

Women's groups say that governments, not recognizing the

point, put more pressure on contraceptive providers to increase their "success" rate, making them less inclined to factor quality reproductive health services into family planning programs and more susceptible to the kind of abuses perpetrated in some countries by local overzealous family planning workers.

"Programs that put demographic objectives ahead of women's rights have not only failed to alleviate pervasive economic and environmental problems," says Jacobson, "but by diminishing the status of women they have further perpetuated the very problem family planning agencies have set out to solve. You can never help women out of the population trap unless you help them out of the poverty trap, and you will never help them out of the poverty trap until you take steps to equalize access to resources."[14]

A small group of radical feminists actually opposes family planning altogether and denies the existence of a population problem. The Population Council's Cynthia Lloyd notes that at its extremes the debate catalyzed by the women's movement has been waged between "those who care more about getting fertility down than helping women, and those who care more about helping women than getting fertility down."[15] More typical is the centrist view that recognizes the contribution family planning is making to the improvement of women's status. By reducing domestic burdens, family planning is a fundamental part of any definition of empowerment. And by helping to space and limit births, family planning programs have made a demonstrable contribution to the health of both children and mothers, saving as many as a million women's lives over the past quarter century, according to some estimates.[16]

Even in Africa, where national fertility surveys have long recorded the desire of African women for families of six or seven or more as a means of providing status, old age security, and insurance against high rates of infant mortality, the Population Council's Nahid Toubia has discovered a latent desire for fertility regulation revealed in a surprisingly high prevalence of abortion.

In research in Ghana, Mali, and the Ivory Coast, Toubia found that between 10 and 15 percent of women have had an abortion.[17]

Toubia believes this indicates that African women want more family planning services, not fewer, perhaps not with the goal of reducing the number of children born but with a clear desire to space their pregnancies. She views the high rate of abortion as "an openly declared need for fertility regulation." Providing better and more accessible services could advance the demographic goal of lowering fertility in Africa; it could also advance what Toubia says should be the primary goal of meeting the individual needs of African women, especially if abortion services are provided as part of family planning programs.

"The reality is that an African woman gets pregnant more times than she wants to," says Toubia. "If you assist her in not having the child she's pregnant with now and link termination services with good post-abortion family planning, she is more likely not to have the six or eight she says she wants."[18]

"Most women's groups would tell you that we want family planning. We just don't want family planning in the way it's been provided," summarizes Sajeda Amin, a young Princeton-trained demographer who works at the Bangladesh Institute of Development Studies in Dhaka. "We want it more on our terms. We want control over our own bodies and good family planning, which includes a choice of contraceptives and greater sensitivity to women's health needs."[19]

In the end it is not abstract arguments but concrete circumstances, like those endured by Dellnoor, a twenty-seven-year-old mother of six who lives in Dhaka, that have buttressed the case that women's groups are making. Dellnoor lives in a country that has a good family planning program. But she proves that more is required to lower family size than just providing good contraceptive services. Without the empowerment that comes with education and the lifting of discriminatory laws and social practices, Dellnoor and many women like her are locked into a cycle of high fertility and frustrated hopes.

Dellnoor lives in the impoverished Gandaria district of Dhaka, a sprawling slum that is home to the poorest of the poor in one of the world's poorest countries. In an otherwise ill-starred life she is lucky in one respect: The bleak ten-by-ten room that is home to her family of eight is a third again as large as the five tiny huts, home to families of equal number, that are arrayed around the squalid courtyard on which it fronts.

Like only 3 percent of girls in Bangladesh, Dellnoor managed to complete all five grades of primary school. At ten, she could dream of completing secondary school. But at thirteen, the dreaming stopped. Her education was cut short to begin a life in *purdah*, a lifetime of virtual confinement to the home defined by the conservative traditions, law, and religion of Bangladesh. Shortly after her first menstruation, she was given over in an arranged marriage to Habib, her senior by nearly a decade. At fourteen she had her first baby. The rest, six in all, have come at regular intervals since. Today, at twenty-seven, only a hint of youth remains on a pretty but prematurely middle-aged face.

A virtual prisoner to the will of Habib, an arrangement still common in the male-dominated realms of the developing world, Dellnoor's life has been a chronicle of disappointment. Once a promising student, she is now confined to the compound, forbidden under the strict rules of *purdah* to venture out except on rare occasions and only then with another adult.

At Habib's command, she was forced to give up her only prized possession, a few small jewels given to her by her mother, for a business venture that failed. Frustrated by his own failures, the on-again, off-again textile worker regularly beats her. Sometimes with his fists. Sometimes with a stick. Once when she was six-months pregnant.

"I don't want my daughter's life to be like mine," she tells a visitor tearfully. "I'm like a prisoner in this house."

As for children, the matter has not been hers to decide. Dellnoor says she has wanted to use contraceptives, which are available at a privately run community health center down the street and distributed regularly door-to-door by women from the government's family planning agency. But Habib is opposed to family planning.

"It's not my decision. It's up to him," she says stoically. "He doesn't want family planning."

For reasons Dellnoor is unable to explain, Habib's opposition to family planning does not extend to abortion. She has had three abortions so far and insists she will have one every time she gets pregnant during the remaining two decades of her reproductive life. Nor can she properly care for the children she has. Because Habib will not let her go to the health center, the children have not been immunized.

After the children are grown, Dellnoor would like to work. But with a sigh she acknowledges that that too will be Habib's decision to make: "If it is my necessity I will not be allowed. If it is his necessity I will be allowed."

With none of the choices enjoyed by women like Ayesha who have broken the bonds of *purdah*, Dellnoor cherishes the only dream remaining: of a better life after Habib is gone. When he dies, she says, she would like to have a small inheritance to live on, including income from the five small shacks across the courtyard that Habib now owns. But even Habib's death will not set Dellnoor free: According to the Koran, she will receive only one-eighth of his estate. The rest will go to their children, with each son receiving twice each daughter's share.

"When Habib is gone and the children are out of the home, I shall pray to God," Dellnoor says quietly of the only option remaining. "I shall spend my time calling God."

Though the fourth-poorest nation on earth, Bangladesh is rich in one remarkable respect. Over the past two decades this Wisconsin-sized country has become a magnet that has drawn social activists from all over the world. Armed with money, ideas, and compassion, they have come here to uplift and educate, train and evangelize, heal and organize.

A stroll through an upper middle-class Dhaka neighborhood like Dhanmondi confirms the impression that Bangladesh has become a kind of reverse Mecca, where outsiders come to *bring* salvation. House after house has become the headquarters for some worthy cause: a health clinic, a literacy training center, the local headquarters of a prestigious overseas donor like the Ford Foundation, whose benign interventions have helped to lift a little the almost crushing burden of Bangladesh's mostly rural poverty.

In all, some 700 private voluntary organizations are registered with the government to receive foreign funds, some 200 of which are currently active, according to foundation sources. More remarkable still are the thousands more that have sprung up locally, operating tiny projects that reach into the remotest villages. Their presence has made Bangladesh an extraordinary laboratory for testing theories of economic and social development. Bangladesh has also become a laboratory for testing the proposition that bringing down population growth rates ultimately depends on breaking the rigid social and religious codes that have embedded gender discrimination in almost every aspect of daily life.

With 120 million people, Bangladesh is already one of the most densely populated countries on earth. Demographers project that its population will double in size within a generation. Though most of the dozens of women-centered projects run by nongovernmental organizations (NGOs) in Bangladesh are not primarily concerned with reversing this threatening demographic trend, many are dedicated to the proposition that tending to the health, status, and educational needs of women makes a significant indirect contribution to lowering fertility.

From an office in a cluster of high-rise apartments in Dhaka, Shamima Islam oversees one small pilot project, designed to help girls living in a rural village 200 miles away advance to secondary school. Barely 2 percent of girls do so currently, which is one reason for Bangladesh's endemic underdevelopment. The reasons why—social customs, the preference given to sons, and poverty—have forced Islam and her tiny Center for Women and Development to be creative.

"Families don't like to send girls to school because it's expensive, because their labor is needed, and because girls are expected to be around the house," says the fifty-two-year-old Michigan State University graduate whose project is funded with contributions solicited from friends in Dhaka.[20]

To circumvent a family's resistance, the Center first defrays the incidental costs of school by providing pens, writing paper, and textbooks to the poorest students. Next comes a personal hygiene kit, including soap, towels, and lice-killing combs to help the girls concentrate in class. The most important contribution is a kit containing five packages of seeds for vitamin-rich plants, including pumpkins and leafy vegetables.

Islam explains: "If a poor household has more access to vegetables and fruits there will be increased food in the household. If there is more food it means the girls will get their fair share to eat. If there is more food it also means her labor is less needed and the family won't mind letting her go off to school."[21]

When the project started, thirty-five girls attended the community secondary school regularly. Today the number has jumped to 155 and is still growing. It represents a small assault on the bastion of *purdah*. Islam insists it also has significant implications for fertility: "If we can help keep a girl in school, the effect will be a positive attitude toward education. And if a girl is exposed to broader ideas it's likely she'll have better attitudes toward family control measures. The smaller family norm will be more acceptable."

A U.S. AID–funded program that provides scholarships to girls in the Sharasti Upazila area has demonstrated the same point on a vastly larger scale.[22] Begun in 1982, it drew more than 20,000 girls into secondary school during the first six years alone, swelling the percentage of female enrollment to twice the national level. Girls who would otherwise have been married off by their parents in their early teens to avoid financial burdens have been able to delay marriage to a much later age. The result has been later pregnancies and greater knowledge of how to use contraceptive methods. What is true in Bangladesh is true universally: Along with family planning, educating girls has the biggest effect on reducing the number of unwanted pregnancies and lowering population growth rates. According to one recent study, countries in which education is least accessible to girls have the highest fertility rates in the world, while those that provide the greatest access have the lowest.[23]

Across town, in Dhanmondi, Nahid Choudhury watches over the operations of a dozen rural clinics run by the Bangladesh Women's Health Coalition. Established over a decade ago, it is designed to fill a gap by providing reproductive health services that are mostly unavailable from government-run clinics.

Although the government provides immunizations and health education, the majority of poor Bangladesh women give birth at home. Twenty-four thousand die in childbirth every year, and 95 percent of the children born to them die within one year. The 750,000 women who sought to terminate their pregnancies in the last year for which reliable information is available—the statistics were compiled by the Center for Disease Control in 1978—fared little better: At least 7,500 of them died and several thousand others were left sterile or seriously injured.[24] Menstrual regulation (MR), or induced menstruation, services are far more widely available now, but the number of women seeking to terminate pregnancies either through MR or unsafe abortions is probably much larger now as well.

Like many women's groups, the BWHC has sought to shift the rationale for family planning from demographic to health objectives. Choudhury says that lower fertility is not the goal but the in-

evitable consequence of efforts to improve women's health. Behind
the determination to be woman-centered and not demographically
driven lies what an official of the BWHC's partner organization,
the International Women's Health Coalition in New York, describes as a fundamental difference in values and programs.

"Are you doing this to achieve demographic goals or to advance
the principles of women's rights and social justice? These can be
fundamentally incompatible," says Gabrielle Ross.[25] "In many
population programs the measurement of success is demographic
goals, such as 'births averted' or the number of contraceptive or
sterilization 'acceptors.' The BWHC's measurement is more qualitative. Are women's health needs being met, including safe abortion? Are women getting education and treatment for reproductive
tract infections? Is there counseling on sexuality and contraceptives, abortion and infertility? Is there pre- and postpregnancy
care? Are clients provided with full information and choices
among contraceptive methods? Are they satisfied with the staff and
services? Is there followup? Are women treated with respect and
compassion?

"One indicator of the success of a family planning agency is to
maximize the number of years of contraceptive protection at minimum cost to the agency," Ross elaborates. "That's why some family planning agencies have been criticized for placing emphasis on
permanent or long-acting methods like sterilization and injectables. The other measure of success is whether women's individual
reproductive goals are being met."

Because its main focus has been women, the BWHC has eschewed funding from U.S. AID (which since 1973 has been barred
from paying for abortion services) and has become a provider of
menstrual regulation within the first ten weeks of pregnancy.

Partly because so many women in Bangladesh have children
when they are very young or very old, and because there is still a
sizable unmet demand for contraceptives, the demand for abortion
is high. But with trained providers of MR reaching only about half

the number of women seeking to terminate pregnancies each year, hundreds of thousands of women are compelled to induce their own abortions or go to untrained providers. That's one reason maternal mortality rates are 100 times higher in Bangladesh than in developed countries.

"Theoretically, MR is available to every woman in Bangladesh, but the health care system is so weak that it doesn't reach all the women who need it," explains Nahid Choudhury. "That's where the BWHC comes in, helping pick up the slack."[26]

Safe abortions save the lives of between 100,000 and 160,000 women in Bangladesh each year, Choudhury estimates. "For us," she says, "the key isn't just providing medicine. It's providing service. It's patient counseling. It's respect for the women. While these things may seem obvious, it's surprising how rarely they're provided."

The case of a third Bangladeshi nongovernmental organization, Concerned Women for Family Planning, demonstrates a similar linkage between improving women's health and economic opportunities and reducing fertility.

Now the largest private family planning agency in Bangladesh, it started when a small band of middle-class housewives fanned out into the slums of Dhaka to immunize women who were forced out of rural areas by the great famine of 1974. Making the rounds of shabby refugee communities, they discovered that the women had no access to family planning services. So on future trips they began bringing pills and condoms they got from the government.

"We were not professionals in those days," says the group's founder, Mufaweza Khan, who is widely credited with pioneering the concept of doorstep delivery of contraceptives in Bangladesh. "All we had going for us was that we wanted to treat the women with love, dignity, and care, not as statistics only."[27]

Braving criticism that they were "social elite do-gooders," they institutionalized family planning services with a staff of five field workers in a neighborhood of 50,000 in Dhaka. Within ten years they were servicing 1.3 million women in and around the capital.

"The idea of women going out to the neighborhoods and into the households was revolutionary," says Peggy Curlin, an American who worked side by side with Khan in the early days and who now heads an NGO of her own, the Centre for Development and Population Activities, in Washington. "The outreach and the women-to-women approach is the thing that's lasted most."[28]

In 1982 the group reached a turning point. In a move that was a harbinger of changes now championed by many women's groups, Concerned Women broadened its approach to include a limited range of maternal and child health care services, including immunizations and pre- and postnatal care.

As Khan explains: "We were only doing family planning. But many of the women we were servicing couldn't take care of their children. Infant mortality is very high here. When you go to the houses and see a woman pregnant, then go back in three months and discover that she's lost her child—that's when we realized that we had a moral obligation to provide help. We learned that if a pregnant woman is taken care of and gives birth to a healthy child, she's more prone to accept family planning. She has more trust in us because we were taking care of her, not just trying to tell her not to have another child. And if she doesn't lose her child she won't want to get pregnant again."[29]

Three years later, Concerned Women broadened its approach even further when it began training courses for family planning acceptors in basic skills like embroidery and pottery making. Two years later, it established four business enterprises, including a laundry, two restaurants, and a catering service, all staffed by women.

Although the effects of such programs on fertility can be measured only by anecdotal evidence, Khan is convinced that they have made a difference. "All the people involved in the skills development program have fewer children. And their children are better educated, which means that the next generation will be more prone to use family planning."[30]

"We can see big changes in the women," Khan continues. "They're confident. They have higher status in the family. A woman goes by herself to the market. She organizes groups. She makes things. She buys her own material. If she is bringing in 500 takas she can decide how to spend it. And she can decide on her own if she wants to use contraceptives. Using only contraceptives you can go to 50 or 60 percent contraceptive prevalence in any given population. To get beyond that you have to come at it from a different direction. That's what we've tried to do."

The idea for the most unorthodox and influential form of women's empowerment in Bangladesh originated with an obscure professor of economics at Chittagong University, near Dhaka. Like Concerned Women, it also grew out of the great famine of 1974.

As Muhammed Yunus, now a legendary figure in the international development community, recounts the story: "I was teaching economics and watching people die on the streets when I began doubting what I had learned from the textbooks. It occurred to me that maybe there was something wrong with economics because it did not solve the problem. So I went to the village [Jobra, near the university] and tried to understand economics from the daily life of people living there. The village became my university."[31]

One of the first people Yunus encountered was an old woman who made small bamboo stools, earning ten annas—about two cents—for each one. "I was shocked that anyone could spend so long making such a beautiful stool and get paid so little."

The reason, Yunus discovered, was that she had to borrow

money to buy the bamboo from a trader. To repay the money she
had to sell the stool back to the trader, who paid her only slightly
more than the cost of the raw materials.

"In other words, her labor came almost free. It was a form of
slavery. I realized she could only get out of this bondage if she
could borrow a small amount of money. Here we were, talking
about big economic theories, when people were languishing in
poverty because they couldn't get a dollar in cash. Her life was
miserable because she could only live in that cycle: borrowing
from the trader and selling it to him. It was such a simple problem.
All you had to do is lend her five takas and it was solved."

After canvassing the village, he found forty-two other residents
who were also engaged in potentially profitable micro-enterprises
and who had a combined capital need of less than thirty dollars. So
he decided to put up the money out of his own pocket. Each of the
borrowers got on their feet financially and each repaid in full.
"That was the beginning," says Yunus.

Convinced that the idea was worth emulating in other villages,
Yunus went to a local bank to raise the needed capital. There, the
limitations of conventional economics were again underscored.
First the bank scoffed because the amounts in question were so
low. Then it said such micro-loans would require collateral. Determined to overcome the bank's resistance, Yunus expanded the loan
program to two villages, then to five, then to an entire district, all
with the same positive results. Finally convinced that the banks
were beyond redemption, he set up his own, the now legendary
Grameen (or "rural") Bank, which was chartered in 1982. Today
the Grameen Bank and BRAC, which also specializes in micro-
enterprise loans, are providing credit to well over a million villagers throughout Bangladesh, mostly impoverished women like
Ayesha, with a repayment rate of over 97 percent.

The idea of enhancing the economic status of women through
the promotion of micro-enterprises is now being emulated in dozens of countries, including the BKK Credit Program in Indonesia,

the Working Women's Forum in India, and the FINCA program in Latin America. It is one reason nearly half of all women in commerce now work in informal enterprises.[32]

"When you teach at a university you feel you know it all. You see the world with a bird's-eye view," Yunus recalled to the *Daily Star*, a Dhaka daily. "But eventually I realized that you're totally blinded by the height. So what I was doing in Jobra was trying to acquire a woman's-eye view, where you face a thing and try to overcome that tiny problem."[33]

"This program is proof," says a buoyant Yunus, "that people who are rejected by society can come back to the mainstream without a handout. If you only give them an equal chance there's no reason why there should be poverty. Poverty can be removed from the whole earth totally and for all time to come if only we re-examine our concepts and the institutions we have created."[34]

As Yunus and F. H. Abed, BRAC's founder and director, both acknowledge, the ultimate purpose—controversial in this traditional Muslim culture—is nothing less than freeing women like Dellnoor from the prison of isolation. "We are opposed to the image of women they have," says Yunus flatly of religious fundamentalists.

Abed elaborates: "We think we have to fight *purdah* and fundamentalist tenets. Many of these women have learned from childhood that *purdah* is good and that you shouldn't oppose men. But if *purdah* is kept, women can't enter the mainstream of economic development. Women in Bangladesh have a lot of potential which, if released from the confines of *purdah*, is going to take Bangladesh out of its dire poverty in the course of time. Bangladesh's real future lies in getting all of these women out of *purdah* and getting them into the mainstream of development."[35]

Determined to speed the process of social change along, Abed and Yunus have energized the small army of female creditors created by BRAC and Grameen with an ambitious consciousness-raising program. BRAC and Grameen women are organized into small peer groups that meet weekly. Regular attendance is a pre-condition to receiving a loan. As one journalist notes, the sessions—like the ones Ayesha has now attended regularly for over seven years—"combine a military-like sense of discipline with the atmosphere of a confessional and the support of a self-help therapy group," instilling the virtues of fiscal prudence, personal hygiene, household cleanliness, education, thrift, and small families.[36]

"The bottom line," says Abed, "is building self-worth in people who do not have a full sense of their worth, and to show them that as a group they can do more to withstand exploitation than if they stand alone."[37]

Precisely how participation in the loan programs affects fertility remains largely a matter of conjecture, as Abed acknowledges.

"I'm sure there's a relationship between empowerment and fertility but I don't think we've actually measured it very well. We know that in some of our project areas fertility is declining. What we don't know is whether fertility is declining because of economic development, the delivery of family planning services, or the fact that women are earning more money."

A direct casual link between financial empowerment and lower fertility has been drawn by three researchers: Sidney Ruth Schuler of the JSI Research and Training Institute in Arlington, Virginia, Penn State sociologist Dominique Meekers, and Syed Hashemi, an economist at Dhaka's Jahangirnagar University. The socialization process that results from membership in Grameen and BRAC, the three reported in 1992, depends on the duration of a woman's participation in the program and the extent to which family planning is emphasized in group meetings and informal inter-actions between program field staff and participants. They found that just over 50 percent of Grameen Bank members were using contraceptives, compared with just under 40 percent in a control group.[38]

"Women who perceive health and family planning as important activities of the local group are much more likely to use modern temporary methods of contraception than women who do not," the trio of researchers reported. "The fact that the program staff encourage members to discuss family planning appears to be enhancing the image of family planning as an accepted social norm."[39]

However unproven the direct effect, few researchers doubt that the indirect effects of credit programs and other forms of empowerment on reproductive behavior, by contributing to mobility, a sense of self-worth, and greater parity in the household, are substantial. As the Population Council's Judith Bruce explains: "Interacting in a wider set of relationships means having access to more objective information on the costs and benefits of having more children. It means more equality in the marital relationship."[40]

But empowerment can often work at a subtler level, as Abed explains and as the case of Ayesha illustrates: "In rural Bangladesh a landless laborer gets work for about 210 days a year. During the days when there is no work the food in the household declines. So the planning cycle becomes a day-to-day matter. But when somebody saves money it means they're planning for the future. To take them from day-to-day planning to longer-term planning like one or two years means there's a kind of evolution of the mind. This is where a savings program begins to contribute to family planning."[41]

"When your planning cycle is two years, then and only then are you thinking of family size," says Abed. "Not that BRAC is making me but because I'm thinking about my own future. Once you do that, if you have three children it will come to you automatically that you don't need any more."

Syed Hashemi elaborates on the cause-and-effect relationship between women's empowerment and lower fertility: "Traditionally, the village set the boundary of a woman's life. If there was a doctor living in the next village a woman couldn't go by herself to see him. If there was a family planning center she couldn't go there without an escort. But BRAC and Grameen are forcing her out of the house.[42]

"Now once a week she has to go to the meetings. She remembers she has to pay back twenty takas each time. She's playing with numbers. She now has to keep track. Maybe she's making errors, but now she's handling cash and has to keep track of it. And that in itself gives her more confidence.

"The first few times the woman is scared. She looks down at the ground. She doesn't look up. She huddles with a few of the other women. But over time she gets used to going out of the house. Before this her whole identity was as someone's mother or wife or daughter. Now she has a different identity. Now she belongs to BRAC or Grameen, something external, something outside. And by being with these women for the first time she sees herself as someone separate from her kin group. She feels confident without a father, husband, or son there. This confidence in being able to live in the public sphere implies she can talk to someone outside of her family without being scared. She can walk into a family planning clinic and seek assistance. She can stand in front of a doctor without being scared out of her mind.

"In the group meetings she finds out that there's a way out of having too many children. She begins to understand the health problems of having too many kids. Slowly, gradually, that translates into a demand on her part for contraceptives. Now she has the ability to access family planning sources without her husband. And that's how empowerment leads to increased access. It's that simple: A woman who is more assertive will seek out contraception far more than a woman who depends on a male member of the family."

In a small Dhaka office that houses one of the country's dozens of women-centered NGOs, five middle-class Bangladeshi women have gathered to evaluate empowerment programs like BRAC and Grameen. Like nearly all Bangladeshi women of social position, they have been educated at the best universities abroad. Places like

Oxford, Chicago, and Princeton have taught them not only the need for female empowerment but also its limits in a society where tradition still outweighs modernity. As Zarine Rahman Khan, who teaches public administration at the University of Dhaka, explains: "The problem is that a woman going out to work in the village is not taken as somebody who is the ideal woman. She is still considered someone who has broken the norm. And that reinforces the whole system. I think this whole thing about us thinking in terms of breaking out of the tradition and going to something modern is limited to a very privileged middle class."[43]

Sajeda Amin of the Bangladesh Institute of Development Studies concurs: "We still don't have the choice between traditional and modern because at a very personal level for most women the only choice is between conforming to tradition and not conforming. Here the opposite of traditional is not conforming. There isn't a positive model alternative that is there for the taking as a whole. That's where the barrier to change lies. It's an option between challenging something that's there for something we don't quite know how to define. The first step is getting out of confinement, but because you've been confined you don't know what's out there."[44]

Even exponents of the feminist critique acknowledge that too little research has been done to establish an airtight cause-and-effect relationship between gender equity and demographic transition. The circumstances that have propelled women like Ayesha into the workforce have clearly made a difference in Bangladesh. But birthrates have plummeted and contraceptive use has increased significantly in dozens of countries—like Egypt, for example—where the status of women remains inferior and where opportunities for employment and education are still restricted. One explanation is that a high level of unmet demand for family planning services exists even in poor countries and among unempowered women.

The limits of female empowerment have been gauged in another way by such analysts as the Population Council's Cynthia Lloyd. She is on the leading edge of research into a hitherto over-looked aspect of empowerment that has led her and others to con-clude that its effects on fertility may not be as clear-cut as once imagined.

The conventional wisdom is that if a woman can retain a fair share of her earnings, she will need and therefore have fewer chil-dren. But researchers like Lloyd are just beginning to understand the extent to which families absorb the fruits of women's labor and to which the burden of family responsibility is being shifted to income-earning mothers. The effect of both developments has been to blunt the effects of empowerment on fertility.

"For twenty years we pursued the issue of women in develop-ment without looking at women in the context of their families," says Lloyd. "There's a growing concern that factors that have not been fully examined yet could attenuate the gains of empower-ment."[45]

The pattern identified by the Council's Susan Greenhalgh in re-search in Ghana, India, and Thailand is that men have reaped the surplus from women's entrepreneurship, either directly for them-selves or indirectly in the form of reduced obligations to other family members.[46]

"We've assumed that as the cost of children rises, the demand for children falls," comments Lloyd. "But that's only true if the person in control of decisionmaking is also the person who bears the rising costs. If the income comes home and gets co-opted away, then it doesn't have the kind of impact we hoped it would have."[47]

Another response to the rising cost of raising children, besides having fewer children, is to invest more in some children than oth-ers. Where there is no legal obligation to be equitable, which is the case in most countries, one way of getting around rising costs is to send one child to school and keep the other at home.

"That's what's happening now in the developing world," says

Lloyd. "If parents feel the pinch they'll say, We'll have a couple of kids plugged into the wider world and we'll keep the rest at home. That's producing a growing inequality in the family, and governments are not saying that's not okay."[48]

"If men's family responsibilities are reduced, women will be left where they were before: dependent on men for essential resources and dependent on children for long-term economic security. Unless men are forced to bear parallel costs, what incentive do they have to cut fertility?"

Despite such findings, research still largely bears out the hopeful assumptions that have guided practitioners like Abed and Yunus. By competing with the value of children as sources of labor, status, and insurance for divorce, old age, and widowhood, the empowerment conferred by higher education and employment and buttressed by family planning services does lead to lower fertility. Empowerment increases the opportunity costs of children, prompting later marriages and increasing the divorce rate, similarly lowering fertility.

Moreover, research abundantly confirms the more pronounced effect employment in nontraditional settings has on reducing fertility. Historically, fertility dropped in Europe when industry evolved out of the house and into factories.[49] More recently, fertility rates plummeted when women went to work in Taiwan and South Korea.[50] When women in the Caribbean Islands of Barbados and Antigua found work in the tourist industry during the 1980s, fertility actually dropped below replacement level (2.1 children).[51] The negative employment-fertility relationship is strong for modern-sector employment and much weaker for informal sector and agricultural sector employment, in which it is easier for women to combine work and child care.

"The connection is clear and the rationale compelling: Fertility falls when women can profit from their work outside the agricultural sector or home," notes Virginia Abernethy, a professor of psychiatry at the Vanderbilt University Medical Center. "A woman with an independent income does not have to marry young or barter sex or childbearing for support."[52]

Stories about women like Ayesha are part of the reason most experts are now convinced that fertility declines fastest when the supply- and demand-side approaches to reducing family size are combined.

Religious beliefs, gender roles, inaccessible villages, high infant mortality, high female illiteracy, and one of the world's poorest economies have combined to make fertility reduction through family planning as unlikely in Bangladesh as any place on earth. Yet despite all the reasons Bangladesh should not be a success story, a family planning program combining inexpensive contraceptives and home visits by 24,000 female outreach workers has made a huge dent in high birthrates. Under the nearly ideal conditions that obtain in an experimental program in the villages of the Matlab region of Bangladesh, intensive household coverage by outreach workers, more comprehensive counseling, and wider contraceptive choice have raised contraceptive prevalence to 60 percent. In some villages fertility has been lowered to below replacement level, hinting at the possibilities for all developing nations once program imperfections are ironed out.[53] Thanks to unexpectedly high levels of latent demand for family planning services, Bangladesh has managed to decrease average family size from seven to four, proving that economic underdevelopment and traditional social norms are not insurmountable obstacles to the acceptance of family planning. Nations like Bangladesh have proved that it is not necessary to wait for social and economic transformation to advance the process of slowing population growth.

But it is unclear whether such success has limits. Like most poor countries with successful family planning programs, Bangladesh has found it difficult to push contraceptive use rates above 50 percent except under experimental conditions. One reason is that most Bangladeshi women still want at least three children and will probably continue to want them until their social and economic circumstances change.[54] That means that even with perfect access to contraception, replacement fertility will be extremely difficult to reach. To bridge the gap to replacement fertility, it will be necessary to reduce the demand for large families. Family planning programs themselves can help in this regard. As Thai demographer Napaporn Havanon notes, the spread of information and ideas about family planning can help the small-family model gain acceptability in a relatively short time.[55] But economic development needs to be part of the equation, as nations like South Korea and Taiwan, which have undergone far more dramatic demographic transitions, demonstrate. Thirty years ago, South Korea was like most low-income countries are today: It had a backward economy and high birthrates. But spectacular economic growth drove per capita income up, creating economic and educational opportunities for women that have significantly lowered the demand for large families. Contraceptive prevalence in South Korea is now close to 80 percent. Fertility has dropped to below replacement level. Family planning programs played an important part, but in the end it wasn't the *means* to limit family size but the *motivation* that was the more powerful engine of change.

In the biggest cities and remotest villages of the developing world, researchers have been quietly gathering new data to gain a better understanding of the factors that shape the motivation to have fewer children. The kind of economic empowerment enjoyed by women like Ayesha is clearly one. But empowerment has other dimensions that influence desired family size.

The most important by far is education, which, second only to access to good-quality family planning services, has the most direct bearing on increased contraceptive use and lower fertility. One of the best examples of the relationship between education and fertility is the Indian state of Kerala, where a female literacy rate of 87 percent has contributed to a fertility rate of 2.3, one of the lowest in the developing world.[56] There are numerous other examples, including Sri Lanka, where female literacy and contraceptive prevalence have risen simultaneously to Western levels.[57] One study in Mexico showed that only 47 pregnancies were recorded for each 1,000 adolescents who had a secondary education, while 219 were recorded for each 1,000 who did not.[58] In Kenya, meanwhile, a huge leap in the percentage of women seeking the means to stop childbearing or delay pregnancy is the partial result of a massive effort to get girls into school. Among women with no formal education in Kenya, contraceptive use is only 15 percent; among women with primary education it is 29 percent; among women with at least some secondary education it is 45 percent.[59]

A 1987 UN study based on data from thirty-eight developing countries showed that education is "strongly related" to fertility. Overall, women who have completed seven or more years of schooling will bear an average of 3.9 children, while women with none will bear an average of 6.9, or 80 percent more, the study found. Fertility differences by education tend to be higher in urban than rural areas.[60]

According to the World Bank, doubling female enrollment rates in a large sampling of developing countries could have translated into nearly 30 million fewer births. Econometric studies by the Bank within individual countries concluded that an extra year of female schooling reduces infant mortality by between 5 and 10 percent, thus indirectly contributing to lower fertility.[61]

Where education reduces fertility, which is nearly everywhere, the trigger point varies according to cultural influences. In the Middle East, for example, even minimal exposure to formal education appears to have an eventual effect on fertility—not because of the content of the education itself but because schooling gets girls who are traditionally confined to the house into a different environment. One Korean researcher confirms that the reason education influences fertility may have little to do with literacy per se: "It is clearly not education as such that prompts an individual to act in an educated way, but it is 'something' that being educated for a certain period of time has created in the individual (certain ways of perceiving, feeling, thinking and acting)."[62]

"The longer people attend school the more likely they are to develop a different sense of time, and some sense of the future," elaborates Stephen Viederman, a former UNFPA official who now heads the Jessie Smith Noyes Foundation in New York. "There's also evidence that schooling provides the individual with a stronger sense of social and personal efficacy, a greater willingness to consider ideas, to put oneself into situations which are new and different, and to place a higher value on science than tradition."[63]

Another reason education usually translates into lower fertility is that it imparts the knowledge and skills to act on the desire for smaller families by seeking out and using family planning methods. As one World Bank official notes, women with more education are more likely use to contraceptives, just as farmers with more education are more likely to adopt new farming techniques.[64] Education may also reduce fertility by improving women's employment opportunities, thereby elevating the opportunity costs of children and diminishing both economic and status needs for children.

"Education changes the value of time for women," says World Bank senior economist Elizabeth King. "It gives them meaningful alternative uses of time outside motherhood and homemaking."[65]

Perhaps the most important way in which education affects fertility is by delaying marriage. By reducing the number of years during which a woman may become pregnant, fewer children are born. Women who have seven or more years of education marry nearly four years later on average than those who do not, according to data compiled by the World Fertility Survey, and their contraceptive use rate is 25 percentage points higher. Education also increases equality in the marriage relationship, giving women more control over decisions concerning family size.[66]

Though the education-fertility link is largely undisputed, low-income countries are struggling to afford the huge expenditures needed to improve and expand literacy, especially at the secondary level.

"You have to look at how education budgets are already being spent and whether it's more important to build another university for the elites or to expand primary and secondary education," says Judith Bruce. "You also have to look at military spending. The pie is not too small unless you're wasting some of it. What donors need to say is, Unless you reduce military spending and devote more to education and other services, we will not assist you in other areas you want."[67]

"If I had to choose between educating all the girls or providing family planning, I'd educate the girls because then they would get the family planning services for themselves," says PAI's Joseph Speidel, who is a strong advocate of family planning. "But the resource needs for family planning are so small and the benefits of education so remarkable that it should not have to be an either/or proposition."[68]

Besides education, there are other social factors that bear on desired family size, one of which—the preference that exists in some parts of the world for sons—is deeply rooted in tradition. Consider Joshai and Ashan, an elderly couple who live in the tiny Bangladeshi village of Pachbaroil. They have spent a lifetime playing the birth lottery. Despite a huge investment, they have come up empty.

Their first three children were answers to their prayers in this socially conservative, economically deprived region where sons are valued and daughters are not. But all three died in childhood. Desperate for more sons to provide for them in their old age, they kept trying. Instead they got only daughters, seven in all, before they finally gave up. Today their impoverished circumstances testify to the price of having no male heirs and to the financial drain of having more daughters than they could afford.

"If I had a son he could go to a far country, maybe the Middle

East, to earn more money. Or he could help me buy land or a new home," says Ashan. "Maybe we could have worked together. If I had a son he would have more [income-earning] choices; if I have a daughter she can't go anywhere."

Joshai's seven daughters are lucky in that they survived to adulthood. But so strong is the demand for sons and so little valued are girls that each year thousands of newborn girls are murdered, mostly in the rural reaches of southern Asia and China, simply because they are female.

In many developing countries, the lack of sons has created the kind of pressures that have forced couples like Joshai and Ashan to eschew the use of contraceptives in favor of having large families. The reasons are complex, but they lie at the root of social conditions that many women insist need to be changed before birthrates can fall. In traditional societies girl children are regarded as investments on which there is no return. Unable to work, they can provide no income to the family. If a dowry is required at marriage, the costs can be catastrophic, wiping out a lifetime of savings. After they have left the family, daughters—like Joshai's and Jashan's—usually have neither the means nor the obligation to help their parents.

If a woman without sons is widowed, she is the ultimate casualty. According to one recent study, 60 percent of women in India over age sixty are widows. But some of India's many castes prohibit widows from returning to the village of their birth or joining the lineage of their married daughters. Abandoned, many are left to beg on the streets for the rest of their lives.[69] "Unless she has adult or married sons, a woman is left virtually on her own," says Marty Chen of the Harvard Institute for International Development in Cambridge, Massachusetts, and the author of the research.[70]

According to an Indian government study cited by the *Washington Post*, of 8,000 abortions performed after amniocentesis in one Bombay clinic, 7,999 were of female fetuses. In China, meanwhile, the incidence of female infanticide increased after Chinese leaders introduced a one-child policy in 1980.[71]

The low value attached to girl children is suggested by Rahima, a laundress who lives in Dhaka. Asked about the size of her family, the twenty-five-year-old responds that she has four children. In fact, Rahima has four sons but also one daughter, whom she considers too insignificant to mention.

"This is typical," comments an interpreter. "Sons are an asset and girls are considered a liability. Daughters will go to another house when they are married. When she is old, only her sons will help."

If the absence of sons can result in higher fertility, the reverse can also be true: The demand for family planning services in some Asian countries has risen in direct proportion to the number of sons a family has.[72] Parents with one or more sons are far more likely to be using family planning than parents who have only daughters, according to a UNFPA study. In rural areas, "families with three or more surviving sons are twice as likely to be using family planning as parents with only one son, and over three times as likely as parents with three or more daughters," says the study, titled *Investing in Women*.[73]

Couples with all boys were from two to six times more likely to use modern contraceptives than were couples with all girls, according to another study,[74] while a third, conducted in Nepal, indicates that most couples don't even begin using contraceptives until they have at least one son.[75] If having boys increases contraceptive use, so too does elevating the status of women, according to research published by Karen Oppenheim Mason of the University of Hawaii's East-West Center. In social settings where a degree of parity exists between men and women and where women have access to productive resources, female children have higher value and the pressure to have more children just to get sons is decreased.[76]

A final factor that affects the number of children desired by developing world couples is infant mortality. One bit of wisdom attributed to former Tanzanian president Julius Nyrere is that the most powerful contraceptive is the knowledge that your children will survive. He would have reason to know. Tanzania is one of dozens of third world countries that have contributed to one of the most troubling of demographic statistics: Fourteen million children under the age of five die each year in developing nations as a result of poverty, disease, and malnutrition.[77]

The conventional wisdom is that the death of a child prompts one of two reactions on the part of parents: Either they will replace the child or, in the words of one Thai villager, actually "overshoot" to compensate for the loss by having more than one additional child. As John Baker of the Population and Community Development Association in Bangkok explains the parental calculation: "You go into a village and ask someone to take pills so that they have fewer children and the village woman looks at you and says, I'm only going to have fewer children when I know that the children I already have are going to survive."[78] According to the "child survival hypothesis," couples who expect that some children will die are more reluctant to practice family planning. Statistics gathered by two World Bank researchers indicate, for example, that because an infant's death normally terminates breastfeeding and triggers the resumption of ovulation, it usually increases the number of births over a woman's reproductive life, especially in areas where family planning programs are not available.[79]

The correlation between infant mortality and fertility has not been well documented. In several African and Middle Eastern nations, infant mortality has declined significantly with no impact on high fertility rates, mostly because of the existing high demand for children.[80] But in most of Asia and Latin America, infant mortality and fertility are declining in tandem. In a few countries, including India, couples that have experienced the death of at least one child were found to be more likely to desire a large family and substantially less likely to practice contraception than couples who have not.[81]

Couples with infant or child deaths have an average of just under 50 percent more births than those who don't, according to the World Bank researchers.[82] Conversely, child survival can help lower fertility by increasing intervals between births. It also combats fatalism, encourages family planning, and gives parents the confidence to invest more in fewer children in lieu of having many children. But if reducing childhood mortality helps to reduce fertility, it is also true that family planning helps to reduce childhood mortality; or conversely, that the absence of family planning can contribute to higher infant mortality. The reason: Family planning helps reduce infant deaths by reducing higher-risk births among younger and older women and births that are spaced at intervals of less than two years. In two of many countries where the correlation has been studied—Indonesia and Pakistan—spacing births at least two years apart lowered infant mortality rates by 16 and 15 percent, respectively.[83] While reducing infant mortality rates is probably required to reach replacement fertility, it does not appear to be needed to increase contraceptive acceptance.

"If the goal is healthier parents and children," the two World Bank researchers argue, "then family planning is the most efficient way to achieve it."[84]

In recent years an old debate between advocates of the supply- and demand-side approaches to reducing population growth has given way to a strong and widening consensus that both family planning and social and economic development have strong independent effects on fertility and that the synergy between them is the most potent factor at work on high birthrates.

"Social science has advanced beyond the either/or kind of thing," says the Population Reference Bureau's Peter Donaldson.

"There is agreement that it would be insane for a policymaker to say, I'm going to push family planning at the expense of everything else. And it would be insane for a policymaker to say, I'm not going to have good quality family planning programs."[85]

From this consensus a rough plan of action has emerged. The Population Council's Judith Bruce summarizes its main points: "that good family planning services are important; that there are many deficiencies in quality that need to be improved; that the private sector and NGOs need to be more involved; that men need more attention; that girls' education is important; that women need more access to resources; that family law has been neglected. In short, population policy should include more actions than it has in the past. It has to mean something more far reaching."[86]

But if the theoretical debate has been settled, the more practical question of where to invest limited resources to cope with high rates of population growth has not. Given the necessity to choose, experts ask, should money be spent on long- or short-term approaches to the task of lowering population growth rates? Reproductive rights groups have put a finer point on the question: Should not more of the money now earmarked for family planning be concentrated on meeting women's reproductive health needs?

"The substantive point is taken. The strategy point is still up in the air," says Judith Bruce. "We're underfunded, so one group says, Let's retain what we can for family planning services. Another group says, Let's expand family planning but also encourage the social agenda, especially those issues that improve women's access to resources, since they create the conditions for fertility decline."[87]

New life has been breathed into the case for family planning by a series of national research surveys undertaken beginning in the early 1970s with funds from the U.S. Agency for International Development. The World Fertility Survey (WFS), the Demographic and Health Surveys (DHS), and the Family Planning Surveys (FPS) have reached into dozens of developing countries during the past twenty years and come up with striking findings. In nearly all developing countries, levels of unwanted fertility are high and growing, as is the demand for family planning services. In most countries surveyed by the Demographic and Health Survey, between 20 percent and 30 percent of married women have an unmet need for family planning, which can be met by providing quality contraceptive services alone.[88]

"Family planning is a very simple process," says Malcolm Potts, who teaches population studies at the University of California at Berkeley. "It's easily deflected by evil people like [North Carolina Senator] Jesse Helms but also by well-intended people who want to use it to solve all the problems in the world. The problem is that we're dragging too much on the coattails of family planning. No one can complain about raising the status of women, but it's not family planning and there isn't the money for it. The way to contribute to female education is by doing family planning as cheaply as possible. Overemphasis on unrealistic services is simply wasting money that would meet the goals of feminists better if it was invested directly."[89]

Despite such controversy over tactics, the evidence that family planning and social and economic development are both required to lower fertility to replacement level is abundant and largely unanswerable. A landmark evaluation of family planning programs conducted by Robert Lapham and W. Parker Mauldin in the late 1980s indicates, for example, that even weak family planning programs in countries with "high" social and economic indicators lead to three times the birthrate reduction as weak programs in countries in the "lower-middle" rank. Conversely, a combination of strong development and strong family planning can have a dramatic effect on fertility, as the case of Thailand demonstrates.[90]

Moreover, calculations reported by the Rockefeller Foundation's Steven Sinding suggest the proportional contribution that could be made by the complementary halves of a successful population policy. Sinding estimates that if the unmet need for family planning were satisfied in developing countries, contraceptive use would increase enough to lower fertility halfway from current to replacement level. The other half can be achieved through continued efforts to alleviate poverty and raise living standards, Sinding says, and by providing women with the education and empowerment needed to delay marriage and childbirth and to enhance access to family planning services. As decades of research have proved beyond any doubt, the latter measure especially will be crucial if developing nations are to stabilize their populations at a manageable level.[91]

"As women get more power and more education, they acquire more modern concepts of life, including the idea of small families," summarizes Abbas Bhuiya of the International Center for Diarrheal Disease Research in Dhaka. "It's as certain as the rising and the setting of the sun."[92]

SIX

"Go Forth and Multiply": Faith and Family Planning

Mexico

Padre Alberto Marquez Aquino's church, a cinderblock rectangle held up by poured-concrete beams, is as nondescript as its address: the corner of Avenues 508 and 518 in the sprawling western reaches of one of the world's largest cities.

On this Saturday morning, the neighborhood of Maria Madre de la Iglesia is relaxed. Mothers cluster to gossip while toddlers orbit the pack like tiny revolving moons. Across the street, half a dozen teenage boys hunch over a broken bicycle. Diagonally across from the church, which bears the neighborhood's name, Videocentro does a brisk trade renting movies like *Lethal Weapon* and *Ghostbusters*.

The neighborhood also bears reminders this day of the troubles faced by a country in which rapid population growth has outpaced economic performance, leaving millions unemployed and anxious. A white banner hung from the churchyard fence announces meetings for A Better Way, Mexico's branch of Alcoholics Anonymous.

Padre Marquez's church is a haven for the several hundred parishioners who comprise a corner of this 30,000-person community of bureaucrats and gardeners, small merchants and mechanics.

They come to praise God and confess their sins, to marry and mourn their dead. And, as on this day, to celebrate the rites of passage that demarcate often difficult lives. A special mass has been held to mark the fifteenth birthday of Teresa, dressed for the occasion in a formal, turquoise taffeta dress. Following the service, she is the center of attention in the small courtyard that abuts the church. Four brothers, uncomfortable in ill-fitting tuxedos, act dutifully as attendants while family and friends look on admiringly and an uncle captures the event on videotape. It is a moment of genuine pride and happiness.

A granite statue of Christ Jesus looks on from an adjacent grassy plot demarcated by a dozen poplar trees and rows of pansies and geraniums, bedraggled but still cheerful in the lukewarm January sun. To the right of the statue is a low-slung building that houses the parish's administrative offices. There secretaries answer phones and type letters under the gaze of two figures who have shaped the Catholicism of modern Mexico. One is a virgin. The other has stern advice for those who aren't.

The virgin is Mary, possessor of a virtue the Church has long considered more conducive to the quest for spiritual perfection than marriage. Legend has it that in 1531, just a decade after the Spanish came to Mexico, she appeared to an Indian on his way to a mission. She asked him to build a church to her memory and performed the first miracle in the New World. She is considered a mother to the Americas, a symbol of the arrival of Christianity in Mexico, the West Indies, and Central America. Her virginity is one of the highest ideals in Catholicism.

The other figure is Pope John-Paul II. A color photo of the peripatetic pontiff shows him stepping off an Aero-Mexico jet during his first visit to Mexico, his white robes blending into fluffy winter clouds behind. On his first papal trip, he retraced the route taken by the first Christian evangelist to the New World, Christopher Columbus, to Mexico and the Dominican Republic. He visited Guadalupe's basilica and pledged to be a voice for the poor and oppressed. When he warned that economic and political rights should never be allowed to take precedence over human rights, few of Mexico's faithful missed the point: Catholics should not use hard economic times as an excuse to resort to modern methods of contraception to limit the size of their families.

In 1979, the year of the papal visit, only 18 percent of Mexican women were using contraceptives. Fifteen years later, at 59 percent, Mexico has one of the highest contraceptive prevalence rates in the developing world.

In a small office lined with wooden bookcases, Padre Marquez, a keeper of the faith, says the pope is right.

"We have to respect nature because that's the voice of God and we cannot alter it. These principles the Church teaches can be seen very clearly by people who have the Christian faith, by people who are pure and understand the dignity of the person. We have to learn to look at how we're going to live life. Are we going to live it righteously or go through life doing what our urges prompt us to do? Do you have sex when you want kids or because you like it?"

Marquez has been a priest for over twenty years. A stalwart, he is popular in this community where the Church retains a strong hold on the peoples' affections and loyalties. He speaks as a man who has no doubt about the Church's position on contraception but who understands the struggles of those who do. He also grasps the surprising fact, borne out by a large body of anecdotal evidence, that despite the Church's well-publicized views on the subject, very many Catholics do not understand the large area of permissibility that enables Catholics to space children and to use natural means of contraception to limit family size.

"The problem regarding the use of contraceptives is that many people don't know what the Church really says," says the soft-spoken cleric. "Many people think that the Church says they should have a lot of kids. Others think that Catholicism is totally against any type of contraception and family planning. Maybe 10 percent know what the Church really feels. And because they don't understand what the Church doctrine is, they don't even think about it and they do what they want to do. Some feel guilty but most are simply ignorant of the Church's true position."

As the senior priest of Maria Madre for the past seven years, Marquez has spent dozens of hours talking to parishioners about birth control. His main target has been engaged couples. In sessions before marriage, he tells them about the Church's position, about the requirements of successful marriage, about managing a domestic economy. A doctor talks about sexual relations. The point is reinforced by examples of couples for whom "natural" family planning methods—various forms of periodic abstinence such as the rhythm method—have worked.

"Too many people think natural forms of birth control don't work. If they really understood that natural methods do work, they would not use artificial contraceptives."

He has no way of knowing how many obey because most no longer confess to using modern contraceptives. But he is worried that the battle is being lost.

"There's an element of laziness. There's a certain discipline associated with natural methods that people are unwilling to accept." The real problem, he says, is "the atmosphere of technology" that has bred trust in artificial means to achieve what is now an almost universal goal in Mexico: smaller families.

"When I can talk with people about this personally they usually understand. The problem is that we can only reach so many people. But the publicity and advertising about artificial contraceptives and the need to limit families reaches everybody. People are hearing it from all sides: governments, contraceptive manufacturers, schools. Can the Church compete with this? I'm not sure we can win, but we're trying."

A sketch of Don Quixote hangs on one wall between two bookcases. If Padre Marquez knows the feeling of an uphill cause, he also has no doubt that the cause is right.

"Using artificial contraceptives is a sin. Sin isn't just performing the act of using artificial contraceptives. It's what you think. You can have a wife who uses a pill or an IUD, but if she's not aware that it's a sin it's not a sin. When she comes to me I ask: Did you know it was a sin? If she says no, it's not a sin even though it's all wrong. All sins are forgiven so long as they know they're wrong and try to correct them. Even abortion can be forgiven under such circumstances if the person feels sincerely repentant."

"It's a problem, but it happens in all different areas of life," Marquez says of the spreading apostasy on the subject of birth control. "People take drugs, people are unjust, people will disobey. The mission of the Church is to tell people what's right but there are always going to be people who will go against that."

Guadelupe is one of those people who do.

If the statistics are accurate, the thirty-two-year-old mother of two represents what Mexico has become: a nation of Catholics who believe themselves faithful despite a breach over the essential issue of contraception.

When they were married in San Jose de los Cedros, a small mountain town on the outskirts of the capital, Guadelupe and her husband, Santiago, nodded when the priest informed them that it was their duty to have all the children God sends. The first one, Julio, now fifteen, came almost immediately.

Then Santiago decided to go back to school to earn an accountant's degree. After calculating that it would be impossible to support a second child on a student's budget, Guadelupe made a fateful decision. After talking to her husband and her doctor—but not her priest—she began using an IUD.

"I was just sixteen when I had my first child. I wasn't sure what to do next and I was very afraid. So I talked to my doctor. He recommended using an IUD. We didn't talk about religion. I was aware of what the Church said. But I was sure it would be better to use an artificial contraceptive because I knew 'natural' methods wouldn't work the way the Church said. I knew my husband wouldn't abstain on the days we weren't supposed to have sex."

Like millions of Mexican women, Guadelupe insists that the decision to use artificial contraceptives has not compromised her loyalties to the Church. "I agree with the Church on everything else," she says. "I still think of myself as a good Catholic. But I can't agree on the subject of birth control. I can't believe that the fact that I only want two children makes me a bad Catholic."

Two years ago a second child, Edgar, was born. After consulting with her husband again, she decided to have a tubal ligation, closing off the possibility of further births. Later she told her parish priest. He told her that what she had done was a sin, then said that what's done is done.

"I told him, I don't care because I don't want to have any more kids. To bring kids into the world and not be able to give them proper food and clothing is not right. I know I'm supposed to do what God wants. But I don't see God. I haven't heard him tell me to have more children. So I feel I've done the right thing. I'm sure that God cannot be angry with me because I want to have only the children I can educate.

"Things are difficult here. A majority of people are having hard times. Jobs are hard to come by. For me the issue is education. You can't give your kids a good education if you have too many of them. With only two kids we can get them farther along in school, and that's what's going to make it possible for them to have good jobs.

"The Church should accept what the people use because there are so many poor people and the Church doesn't help them. The Church says not to use contraceptives, that it's a sin, but they don't come here and say, I see you have all these kids and I'll help you.

"I'm still a Catholic," says the namesake of her country's patron saint. "But birth control is a whole different issue."

———

If there is any institution that symbolizes conservative resistance to the use of modern contraception, it is the Roman Catholic Church. The opposition is so powerful that, when surveyed in 1992, one distinguished group of academics and government officials judged that changing the Vatican's position was one of the most urgent measures needed to solve one of the world's most urgent problems: rapid population growth.[1]

But as the case of Guadelupe illustrates, the reality behind the perception is changing fast. Across Mexico and around the Catholic world, a historic transformation of lay attitudes toward contraception is taking place as the relentless pace of modernization is forcing millions of believers to revise their ideas about what is morally correct and religiously acceptable. In Latin America, where half the world's 800 million Catholics reside, this transformation has already produced significant demographic changes: A continent that used to be the object of gloomy demographic predictions, similar to those now made about Africa, is now a notable, if not uniform, family planning success story.

"In terms of attitudes toward family planning, Latin America is like Berlin after the Wall came down," says Paul Burgess, a former priest and Vatican official who is an expert on population issues. "It's a whole new era."[2]

At least since the sixteenth century, the Catholic Church has approved the concept of "responsible parenthood," meaning that it is acceptable for Catholic couples to limit births for legitimate medical, economic, and social reasons. The main sticking point is the means, and it is over the question of using "modern" contraceptives that the issue between Rome and the Catholic faithful worldwide has been joined. In many individual countries, Catholics use contraceptives at rates equal to or higher than do adherents of other faiths.[3] Of those who do not, religion is usually now the main reason.[4] Meanwhile, despite pressure from the Church, governments in most Catholic countries are now committed to family planning and have invested large sums of money to make contraceptives widely available.

In Mexico, the magazine *Excelsior* recently sampled public attitudes on a range of matters in which the Church's views have long held sway. Among other things, 93 percent of respondents said that they approved of family planning; only 7 percent disapproved.[5]

On the matter of specific contraceptive choice, public attitudes in Mexico and across Latin America are also largely at variance with the teachings of the Church. Despite the Church's 1975 ban on sterilization, 20 percent of Latin American couples of reproductive age use sterilization and the proportion is rising fast, according to one UN study. Fully one fourth of reproductive age married women in Brazil are sterilized, one third in Panama and El Salvador, and 40 percent in Puerto Rico, the highest rate in the world. And these trends show no sign of leveling off. Among women in their later thirties and early forties, the figures are higher still.[6]

As for the pill, banned in the Church's definitive 1968 encyclical *Humanae Vitae*, only northern and western Europe surpass Catholic Latin America in its use. Together, the pill and female sterilization account for two-thirds of all contraceptive use in Latin America and the Caribbean.[7]

The defection from Church strictures even extends to the baseline issue of abortion, which in the face of the widespread use of contraceptives has become a more crucial litmus test of fidelity. In Mexico, as in most Latin American countries, induced abortion is illegal, permitted only if the life of the mother is endangered or if a woman is a victim of rape or incest. Even so, in a 1991 Mexican Gallup poll, 75 percent of respondents said the decision whether to have an abortion belongs to the woman alone (40 percent) or should be made by the couple together (35 percent). The poll showed that 43 percent of women and a surprising 54 percent of men believe that women should not have to consult the Church when deciding whether to have an abortion.[8]

In practice, the Church's partial success in restricting the availability of contraceptives, and thus increasing the number of unwanted pregnancies, has resulted in higher rates of abortion throughout Latin America. A quarter of all pregnancies in Latin America have been intentionally aborted during the past two decades, compared with estimates of less than 10 percent in Africa and between 15 and 20 percent in South and Southeast Asia, according to the International Planned Parenthood Federation.[9] In a U.S. survey conducted by the Alan Guttmacher Institute in 1987, Catholic women were found to be 30 percent more likely to have an abortion than Protestant women.[10]

The diminishing influence of religion on fertility is also suggested by the fact that the gap between desired fertility and actual fertility—that is, the percentage of unwanted births—is higher in Latin America than any region of the globe. Among women in Latin America who do not want children and who do not use contraceptives, only a small minority cite religious beliefs as their reason for not practicing family planning, according to the IPPF.[11]

Latin America, of course, is not the only predominantly Catholic region swept by the revolution in contraceptive use. The use of modern birth control devices is widespread in other Catholic nations, testifying to the prevalence of what Pope John Paul II has described as the "contraceptive mentality." The prime example lies outside the pope's front door. Italy, where condoms can be purchased within sight of the Vatican, has the highest contraceptive prevalence rate (nearly 80 percent) and the lowest fertility rate (1.3 children per woman) ever recorded. According to the World Health Organization, the country's birthrate has declined by half since the early 1960s. It now produces fewer children in relation to its population than any country in the world.[12]

Nor is Catholicism the only religion buffeted by the contraceptive revolution. Millions of Muslims have responded as well by accenting a more permissive side of their theology. In the process they have removed one barrier to reducing fertility in the Muslim crescent of South Asia and the Arab world, where birthrates are among the highest in the world. There are signs of change even in that bastion of religious fundamentalism Iran, where a belated recognition of the economic consequences of runaway population growth has led government officials to begin aggressively promoting family planning.

The ethics of reproduction are also changing in Hindu nations. Like most of the world's major faiths, Hinduism is pronatalist and patriarchal. Sons are extremely important, among other reasons, because males are responsible for the funeral rites that ensure the survival of the souls of the departed.[13] In rural Nepal, the emphasis on sons has been so great that couples traditionally have as many as six children to ensure two surviving sons, according to research conducted by the Ford Foundation's James Ross.[14]

But in Nepal, as elsewhere, new factors have altered the calculus of reproduction. With less and less agricultural land to divide among heirs, the economics of having large families has been altered. As a result, religious considerations that favor large families have taken a backseat to the necessity of having fewer children who can be educated for salaried jobs. The trend toward smaller families in Nepal has been abetted by the increasing availability of health care services, which have raised child survival rates, and by the provision of basic family planning services by the government.

"In all religions there are strong culturally pronatalist values, but they are amenable to variation," says Ross, who is the Ford Foundation's representative in Bangladesh.

In nearly every region of the world, similar circumstances have prompted millions of believers to separate their reproductive decisions from their religious faith.

The recent dramatic growth of urban areas has been one powerful catalyst for change. In the face of the idle hours of unemployment, shacks made from scrounged debris, and the brutal environment of exploding mega-slums, the admonition of one recent pope that "large families are most blessed by God" has lost much of its appeal.[15]

The evolving role of women has also had a large effect, as the gradual expansion of economic and educational opportunities has catapulted millions of women out of traditional roles that are often reinforced by religious doctrines.

Conservative religious teachings have also lost ground to the full-scale public information campaigns mounted by scores of government and private family planning agencies, which have relentlessly spread the new gospel of smaller families to the remotest corners of the world.

Bruce Harris is head of the Mexico City office of Covenant House, a Catholic charity that helps street children. His observation on Latin America has universal application. "It's simple," he says. "With more kids, more mouths to feed, and an urban economy that's not growing at a rate where kids can be absorbed into it, you'll have an excess number of kids who won't have enough to eat. If you're living on the edge of survival, economic decisions outweigh the Church."[16]

Demographers and other academic experts have debated for years just how—or even whether—religious beliefs influence reproductive behavior.

During the 1950s and 1960s, the conventional wisdom was that Church doctrine made a big difference in fertility rates and contraceptive practices. This commonsensical-sounding notion of "particularized theology" held that couples whose religion banned abortion and contraceptives and promoted large families were likely to have more children.

Nowadays demographers are much less certain whether this cause-and-effect relationship actually exists and are much more inclined to attribute the high birthrates of earlier eras to factors other than religion. In fact, women may have had their own reason for wanting larger families, a desire that was far more prevalent in premodern rural societies. Or large families may have simply resulted from the fact that modern contraceptives were unavailable.

Joseph Chamie is a UN official whose book *Religion and Fertility* examines the influence of religious beliefs on reproductive behavior in Lebanon.[17]

"Forty years ago it seemed that if Catholics had higher fertility than Jews, religion must be the reason," he says. "The problem is that correlations don't prove causality. Very few people have eight or ten kids because of religion."[18]

In fact, the synergism between religious belief and fertility is complex. To understand it, it is necessary to make a distinction between the direct and indirect influence religion has on reproductive behavior.

Most researchers doubt that there has ever been a strong direct correlation between Church policy and individual family planning decisions. If they are right, plummeting fertility in the Catholic world (and elsewhere, for that matter) may have little to do with the declining influence of the Church. Modernization, urbanization, higher levels of education, expanding economic opportunities for women, and the sheer availability of contraception may be more important factors.

Bolivia and Peru are cases in point. According to recent studies, a majority of women in these countries use "natural" methods of contraception—not because the Church tells them to, but because they can't obtain more modern methods. The fact that 90 percent of Peruvian and Bolivian women say they do not want another child is stronger evidence that fealty to the Church is not their primary motive. Indeed, Peru has the highest level of unmet demand for modern contraceptives in the world.[19]

Research conducted in 1987 by the Mexican Institute for Family and Population Research confirms the absence of any significant direct Church influence on reproductive behavior. The study examined factors that form attitudes and shape behavior on the subject of family planning. The key variable turned out to be the relationship women had with their sexual partners. Out of 1,500 women interviewed, only one cited the Church's position as her reason for not using artificial contraception.[20]

Evidence from Colombia reinforces the point. A survey there questioned sexually active women who said they did not want to become pregnant, yet did not use artificial contraception. Fewer than one in 200 cited religious beliefs as their reason for not practicing family planning.[21] Similar conclusions, based on anecdotal evidence, come from a series of interviews the Mexican Institute conducted with Mexican women whose reproductive years predated the widespread availability of modern family planning methods.

"Women have always wanted family planning in this country; they have always wanted to stop having so many children," says the Institute's Susan Pick de Weiss. "But women were afraid to talk about it. It wasn't socially acceptable. . . . It's not that *attitudes* have changed. It's *behavior* that's changed because now it's possible to get information about family planning and access to contraceptives."[22]

"There has never been a period when a majority of Catholic women took the Church's position on birth control seriously. The Church's position has never been a determining factor for most women," adds Frances Kissling, president of the Washington-based Catholics for a Free Choice. "What has changed is sexual attitudes and the availability of contraceptives."[23]

The evidence suggests, then, that the direct influence of religious doctrine on individual reproductive decisions is weak. But indirect or oblique influence is another matter, and in many countries this has been sufficient to slow the transition from high to low fertility. One example of such influence is the way religious authorities have restricted access to modern contraceptives, often through direct intervention in the political process. Their main targets have been sterilization, which is restricted in most Catholic and Islamic nations, and abortion, which is widely practiced but legally banned except to save the life of the mother in the Catholic nations of Eastern Europe, in Francophone Africa, and everywhere in Latin America except for Cuba and Nicaragua.

But even temporary birth control methods have come under religious censure. The Church has attacked the pill, IUDs, and other modern contraceptives for being "abortifacients," since on very rare occasions they act to prevent implantation of a fertilized egg. In lieu of such "artificial" means it has promoted "natural" methods like breastfeeding and periodic abstinence, which have a higher failure rate.

Limits on contraceptive choices can also be self-imposed for religious reasons. Two American scholars published research in the late 1980s indicating that American Catholics have a somewhat greater tendency to use the anonymous condom rather than IUDS and diaphragms, which require the intervention of a physician.[24]

Another example is the influence religion has on the cultural values that bear on fertility, including attitudes toward children, family size, and the role of women in society. Sylvia Marcos, a clinical psychologist from Guernavaca and director of the Mexican branch of Catholics for the Right to Decide, explains: "The Church is a determinant in a larger sense than just faith. The morals of Mexico are Catholic morals. It's not that people have religious attitudes but that it's a Catholic, pronatalist culture with no public life for women."[25]

This phenomenon can manifest itself in ways that seem contradictory. One Mexican doctor explains that in her small village, fear of using contraceptives often outweighs the fear of getting pregnant.

"There's less stigma for a girl who has premarital sex without contraceptives and gets pregnant than one who uses contraceptives and doesn't. If you use birth control, people assume you're sleeping with several people."[26]

The Mexican Institute, for its part, found in research conducted in 1990 that religious values did have a significant bearing on the sexual behavior of Mexican adolescents. At least one important personality trait—submissiveness—distinguished between teenagers who had sex and those who did not; between those who used contraceptives and those who did not; and between those who got pregnant and those who did not.

"The strong influence of the Church is indirect. It's cultural and educational. The submissiveness is a kind of passiveness, a lack of initiative, a tendency to obey authority—men, adults, parents, the Church. It's in this sense that the influence of the Church is important—this submissiveness and the guilt it teaches us we should have," says the Institute's de Weiss.[27]

"We are taught that we should obey what is expected of us and not think in terms of what we need," de Weiss continues. "We are expected to be traditional in our ways. One aspect of this is to have sex for reproductive reasons, not to have sex for pleasure.

"An enormous amount of the education we get and the motivation we have in our day-to-day actions is based on guilt. If I don't do this I get punished. If I do this I get rewarded. We are not internally controlled in our actions but more externally controlled, and one of the external factors is the guilt. And I think that is transmitted through the Church."

In the Muslim world, the line between religion and conservative social traditions is harder to draw. But the effect of Catholic values has its counterpart. Despite the pressures of overcrowding in cities like Cairo and Algiers, couples are still urged by families and friends to have children early and often.

"The normal thing is, after you get married, people begin to ask: Any good news? Anything coming along yet?" says one young Cairene who decided to delay her first pregnancy.

High fertility rates are buttressed by the less than egalitarian view of women that prevails in many Muslim nations. Attitudes toward marriage (early), divorce (easy for a man; nearly impossible for a woman), and polygamy (permitted conditionally in the Koran and still legal even in more modernized Muslim countries like Egypt) reinforce a woman's dependence on children for status and economic security. In Muslim as in most third world societies, the primary role of women is to serve and obey men and to bear them children.

The strength of such attitudes has forced family planning agencies to be highly sensitive to religious opinion and cultural views. A new employee's manual issued by Egypt's Ministry of Health containing instructions on dealing with patients, for example, strikes a fine balance between the sacred and profane in making the case that mothers should breastfeed as a means of spacing births: "She will please her God, who has ordained breastfeeding. She will [also] protect her baby's life and get rid of fats accumulated during pregnancy, thus preserving her figure."[28]

In Latin America, family planning agencies have also had to base their arguments for child-spacing on the need to protect the health of mother and child, without reference to limiting family size. In several notable cases, including Colombia, they have made a virtue of necessity to gain the reluctant acquiescence of Church authorities. They have argued that if the Church is serious about stopping abortion, then Church officials must back—or at least not publicly oppose—family planning to reduce the number of unwanted pregnancies.

The strongest influence religion has on slowing the transition to low fertility is among poor and uneducated women in rural areas. The example of one woman living in a village in rural Bangladesh illustrates the point.

Influenced by the steady drumbeat of family planning messages broadcast by the government and endorsed by the country's Muslim hierarchy, the woman decided to get sterilized, but without her husband's permission. "A few days after she was sterilized she slipped and fell down and has not felt well since," note Sidney Ruth Schuler and Syed M. Hashemi, the two researchers who interviewed her. "Her husband consulted the local *maulavis*, and she became worried about whether she would receive a proper burial. She recalled that, a month after her sister-in-law was sterilized, a goat died all of a sudden. She confided to the interviewer her fear that punishment might suddenly be meted out to her as well."

"There is punishment for not seeking one's husband's permission," she told the researchers. "Sin I have committed, no doubt, and my heart throbs constantly with premonitions and fears."[29]

The woman's experience illustrates what Schuler and Hashemi describe as the struggle taking place in rural Bangladesh between "traditional" and "modern" views of the religious status of contraception. This struggle remains intense in rural and poor settings. But there is now abundant evidence that the resistance of religion and tradition give way quickly in the presence of opportunities for higher education and gainful employment.

Fertility rates are relatively low in Muslim countries such as Tunisia and Turkey that provide greater access for women to education and jobs, according to one study. Rates remain high in Muslim nations where such opportunities are largely unavailable, such as Algeria and Pakistan. The results suggest that fertility rates are a function not so much of religion as of education and employment. These secular concerns influence age at marriage, equality within marriage, and the confidence to use family planning services.[30]

The conclusion that socioeconomic factors outweigh religion when it comes to reproductive choices is supported by another study, conducted in Bangladesh. The research showed no significant differences in the use of contraceptives between Muslims and Hindus at higher levels of education. At lower levels of education, contraceptive use among Hindus was significantly higher than among Muslims.[31]

Whether they like it or not, the world's major religions have had to take steps to accommodate the contraceptive revolution that has swept the world since the 1960s. In many ways Islam has adapted more gracefully to these changing circumstances.

There are differences of opinion among Islamic leaders over the propriety of modern family planning methods. But these tend to be vertical, between conservatives who cling to old ways and liberals who believe that the religion needs to be responsive to changing circumstances. In the Catholic Church, the division is more strictly horizontal, as parishioners and many local clerics, faced daily with the grim consequences of rapid urbanization and population growth in Latin America and Africa, have parted ways with the strict mandates of Rome.

"Is the Roman Catholic Church against family planning?" asks the former priest Paul Burgess. "If by the Church you mean the hierarchy and the bishops in Rome, the answer is yes. If by the Church you mean the clergy and the laity, the answer is no. At the level where it counts, the Catholic Church practices birth control."[32]

The history of the Catholic Church's position on contraception can be divided into two distinct phases.[33] During the first, which lasted until the Reformation in the sixteenth century, a rigidly restrictive doctrine evolved in response to one set of historical circumstances, including the plagues and famines lasting through the Middle Ages, that decimated Catholic populations in Europe.

"We are not dealing with a doctrine invented by man," said Pope John Paul II of the teaching. It is a doctrine "written by the creative hand of God in the nature of the human person."[34]

The second phase has been one of a halting, reluctant, limited accommodation to another set of historical circumstances: the improving status of women, greater scientific knowledge of the reproductive function, the rise of the birth control movement, and the population crisis itself—the combination of which has produced a slight relaxation in the Church's absolute standard.

The Church's dim view of contraception began as a reaction to the sexual dissipation of the Roman empire, where the Church was born. It drew strength from the Genesis injunction to "go forth and multiply," prompting one early pope to insist that procreation was not merely good but sacred, since it furthered the work of God. Grounded on the point, early Catholic theologians concluded that procreation could be the only legitimate reason for conjugal intercourse.[35] To survive in the face of the pagan vices of the Greco-Roman world, writes former Vatican official Francis X. Murphy, "the Church had to insist on the value of life and its transmission, and the positive aspects of love and human dignity."[36]

The next intellectual building block was supplied by St. Augustine, who in the fifth century posited the notion that dominated all of Christianity until the twentieth: that contraception was evil since it violated the primary purpose of marital intercourse—namely, to produce children. In Augustine's scheme, contraception was an instrument of the sin of lust, turning the wife into a "harlot" and the husband into an "adulterer." Couples who used an "evil appliance" to stop contraception, Augustine warned, were guilty of mortal sin.[37] The first actual papal injunction against birth control, issued by Gregory IX in 1230, reflected a further concern that contraception opened the door to promiscuity, threatening the sanctity of marriage. The first papal legislation on the subject, enacted by Gregory X in 1272, voided a marriage that was entered into with the intention of not having children.[38]

By the advent of the modern age, the fundamental premise of the Church's position was firmly in place: that sexual intercourse was not legitimate without reproductive intent. As a result, the Church's first reaction to the growing practice of contraception, championed by the birth control movement that originated in nineteenth-century England and America, was defensive.

"Any use whatsoever of matrimony exercised in such a way that the act is frustrated in its natural power to guarantee life is an offense against the law of God and nature, and those who indulge in such are branded with the guilt of grave sin," a defiant Pope Pius XI declared in a landmark encyclical in 1930.[39]

The document makes clear that the Church's pronatalism was not entirely disinterested. It is the duty of Christian couples, it said, "to raise up . . . members of God's household, that the worshipers of God and of Our Savior may daily increase."[40] But in one of the first compromises of its kind, the same Pope Pius XI recognized the legitimacy of intercourse during the infertile period, if not for family planning then at least as a means of satisfying the secondary ends of marriage: "mutual aid, the cultivation of mutual love, and the quieting of concupiscence."[41]

Two decades later, in 1951, Pope Pius XII went further, recognizing the legitimacy of natural family planning under certain circumstances but within the context of a general obligation on the part of married couples to have children.[42] Pius endorsed the principle, implied in earlier Church teachings, that acceptable medical, economic, and social grounds exist for avoiding procreation. The position, which still pertains, is as close as the Church has ever come to legitimizing family planning.

The high-water mark of dissent occurred when, spurred by the advent of the pill and runaway population growth in the developing world, a movement formed within the Church to legitimize all forms of contraception. In 1963, during the Second Vatican Council, Pope John XXIII bowed to the gathering forces of change and agreed to create a commission to review the Church's position on family planning. After deliberating for two years, a body of sixty-four laymen and theologians endorsed a plan to revise Church policy by allowing the use of artificial contraceptives. Of the fifteen cardinals who took part in the final session, only six voted to maintain the Church's hard-line position. The commission even prepared an explanatory note laying the intellectual groundwork for what would have been a historic turnabout comparable to those made by the Church in earlier years on the subjects of slavery and usury.

"They left convinced that the position was going to change," explains Father Murphy, whose reports from Vatican II were published in *The New Yorker* under the *nom de plume* Xavier Rynne.[43] But at the last minute a small group of conservative bishops intervened with Paul VI, who had acceded to the papacy after John's death in 1963. They convinced him that to change positions after so long would undermine the Church's magisterial authority. "If the Church had been wrong, what would that mean for the souls sent to Hell for violating the ban?" one Spanish Jesuit asked, getting to the heart of the matter.[44]

After a long period of deliberation, during which one cardinal personally entreated the pope not to create "another Galileo case" by keeping the Church out of sync with the times, the pontiff decided to close the door on reform.[45] In a strongly worded encyclical, *Humanae Vitae*, issued in 1968, he categorically reaffirmed the Church's prohibition on all but natural forms of contraception. The Church's teaching is founded on nothing less, he said, than "the inseparable connection, established by God and unable to be broken by man on his own initiative, between the unitive and the procreative meanings" of the conjugal act.[46]

The ban on artificial methods was reaffirmed in 1992 in the first new universal catechism issued by the Church since the mid-sixteenth century.[47] In 1993 it was again reaffirmed in the encyclical *Veritatis Splendor*,[48] issued by Paul's successor, John Paul II, who early in his papacy attacked the "irrational control of births preventing the access of new mouths at the banquet of the Lord."[49]

Like the pope, defenders of *Humanae Vitae* see the ban on artificial contraception as part of a larger war against the onslaught of materialism, secularism, and sexual permissiveness. Defenders also insist that the Church is not ignoring the real problem, which is not rapid population growth but political and economic systems that inequitably distribute the world's resources.

"We can't take a mechanistic approach to the solution of poverty and finding jobs," explains one Mexican Church official. "We can't lump all this into the population bottle. We can't say that if we just give enough people enough pills and IUDs that somehow justice will suddenly emerge. We've had family planning programs in Mexico for twenty years. We've reduced fertility rates. But our people still do not have more jobs, are not wealthier, do not have better jobs than when fertility rates were higher."[50]

But in other quarters *Humanae Vitae* was greeted with consternation, opening the door to a dissident view that is now so widespread within the Church as to bear quasilegitimacy in the eyes of many Catholic clerics and laity. Twenty-five years later, one priest describes the encyclical as "probably the papacy's most controversial . . . and also probably its most ineffective document."[51]

When *Humanae Vitae* was handed down, hundreds of theologians and Catholic scholars around the world respectfully but firmly dissented. A majority of the national bishops' conferences "mitigated" the encyclical by pointing to another Church doctrine—freedom of conscience—that confers upon Catholics the right to make their own decisions. A large minority of bishops at a 1980 synod on the family, meanwhile, asked that the encyclical be reconsidered.[52]

Many clerics and lay Catholics have challenged the notion, advanced by the Church for centuries, that contraception violates "natural law," a controversial concept that is usually interpreted to mean whatever the authorities in Rome say it means. Others now protest that in an era of AIDS, and in the face of the vast number of unsafe abortions resulting from unwanted pregnancies in Catholic countries each year, the Church's views on contraception are at variance with its own doctrine regarding the sanctity of human life.

Another objection has been the element of confusion that, critics charge, continues to surround the Church's position. Since the 1920s it has been known that a woman can get pregnant only three days or so of every month. Such knowledge has rendered meaningless the notion that every conjugal act should be open to the transfer of life. If, say the critics, it is acceptable to take advantage of such long infertile periods, as the encyclical indicates, then it is disingenuous to insist, as *Humanae Vitae* also does, that all sex acts remain open to the transmission of life. And if economic and educational considerations constitute valid moral reasons for limiting family size—a notion first legitimized by the Church in the sixteenth century—then why does it matter whether natural or artificial means are used? Why, in short, is one form of contraception (natural) a form of obedience to the law of God, while another (artificial) is a sin, when the usual motive behind the use of either—child-spacing and family limitation—is acceptable to the Church?

The answer, given overwhelmingly by Catholics around the world, reflects significant global value changes that have left the Church and its adherents at a crucial impass. Church officials show no signs of backing down. Individual Catholics continue to use modern contraceptives at rates equal to or higher than non-Catholics. The issue is joined, and no compromise is in sight.

While Roman Catholicism is restrictive at the top and permissive at the bottom, just the reverse is true in Muslim nations, where birthrates are among the highest in the world.

Mohammad Sayyid Tantawi's office overlooks one of the infamous landmarks of Cairo: a cemetery—the "City of the Dead"—which is home to half a million living Cairenes. A government-appointed *mufti*, or religious scholar, he speaks with authority as a keeper of doctrine for the world's 850 million Sunni Muslims.

"Islam provides no opposition to controlling birth. There is no Koranic verse which forbids family planning," says the bearded cleric. "I personally, if I were to have a meeting with the pope at the Vatican, would explain to him that the Shari'a of Islam does not forbid family planning as long as the couple sees that there is a necessity for it."[53]

Across town, inside an ornate 300-year-old mosque, three wiz-
ened sheikhs ponder the same subject while waiting for the start of
afternoon prayers.

"Contraception is killing," says one, as his bearded colleagues
nod in agreement. "Because God the Almighty is the one who creates the being, so we do not kill it."

"The only people who say contraception is okay are the sheikhs
of the government," proclaims another, in an obvious reference to
Tantawi. "All other sheikhs say it's sacrilegious. The Koran says
you can't limit the size of your family."

Just what is and what is not allowed under Muslim law, it seems,
is a matter of debate. Throughout the 1,400-year history of Islam,
the world's second-largest faith, children have been considered one
of the greatest blessings of God. The religion's long tradition,
based on the Prophet Muhammad's injunction to "marry and have
children"—the Islamic equivalent of the Genesis admonition to
"go forth and multiply"—is one reason why large families have
been the rule in Muslim nations. But in the Muslim world, as in
Catholic nations, old teachings are bumping up against the hard
realities of population trends that have fundamentally altered daily
life. The result has been a sweeping redefinition of permissible reproductive behavior that has opened the door to family planning
progress in Muslim countries around the world.

The implications of high birthrates in the Arab world dawned
first among politicians, whose jobs depend on keeping up with spiraling demands for jobs, food, and housing. More than three decades ago, Tunisia's president Habib Bourghiba warned of "a
human tidal wave that is implacably rising—rising more quickly
than our capacity to support ourselves."

"What good is it to increase our agricultural production and
our mineral wealth if the population continues its anarchic and de-
mential growth?" Bourghiba asked rhetorically as he established
the region's first successful family planning program.[54]

Thirty years later, the logic of family planning extends even to that bastion of Shiite orthodoxy, Iran. When they seized control of the country from the Shah in 1979, the country's Islamic rulers sneered at birth control, condemning it as a Western plot. Fifteen years later, with twice the population but the same fixed, oil-based annual income, the mullahs have caught the spirit. With the zeal of converts, they have erected the structure of a family planning program that includes everything from aggressive public education to free vasectomies to financial disincentives for couples having over three children.[55]

As the case of Indonesia, the Muslim world's greatest success story, demonstrates, translating the desire to slow population growth into a successful family planning program involves more than creating a government bureaucracy. It also requires winning the support of the country's Islamic establishment.

"You can't disregard the fact that you have to get Islamic support," says Aziza Hussein, who should know. She is the founder and chairperson of the Cairo Family Planning Association, a leading private group that has devoted long hours to cultivating clerical support for Egypt's family planning efforts. "If Islamic leaders know the size of the problem they have to back family planning," Hussein says, "because Islam says you have to do what's in the interest of the community."[56]

Such support has been forthcoming in many Islamic nations because, with the Koran silent on the subject of family planning, the issue has essentially been a matter of local option.

Tantawi explains: "When it comes to rituals, they are required to be performed the same way in Egypt as in Saudi Arabia. But there is nothing in the Koran about family planning, so in these matters we improvise.

"Family planning is permitted in the Islamic Shari'a whenever there is a necessity for it. And this question varies from one circumstance to another, from one state to another. Where family planning might be a duty in Egypt it could be unnecessary in Libya, for example, because Libya's area is greater than that of

Egypt and its population is only 4 million. A *fatwa* [religious edict] there would be different than a *fatwa* here, even if set by the same man."[57]

Another reason for Islam's adaptability is that the faith contains parallel traditions, one that provides an elaborate justification for large families, the other of which, now in vogue, justifies precisely the opposite. The first tradition stems from the notion, a tenet of nearly every major faith, that children are the gifts of God and that it is a religious duty to multiply. For generations the sacred admonition to "marry and multiply, for I will make a display of you on the Day of Judgment," has been reinforced by secular circumstances—namely, the need for many children to earn and protect wealth, gain honor, and demonstrate a man's virility. If it is right to propagate, then the reverse is also true: that to thwart pregnancy—even for economic reasons—is to thwart the will of God and to doubt his ability to provide.

"What creature living on earth does not God look after?" asks one of the Egyptian sheikhs. "You do not kill your children for the fear of poverty, because God provides."

The resistance to family planning stems also from the fatalistic notion that, with or without contraceptives, God will settle the issue of family size.

"To God is ownership of the skies and heaven," says another of the sheikhs. "God can make a woman pregnant or make a man sterile. It is all God's decision."

An entirely different strain of Islamic thought is elucidated in Tantawi's 1989 *fatwa*, which has been indispensable to the Egyptian government's efforts to slow the country's population growth rate. The more liberal view laid out in the *fatwa* draws on the Koran's counsel to parents to have no more children than they can provide for physically and economically. The corollary—that preventing economic hardship nurtures piety—also speaks to the burden of large families on parents. "The most grueling trial," the tradition of the Prophet has it, "is to have plenty of children with no adequate means."[58] Nor are weak multitudes advantageous to the prosperity of Islam itself, as one official statement issued by the *mufti* proclaims: "Such a multitude cannot be considered as a source of pride for the noble Prophet, peace be upon him. On the contrary, Islam abhors and despises such a multitude as pointed out by the Prophet: '. . . You will be in great numbers, but you will be worthless like the bubbles of water driven ahead by torrents.' "[59]

The most important tenet of this more permissive interpretation is its endorsement of contraception, based on the Hadith, or commentaries on the Prophet written by Muhammad's contemporaries, including Jabir Ibn Abdullah: "We used to practice coitus interruptus ['*azl*] during the time of the Prophet. The Prophet came to know about it, but did not forbid us. If this were something to be prohibited, the Koran would have forbidden us to do it."[60]

Using argument by analogy—the third source of law after the Koran and the Hadith—Muslim scholars have reasoned that if '*azl* was acceptable to the Prophet, modern contraceptives are acceptable today.

An earlier *fatwa*, handed down in 1964, elucidates the context in which the issue of contraception has been re-evaluated. In an earlier period in history, it notes, Muslims had to multiply to generate the manpower needed to defend Islam against powerful adversaries. "But now," it says, "we find that conditions have changed. We find that the density of population in the world threatens seriously to reduce the living standards of mankind to the extent that many men of thought have been prompted to seek family planning in every country, so that the resources may not fall short of ensuring a decent living for its people."[61]

Although family planning has been the subject of debate among Islamic scholars for centuries, the more permissive view has been buttressed by the impact of unprecedented population growth rates.

"Fifty years ago, the *mufti* would have said that family planning is infidelism and paganism, going against the will of God. Talking about family planning would have been impossible," says Tantawi. "But the world has changed in the past fifty years more than it has in the thousand years before. Fifty years ago, the population of Egypt was 6 million and there were 6 million fedans of land. Today there are 60 million Egyptians and the land is still 6 million. So family planning is necessary. You must take the measures by which you minimize the numbers of population so that Egypt can progress."[62]

But if such adaptability has enabled governments like Egypt to harness the Muslim establishment to its policy of reducing population growth, the message has been slow to trickle down to the local mosque *imams*, or preachers, many of whom—to the consternation of family planning agencies—still counsel that limiting family size contravenes the will of God.

The problem, explains Abdel Omran in his book *Family Planning in the Legacy of Islam*, is that with family planning acceptable in Islam only by implication, the latitude for disagreement is wide: "It's not like prayer, which you have to do. In Islam family planning is permissible but it's optional. That opens the door to controversy. Islam is definitely not a hindrance to family planning, but grassroots Muslim leaders sometimes oppose family planning because of their own misunderstanding."[63]

The traditional, antimodernist outlook of many local *imams* has been reinforced by the resurgence of Muslim fundamentalism, which views family planning as a Western plot to weaken Islam by keeping Muslim nations underpopulated.

"The correct interpretation [of Islam on family planning] will win out in the end," says Tantawi. "The people who have brains are aware of it. Thanks be to God, the people who have brains are becoming more numerous than those without."[64]

On January 30, 1993, news of an unusual incident crossed the Associated Press news wire. It concerned the death of an Italian housewife, Carla Ardenghi. Stricken with cancer, the twenty-eight-year-old Ardenghi decided to stop treatments during her pregnancy to protect her unborn child. Eight hours after the baby's premature birth, Carla Ardenghi died.

"Every day in my life is another day for the child I have inside," reads an entry from her diary, released by her husband.[65]

Ardenghi's death, which was front-page news in Italy, triggered a lively public debate over the terrible ethical dilemmas involved in weighing the life of a mother against that of an unborn child. Inside the Vatican, it was an easy call. One Church spokesman praised Ardenghi posthumously for her "heroic" decision not to have an abortion, a decision, said another, that has given meaning to "all of our lives." A month earlier the Vatican beatified Gianna Beretta Molla, advancing to the verge of sainthood another Italian woman who died in 1962 after giving birth.[66]

The Vatican's swift, unqualified response to Ardenghi's death provides an instructive glimpse of the Church's continuing determination to stem the global tide of apostasy on matters of abortion and contraception. Having lost the battle for the hearts and minds of the vast majority of Catholic faithful, Church leaders by the mid-1970s had adopted the only available alternative strategy, stepping up efforts to win their governments with the objectives of keeping abortion illegal, modern contraceptives scarce, and sex education out of the classroom.

"In terms of [contraceptive] practice, Catholicism has little influence at the parochial level," says Thomas Merrick, senior population adviser at the World Bank in Washington. "But politically the Church is a force in Latin America. At that level the Church has often been a player in the question of whether or not a country should have family planning."[67]

In spirited attacks, Latin American bishops have scorned the relentless inroads made by family planning agencies as a form of "contraceptive imperialism" designed to impose alien traditions on their countries. In Mexico, Church officials have denounced family planning as a "smokescreen" intended, according to various interpretations, to keep Mexico's population low to slow the rate of immigration to the United States; to contribute to the prosperity that would enable Mexicans to buy more consumer goods from the United States; or simply to keep Mexico weak.[68] One particularly blunt papal message juxtaposes the "culture of death," which equates contraception with drugs and murder, with the "culture of life" championed by the Church.[69]

Beyond mere rhetoric, Church leaders have skillfully capitalized on their formidable influence in Catholic countries. In the unusual case of Mexico, the Church has pressed its case from a position of newfound strength. For decades successive Mexican governments have shunned the Church, refusing to recognize it officially and barring clerics from voting or holding land. Relegated to the political sidelines, Church officials were unable to mount any significant resistance to the establishment of the country's ambitious family planning program that was begun in the early 1970s.[70]

But worried by the gathering strength of two opposition parties that have close ties to the Church, President Carlos Salinas de Gortari, the head of Mexico's governing Revolutionary Independent Party (PRI), moved in 1991 to broaden Catholic support by restoring the Church's legal position.

"It was clear to the PRI that if it wanted to maintain political power it would need a stronger constituency," says a Mexican source familiar with the workings of the party. "If it recognized the Church at the official level, it would be likelier to say good things about the PRI in time for the next election."[71]

The deal, closed in 1992, brought Mexico into the community of more than sixty nations that maintain diplomatic ties with the Vatican. Although it merely formalized a tacit arrangement, it gave the Church—and other religions recognized under the same statute—its first free access to Mexican radio, television, and the press.

The political power of the Church had been demonstrated two

years earlier after lawmakers in the Mexican state of Chiapas, in a surprise move, sought to decriminalize abortion for poor and single women and in cases where the decision had the consent of both husband and wife. Faced with such an unprecedented threat, Church leaders sprang into action. Priests were instructed to preach against the measure. One influential local bishop warned that women who sought abortion would be excommunicated. Within two weeks 200,000 signatures were gathered against the measure, forcing the legislature to back down.[72]

A year later the Church again flexed its political muscle when it pressured the provisional governor of the state of San Luis Potosi to expel Mexfam, the twenty-seven-year-old affiliate of the IPPF, for corrupting the morals of young people and encouraging abortion—charges that Mexfam has hotly denied.[73]

"This could not have happened two years ago," says Mexfam's president, Alfonso Lopez Juárez. "This is possible now because of the new courage the Church has to be more bold and to act more officially against things which are against its doctrine. I think the situation is radically changed now from two years ago because of Mexico's recognition of the Church."[74]

The Church's new assertiveness has been encouraged by the papal *nuncio*, or ambassador, dispatched after diplomatic relations with Mexico were officially restored in 1992. As the eyes and ears of the pope and the dispenser of papal perks, including promotions and membership on prized Vatican commissions, the *nuncio* has had the clout to convince local bishops to hold the government's feet to the fire on the issues that matter: abortion, contraception, and sex education.

"Before relations with the Vatican were resumed, individual bishops had much more latitude in terms of the extent to which they hewed to the Vatican line," says a Mexican source who asked not to be identified. "Now that the *nuncio* is here to bring the commands of Rome, they have to be more publicly vigilant and not let deviations arise within the Catholic community.

"The *nuncio* is saying to the bishops: Don't you think you should be commenting to the government and preaching to the people about the increased use of money by the government for family planning? Don't you think you should be insisting on more money for natural family planning? Don't you think you should be decrying the attempt to bring abortion into the country?"[75]

The elevation of the Church's status has also energized the work of socially conservative private groups including Pro-Vida (Pro Life), a shadowy, twenty-year-old organization that has been on the front lines of efforts to restore lost Catholic virtues to Mexico.

One Mexican official likens Pro-Vida to the Heritage Foundation in Washington, which was ideologically close to the Reagan administration during the 1980s without actually being a part of it.[76] Another Mexican, a journalist, compares Pro-Vida to the American gun lobby, which has great influence even though its views are out of sync with those of the vast majority of Americans.[77]

Working with other socially conservative private groups, and frequently with the tacit support of Church officials, Pro-Vida has used newspaper and radio advertisements and direct lobbying to put heat on local government officials to ban sex education for adolescents, whose birthrates remain high and who have been largely overlooked in the otherwise successful twenty-year Mexican campaign to lower birthrates.

"In Chiapas and elsewhere, Pro-Vida and the Roman Catholic Church were working hand in hand. They were lobbying with the quiet support of the Church," notes Edgar Gonzales, a Mexican journalist who has written extensively about Pro-Vida.[78]

One recent newspaper advertisement paid for by Pro-Vida accuses Mexico's education minister of "pushing young people toward sexual promiscuity, which lays a foundation of falsehood and corruption," and for refusing to ban advertisements encouraging the use of condoms. The ad refers to birth control pills as "mini-abortions."[79]

Encouraged meanwhile by their victory in expelling Mexfam from San Luis Potosi, Pro-Vida lobbyists have started targeting other Mexfam chapters armed with a logic that has befuddled family planners.

"Contraception is one step away from abortion," Pro-Vida's president, Jorge Serrano Limon, told the *Miami Herald*. "It encourages couples to have sexual relations for reasons other than having children. Then, when the contraceptives fail, a woman may feel she has no recourse but to abort."[80]

Some Mexican family planning administrators acknowledge privately that the campaign against family planning and sex education is making it harder to operate. They say that local field workers now worry about being excommunicated by the Church. Meanwhile, board members of groups like Mexfam, often prominent personalities in the Mexican business and government establishment, have been stung by the adverse publicity blaming family planning for the corruption of public morals. After one recent ad campaign the chairman of Mexfam stepped down, insisting that Mexfam adopt a lower profile. Following a summit meeting arranged in 1992 between Mexfam and Pro-Vida, Mexfam agreed to be less explicit in future advertising about how to use contraceptives.

"The problem is that we need support from boards, governments, heads of schools, and they are now scared by the Church," notes Lopez, who says one third of his time is now spent warding off attacks and publishing rebuttals.[81] The consequence, he says, is that Mexfam has to channel its resources and energy to fight an adversary that was not in the arena two years ago, or that was present but not on the offensive. The Church knows that it can't change attitudes toward contraception, so the goal is now to harass family planning organizations and to have the government ban Mexfam in every state, says Lopez.

Nor is Mexfam the only object of the Church's interest. In countries around the Catholic world, Church officials have capitalized on local circumstances to slow the spread of artificial contraception. When Peru mounted its first serious effort to erect a family planning program in the 1980s, the archbishop of Lima publicly warned that women who used artificial contraception risked not going to heaven.[82]

In Brazil pressure from the Church has deterred the government from providing federal funding for family planning services altogether. During a 1991 visit, Pope John Paul II condemned the country's privately operated family planning programs as "gravely illicit" and urged couples to have more children to help remedy a national shortage of priests.[83]

In Poland, where the Church's decision to back the Solidarity labor movement marked the beginning of the end of four decades of communist rule, its political influence has been translated into social policy. Family planning programs set up under the communist government have been weakened. Some oral contraceptives have been banned. Those remaining lost their government subsidy, making them too expensive for many women to use. In 1990 sex education in Polish public schools was replaced with classes in Catholicism.[84]

"With little in the way of a private family planning network and with virtually no government support, contraceptive information and services are now almost nonexistent," notes a recent report issued by Population Action International. "With safe abortion services also disappearing, Polish couples, most of whom prefer small families, face an impossible dilemma."[85]

In the Philippines, meanwhile, where fertility is twice the East Asian average, family planning is only slowly recovering from cutbacks pressed by the Catholic Church in the aftermath of the key role it played in the 1981 revolution that overthrew Ferdinand Marcos. Under pressure from the Church, family planning budgets and staff were cut by a third, while the government of Marcos's successor, President Cory Aquino, shifted from an aggressive policy of limiting births through family planning to one that emphasized "the improvement of the quality of human life." The new policy abandoned references to the responsibility of the state to achieve demographic goals.[86] Following a dialogue between Church and government leaders in August 1990, the Church agreed to the principle that in a pluralistic society couples should have access to contraceptives.[87] In return, the government agreed to prohibit contraceptives that induce abortion. But the deal was short-lived. In October the Church issued a pastoral letter that attacked the government's family planning program and urged the government's 7,000 health workers to exercise their freedom of conscience to subvert it.[88]

After the 1992 election of Fidel Ramos, a Protestant who is a strong advocate of family planning, the Church stepped up its attack, staging "down with condom" prayer rallies and challenging the constitutionality of the country's family planning program in the Supreme Court.[89] Church leaders also produced a copy of a 1974 study by the U.S. National Security Council that they said proved that "demographic imperialism" was behind Washington's financial support for the Philippine family planning program. The document, prepared during the Nixon and Ford administrations, said that rapid population growth could contribute to political instability in several strategically important countries, including the Philippines, and recommended family planning assistance.[90]

The Philippine Church's "guiding principles" on population matters urge parents to bring children into the world "generously" and decry "the attitude that selfishly avoids the procreation of offspring solely because couples do not want to bear the responsibility that comes with having a child."[91]

The Roman Catholic Church's most notable political successes occurred in 1984, when the Reagan administration announced that it was withdrawing funding from UNFPA and IPPF; and later, on the eve of the 1992 UN Conference on Environment and Development (UNCED) in Rio, when the Vatican delegation and allied negotiators succeeded in keeping population off the final Earth Summit agenda.

At Rio, Church representatives capitalized on the conviction of developing nations that Northern consumption patterns, not third world population growth, was the primary cause of global environmental degradation. In the runup to the Rio conference, Southern nations held the population issue hostage to Northern concessions on foreign aid and global economic reform, other issues championed by the Church. Tapping into such discontent, representatives of three Latin American nations took the lead during the fourth and final preparatory committee of UN member nations—or "prepcom," for short—in watering down the draft language on population that was ultimately approved at Rio.

As one UN official who was present at the fourth prepcom explains, agreement had been reached between the UNCED secretariat and representatives of the "Group of 77" developing nations on language calling for the right of couples to determine the size and spacing of their families and to have access to the information and means to do so. But as the prepcom dragged on the language was quietly altered, a phrase here, a phrase there, until all mention of family planning was deleted.

"We were asleep at the switch," says the official. "We thought the deal was done, and the Vatican undid it. We totally underestimated what the Vatican was up to."[92]

"The pressures from the North were overruled by the diplomatic power of the Vatican, backed by the total support of the South," a Vatican delegate in Rio confirmed to an American journalist.[93]

The final language of the chapter on demography, approved at the fourth prepcom, called for ensuring access to the "information, education, and means" to enable couples to decide the number and spacing of children, but with the cumbersome caveat that such decisions were to be "in keeping with freedom, dignity,

and personally held values and taking into account ethical and cultural considerations." All references to modern contraceptives
were struck.[94]

The outcome of Rio was not radically altered by the Church's
successful effort to attenuate the language on family planning. But
the Vatican succeeded in creating an awkward gap between the
public statements of conference officials and their final written
declaration regarding the importance of the population issue. The
weakness of the language also made population an easier issue for
journalists to ignore. As Rio demonstrated again, the Church is
uniquely positioned to lobby for the causes it holds dear.

"The Vatican can sit in the UN with permanent observer status
and influence the entire negotiation of the Rio treaty as it relates
to the question of what it's going to say about population, family
planning, and abortion," notes Frances Kissling. "It's a situation
that no other religion is in. Methodists, Jews, Hindus do not have
this privileged status in global politics."[95]

Effective lobbying can take the Church only so far. It has had partial success in changing laws and decrees at the top but has had little success where it counts most: in changing the attitudes of
millions of rank-and-file Catholics who, like Guadelupe, have
parted ways with Rome on the crucial issue of contraception.

For most lay Catholics, the debate over Church policy has long
since passed into irrelevance. Most have learned to live with the
contradiction between the demands of modernization and the law
of the Church. Many, like Guadelupe, have simply done an end
run around the Church's strictures on contraception, either by not
confessing to the use of contraceptives or by seeking out priests
with more permissive views. For their part, many priests have simply learned to look the other way rather than engage in a quixotic
contest over the issue. In the end, the Church has become the vic-

tim of an era in which the ethics of reproduction have become mostly situational.

"The Catholic Church is certainly a very big force here in Mexico," notes Graciela Duce, who heads the United Nations Population Fund office in Mexico. "But it's a spiritual force that people do not get confused with pragmatic things like how many children they want or whether they should practice family planning. These are issues that are not related to thinking about the other world. When it comes to issues like family planning, they go by elements in the culture other than religion. They select a method and go ahead. All questions about religion are at another level of consciousness."[96]

In their standoff with the Vatican, the vast majority of lay Catholics have put Church doctrine to a pragmatic test, which its position on modern contraception has failed. Most Catholics are respectful of the Church's views but most are selectively disobedient: The responsibilities of parenthood under conditions of modernity have been given greater weight than the revealed wisdom in Rome. The Vatican and most of its 700 million followers are joined in a contest of wills. It is a contest that the Vatican will not soon abandon but that it will not soon win.

"The Church takes care of people who inherited original sin and who are sinners," concludes Father Murphy. "As a redemptive organization, it brings God's grace. It's just that the Church and the laity are out of sync on what needs to be redeemed. They have agreed to disagree."[97]

SEVEN

"A World Population Plan of Action": The International Policy Response

The United States

Through most of his term as president, Dwight D. Eisenhower thought population growth in Latin America and the newly independent nations of Africa and Asia was not a problem the United States needed to address. Advised to include family planning assistance in U.S. foreign aid programs, he declined, saying he wanted to keep the government out of the bedroom.

Then, in the waning months of his presidency, he traveled to India. There he saw a poverty-wracked country that was growing by nearly 10 million people a year. He realized then that all plans for India's progress would fail unless measures to limit population growth were adopted. "It was people, people, and more people everywhere—people in such numbers, always increasing, that every plan and program for their betterment invariably set up goals too modest to assure progress as rapid as population growth," Eisenhower later wrote in his memoir, *Waging Peace*. "My trip to India convinced me that we could not stand aloof if requested to help."[1]

Eisenhower's evolution mirrored that of the nation. In the early years of the cold war, assistance to limit population growth in developing nations was a sensitive political topic, opposed by conservative lawmakers and the Catholic Church. But from the early 1960s onward, the bad demographic news rolling out of the third world made it clear that such aid was needed and that it would have to come from the rich industrialized nations of the West.

With the notable exception of the United States during the 1980s, the period since the early 1960s has been characterized by a growing global awareness of the population problem and a growing commitment on the part of national governments, the United Nations, and various private organizations to solve it. As a result, the forces opposed to family planning have gradually weakened. As the turn of the century approaches, an unprecedented opportunity exists to rein in the growth in human numbers that has continued, sometimes at dramatic rates, since the dawn of the modern world.

Birth control is not a phenomenon of the twentieth century. Mankind has sought to prevent unwanted pregnancy since ancient times, when "contraception" meant the use of such mystical methods as tying knots at bridal ceremonies or eating dead bees. The Egyptian Petri Papyrus, dated to 1850 B.C., contains medical recipes then thought to have contraceptive properties. The Greek gynecologist Soranus of Ephesus wrote in detail of birth control and methods to induce abortion in the second century A.D., spreading knowledge that remained the basis for medical contraception in Europe until the late seventeenth century.[2]

Only a tiny fraction of the world's population had access to these early methods, however. Contraception on a scale large enough to affect national birthrates did not occur until the turn of the seventeenth century, in France, when rural peasants adopted contraceptive practices then in use by the country's elite. The French birthrate declined 17 percent between 1750 and 1800, an event demographer Alfred Sauvy called "the most important fact in all France's history."[3]

At the dawn of the industrial revolution, birth control technology was still relatively crude. Condoms, generally made of hemmed animal gut or fish membrane, were unreliable, as was coitus interruptus (withdrawal) and other "nonappliance" methods. Sponges, wool, and other vaginal blocking devices were little better.

Then came vulcanized rubber in 1843, and birth control was never the same. More comfortable and effective condoms were quickly introduced, as well as early diaphragms known as "Dutch caps" due to their popularity in the Netherlands. Perhaps more important, better technology was accompanied by theoretical justification for its use. The seventeenth-century French fertility decline had been the result of somewhat spontaneous contraceptive use. But beginning in the nineteenth century, an organized birth control movement arose for the first time, gaining particular strength in England and the United States as it proselytized on the moral and social virtues of limiting family size.

English radical neo-Malthusians were the modern birth control movement's founding members. Like their namesake, Thomas Malthus, neo-Malthusians such as the English reformers Jeremy Bentham and Francis Place believed that unrestrained population growth could lead the world to disaster. But they rejected Malthus's prescription of late marriage and sexual abstinence as harsh and unrealistic. They advised instead the use of precautionary means against pregnancy—an attitude that was controversial, to say the least, considering the era's sexual conservatism.

Neo-Malthusian aims were only furthered by the occasional arrest and imprisonment of leaders on the grounds that their how-to contraceptive manuals were pornographic. A particular target of the authorities was *The Fruits of Philosophy: or, The Private Companion of Young Married People*, written by Charles Knowlton in the 1830s. The book contained highly detailed contraceptive advice, and Knowlton was eventually imprisoned for a short while in England after its publication there in 1834. In 1876 a further prosecution of a Bristol bookseller for carrying *Fruits of Philosophy* became a *cause célèbre* for free thinkers and led to a bitter trial that gained birth control widespread publicity. Malthusian leagues spread throughout France, Germany, and Holland. They also took root in the United States—where, within the ever-receding frontiers of the wide-open New World, the birth control movement was destined to change into something different and more radical.

Robert Dale Owen, son of a British reformer by the same name, first carried neo-Malthusianism to U.S. shores in the early years of the nineteenth century. He found there a country whose characteristics cast the philosophy of birth control in a new light. Clearly, here was open land able to absorb vast numbers of people. There were no masses of poor crushed together in fetid slums, scrabbling for every crust. Instead, the open land seemed to cry out for increased numbers to develop resources and increase the wealth of all.

But as Betsy Hartmann notes in her account of the beginnings of birth control ideology, the United States was also a country of ideals, and it was home to a strain of social reformers who believed in utopia. Perfect society, they thought, was possible if individuals were perfected; and crucial to that perfection was women's rights. After all, women were (and are) half of humanity.[4]

Owen came to champion birth control as a matter of female self-determination, and it was in this form that birth control philosophy took root in America. In the face of strait-laced opposition symbolized by the 1873 Comstock Act, which attempted to circumscribe the availability of contraception, birth control became a tenet of American radicals. In the early twentieth century, with the social rebellion of working-class militancy in the air, the United States seemed ripe for a birth control revolution—and a young socialist activist named Margaret Sanger was determined to lead it.

Margaret Higgins was born in Corning, New York, on September 14, 1883. She was herself the sixth of eleven children born to a tubercular mother and unsuccessful father, and so early on she knew something of the miserable economic pressures large family size can entail. Married to William Sanger when she was seventeen (they were later divorced), she became a nurse in New York City's Lower East Side, where she saw graphic examples of the relationship between poverty and high rates of fertility. She became a feminist who believed passionately that women had the right to plan the size of their own families.

Her first forum was a paper she founded in 1914 named *Woman Rebel*. Backed by the Socialist party as well as radical unions and anarchists, *Woman Rebel* at first melded staunch support of birth control with general working-class militancy. Eventually birth control theory came to dominate the journal's pages, and the Post Office moved to close it down. Though Sanger fled the country for Europe, she was indicted for distributing obscene material. These charges were dropped in 1916, but by then Sanger was looking toward more direct action. Later that year she opened a birth control clinic in Brooklyn. She was charged with maintaining a "public nuisance" and served thirty days in a workhouse in 1917.

Prosecution only fed a growing public sympathy for her and her cause. By the end of World War I, however, she faced a widening split with her radical allies. Many left-wing activists thought their energy should be focused on class rather than gender problems. In addition, the postwar political climate was poisonously antiradical. Birth control advocates began to think they could gain more public acceptance on their own.

Thus Sanger and her paper, now named *Birth Control Review*, parted ways with her former financial backers. As she moved toward the right in the political spectrum, she and her newly formed American Birth Control League (ABCL) began to attract support from a handful of free-thinking doctors. In return, Sanger threw her support behind legislation that would give doctors the sole right to disseminate contraceptive prescriptions—a move that dismayed her more liberal colleagues.

More dangerous allies came from the eugenics movement,

which aimed at "improving" the human race through manipulation of mating. Many eugenicists thought the poor genetically inferior to the rich, whites genetically superior to blacks, and themselves most genetically fit of all. They pushed for state laws on compulsory sterilization of criminals and the physically defective, with some success. Rich Americans such as Andrew Carnegie helped fund eugenics studies and gave the movement both respectability and some social panache during the 1920s.

Throughout the 1930s the Sanger-led ABCL and eugenics leaders drew closer together. The ABCL eventually came to advocate some thinly veiled racist positions, while eugenicists saw in birth control a means to their ends. Ironically, some eugenics leaders were uneasy about their alliance because they felt it could compromise their then-respectable public image. Then came World War II and the eugenics experiments of Adolf Hitler, which included hundreds of thousands of forced sterilizations side by side with Nazi gas chambers. In the United States eugenics became almost completely discredited.

Meanwhile, the birth control movement was becoming more respectable. Sanger's efforts were attracting the attention of rich philanthropists. In 1939 the ABCL made peace with the various other voluntary birth control groups and formed an umbrella organization named the Birth Control Federation of America. Yet as birth control moved into the main channel of U.S. public life, the woman who had almost single-handedly founded the movement was nudged aside. In 1942, to Sanger's dismay, the umbrella group changed its name to Planned Parenthood. Implicit in the name was a new focus on spacing, rather than limiting, families.

This transformation of a once-radical social movement gained momentum after the end of World War II. The old rubric "birth control" changed to the broader, softer-sounding one of "family planning," as a new generation of establishment figures took control. Margaret Sanger had courted notoriety and even jail; she was replaced by men more familiar with Wall Street than the Bowery.

The new family planning leadership was interested in economics, not biology, and saw in control of births a means to help solve pressing global problems of poverty and development. Usually men of business, often schooled in high government positions during the war, they were used to responsibility and authority. They thought problems existed to be solved. Liberal democracy had defeated the threat of Nazi Germany; surely it could help the starving of the world. Pre-eminent among this leadership was a man who carried perhaps the most respectable surname in America, if not the globe: Rockefeller.

John D. Rockefeller III had in fact been interested in the implications of population pressure for years. In a letter to his father written in 1934, he talked of population as the field in which he wanted "to concentrate his own giving." Decades later he was to say that concern about the seriousness of population growth was one of only two convictions he had never changed his mind about—the other being that the enrichment of human existence is the objective of life.[5]

While on a trip to Asia in 1948, Rockefeller became concerned about population growth in the region, especially in Japan. Upon his return he found that his family's own Rockefeller Foundation was not eager to launch an in-depth study of the situation, nor indeed of any aspect of the growing problem of rapid population growth. The objections of the Catholic Church to such work still resounded strongly in America in the immediate postwar years, and the Foundation's conservative leadership wanted no part of anything remotely controversial.

So Rockefeller organized his own scientific expedition to the region: a small team of demographic scientists and health professionals. Brought face to face with the unknowns of population planning, regional politics, and contraceptive technology, the team recommended in its final report that "study rather than action" was the most pressing need in the years ahead. In light of the

Foundation's continued resistance, Rockefeller decided to press forward on his own.

In June 1952, partly at Rockefeller's urging, the National Academy of Sciences sponsored a sweeping population conference in Williamsburg, Virginia. The old colonial capital then being rebuilt with Rockefeller family funds reverberated with the sounds of hammers and saws and the arguments of health experts, planned parenthood advocates, demographers, and economists. The participants' most significant conclusion was a prosaic one: that a nongovernmental international organization should be founded to carry on their work. Later that year the Population Council was born, with Rockefeller himself serving as its chairman.

The Council in its first years had a twofold impact on the population movement. First, it began to convince health professionals and other scientists of the necessity for action on population. Medical organizations that had declined to work with Planned Parenthood found the Population Council an acceptable partner for the study of fertility and its regulation. Second, the Council made the subject of population more respectable for the giant American foundations. The Ford Foundation's first major grants in the field went to the Rockefeller-led organization; indeed, throughout the decade of the 1950s, the Ford Foundation made almost all its population-oriented grants to the Council.

As the 1950s drew to a close, the Council involved itself more and more in action as opposed to study, helping, for instance, to set up government family planning programs in Pakistan. But its primary reason for existence remained its service as a clearinghouse for ideas and study. The population problem was as large as the globe, and it seemed obvious that it would take involvement on the scale of a U.S. government program to make much progress. In fits and starts, that involvement was coming.

The man who first pushed strongly for it at high levels of the U.S. government was in his own way as establishment-oriented as

Rockefeller, though his name is less well known today. General William H. Draper, Jr., had served in high-level posts directing European reconstruction after the war. A New York banker by trade, he had business experience in developing countries. When in 1958 congressional pressure led President Eisenhower to form a commission to study the U.S. Military Assistance Program overseas, Draper seemed a natural to head it up. His fellow commissioners included such famous figures as John J. McCloy and Admiral Arthur Radford, a former chairman of the Joint Chiefs of Staff.

The panel's stated purpose was to investige whether U.S. postwar aid was too heavily concentrated on military assistance and too lightly on economic help. It took some unusual exhortations and the personal interest of Draper himself to focus the group on population issues. One of the first pieces of advice the commissioners received was a wire from Hugh Moore, founder of the Dixie Cup Corporation and an ardent advocate of family planning. "If your committee does not look into the impact and implications of the population explosion, you will be derelict in your duty," it said.[6]

More serious was a quiet reminder from Ike himself. Draper later recalled that at a National Security Council meeting in December of 1958, the president told him not to forget the population problem, as it was a serious one in some of the countries included in his study.

Through his travels Draper had seen firsthand how sharp cuts in population growth rates had helped Japan recover from the war's devastation. Now he urged the logic of family planning on his commission, over the bitter opposition of most of its staff and many of its members. The report's 1959 conclusions reflected Draper's beliefs.

"We found . . . that in most of the developing countries their rate of population growth was such that it was interfering seriously with their economic development, particularly with any improvement in their per capita income," Draper remembered in an interview recorded by the Truman Library in 1974.[7]

Eventually the panel recommended to Eisenhower that the U.S. aid program include funds for the population programs of foreign governments, at their request. Photos of Draper displaying charts predicting dire world population growth ran in many American newspapers. But to Draper's surprise, Ike did not accept the panel's family planning aid suggestion. A presidential election was looming in 1960, and Eisenhower believed correctly that Massachusetts Senator John F. Kennedy would be a candidate.

"President Eisenhower feared that if he approved our recommendation and if Kennedy, as a Catholic, attacked it, this might split the American people on a religious issue in a national political campaign; and he thought this would be bad for the American people," recalled Draper in an oral history interview.[8]

In later years Eisenhower said that in declining to back strong population programs he made a mistake. With fellow ex-president Harry Truman, he was eventually made an honorary co-chair of Planned Parenthood, at Draper's request.

"Their names and their influence and their later statements . . . were of tremendous help in raising the whole level of the Planned Parenthood and world population movement to a much higher level," said Draper.[9]

Through the first fifteen years of the postwar period, the U.S. government and establishment slowly gained interest in population growth. Such a gradual awakening was also occurring at the United Nations, as the new international body acquired the technical expertise to measure and judge population changes.

The UN's first step in this direction was taken in 1946, when a Population Commission was established in the Secretariat to compile global demographic data. In 1949 the commission produced the first Demographic Yearbook, which assembled in one volume much of the world's current demographic information. Before then demographers were mostly focused on population declines in the developed world. Now the UN turned the world's attention to population growth in the developing world. When it compiled the results of a comprehensive survey of postwar demographic trends in 1952, it confirmed a growing suspicion: that deathrates were falling so fast in the developing world that it was on the verge of a period of unprecedented population growth.

Within the commission there were deep divisions about what to do about the data. The controversy was a microcosm of the struggles over population policy in Washington and at the UN that characterized the twenty-year gestation period before the U.S. and UN finally plunged into the business of providing technical and financial help to curb population growth.

Julia Henderson was then head of the UN's Bureau of Social Affairs, which included the commission, and the highest-ranking woman in the UN system. She describes the debate that grew hotter as the population figures soared higher.

"Some of the demographers [in the commission] said there's not much we can do about it. This is not an action group. We're here just to let people know what's happening. Others said the UN should be taking action to help developing countries deal with the population issue. There were lots of fights between the demographers and the statisticians. It went on for years before the tide turned."[10]

The tide turned in response to building pressure from the places that counted: the very third world countries that were feeling the effects of rapid population growth the most and that most needed help. "The Indians kept coming and talking to me about how hard population was to deal with," recalls Henderson, who later served for ten years as president of the International Planned Parenthood Federation. "They were saying we need help from the UN to organize and train our people to get family planning programs going." But the tide turned slowly because of opposition from Catholic countries, some of which, like Argentina and Ireland, threatened to stop paying their dues if the world body actively promoted family planning.

While Catholic opposition was instrumental in keeping agencies like the World Health Organization (WHO) and the United Nations International Children's Emergency Fund (UNICEF) out of family planning, support for a more activist population policy was gaining strength within the UN itself. One reason was the backing eventually provided by some of the former colonial powers, like Great Britain, which began to see what population growth was doing to retard development in their former domains in Africa and Asia. A turning point came in 1961 when France, which had staunchly opposed an activist role for the UN, made a huge tactical error.

"The French said they didn't think third world countries really wanted assistance," Henderson remembers. "They said this was all generated within the UN. So they proposed that a questionnaire go out to all the countries to ask them: Did they have population problems? Would they welcome help from the outside? When the questionnaires all came back they overwhelmingly said yes, we have serious problems. Cities were beginning to explode. They didn't know what to do about health, jobs, and education."

Within the developing world the only solid resistance came from African nations, newly freed from colonial rule and suspicious of the motives of the former colonial powers. But Asian nations pressed the case and were joined by several countries in Latin America, where urban growth was rapidly accelerating. By the mid-1960s many third world nations had taken their second postwar census. The results confirmed that population growth had dramatically increased and helped to dispel much of the remaining resistance to attempts to address it.

One final hurdle had to be cleared before the UN could embrace an activist policy. John F. Kennedy, a Catholic president, was now in the White House. Of all postwar occupants of the Oval Office, he seemed least likely to countenance any change in U.S. population policy. As it happened, the population issue provided Kennedy with an ideal vehicle to redeem a campaign pledge not to be captive to the wishes of Rome. Henderson describes a key meeting in New York with a top Kennedy State Department appointee, Richard Gardner, who was deputy director of international programs under Harlan Cleveland.

"He came to me and said, I know we've been lying low on this issue, but Harlan and I think we can get Kennedy to sign off on it, to say that the UN should help countries that need help in this field, to take a positive attitude toward an action program. Gardner asked me for a demographer to write a paper for the president. He came back within a week beaming and said, We've got the signature, we can go ahead."

Instructions were sent to the State Department to change U.S. policy by encouraging the UN to take a more active role in helping third world nations to lower population growth rates. "Once the Americans got into the water they carried a lot of weight," Henderson remembers. Within three years—by 1966—the General Assembly had passed a resolution authorizing UN agencies to respond to calls for help with technical and financial assistance to set up family planning programs. Three years later the United Nations Fund for Population Activities—now called the UN Population Fund but still bearing the acronym UNFPA—was created. Not by accident its first director was a Catholic—Rafael Salas, from the Philippines—who became an energetic cheerleader and fundraiser on behalf of family planning.

By the mid-1960s it was clear that family planning was coming of age. With a Catholic U.S. president supporting efforts to curb the press of population, the issue gained visibility and political support. Kennedy's former rival within the Democratic party, Adlai

Stevenson, made public speeches on the need for population policy. His former electoral opponent, Richard Nixon, complained that population growth undermined the worth of U.S. foreign aid and said this "immensely controversial" subject shouldn't be swept under the carpet. Activists such as General Draper were instrumental in getting Congress to earmark money in the budget of the Department of Health, Education and Welfare for contraceptive research. The mood of the country was not yet such that large sums could be voted for family planning. But in December 1963, shortly after Kennedy's assassination, Congress, at the behest of Arkansas Senator J. William Fulbright, quietly passed legislation that approved government funds for research into population growth.

At first things moved slowly. Part of the reason was that many in the government were still leery of opposition from the hierarchy of the Catholic Church. Another reason was that the arm of the bureaucracy charged with disseminating foreign assistance, the Agency for International Development (AID), was itself still in its infancy. Its staff members were new and inexperienced and unsure of what the White House and the Congress expected of them.

With the support of such key legislators as Senator Fulbright, a few activists within the AID system began pressing for change. In June 1964, the agency established a Population Reference and Research branch. AID country officers were allowed to respond to requests for demographic and population information. In fiscal 1964 AID made its first population-related grants: $100,000 for a Chilean demographic training center and $40,000 for a similar project by the Pan American Health Organization. But agency officials were fully aware of the sensitivity of the population issue on Capitol Hill and prohibited any dissemination of manufactured contraceptives.

Then in 1965, three developments coalesced to push population higher on the AID agenda, as Phyllis Piotrow describes in her book on the development of U.S. population policy.[11] The first was political: At the urging of some of his closest advisers, President Johnson made reference to the population problem in his State of the Union address. The reference was only one sentence long and said simply that the United States would try to use its knowledge to help deal with the explosion in world numbers. But it was a more explicit endorsement of action than any White House had ever made, and activists seized on it as justification for their population work.

The second development was technological. By 1965 scientists had made great advances in contraceptive technology with birth control pills and the intrauterine device (IUD). In the United States 4 million women were already taking the pill; IUDs were being adopted by Pakistan, India, and other hard-pressed nations for their own population programs.

The third development was a disaster. A food shortage caused by bad weather, bad management, and perhaps population growth hit many parts of the developing world in the summer of 1965. Monsoon rains fell in India, exacerbating the crisis. The president and Congress moved to provide emergency food aid while urging attention to population as part of the solution. By the beginning of 1966, at least fifteen countries had asked AID for help in starting population programs.

Into this situation stepped a new AID population chief whose abrasive leadership was to do much to further the family planning agenda. Dr. Remiert T. Ravenholt was an epidemiologist from the University of Washington, in Seattle. Brought in to head the Population Branch, he was at first appalled by his lack of power and resources, referring to the branch as a "twig."[12] Impatient with bureaucratic procedure and the niceties of intragovernment relations, he quickly decided that AID's ban on handing out contraceptives was a major impediment to progress.

In 1967 congressional allies, notably Senator Fulbright, helped put language into foreign aid legislation that specifically allocated $20 million for family planning assistance. AID officials interpreted the bill's intent as allowing contraceptive distribution. In May of that year, contraceptives were removed from AID's list of prohibited items for the first time.

Finally things were in place. With money, leadership, and high-level political backing, U.S. family planning assistance forged ahead. In 1969 Congress allocated $50 million for population, although overall foreign aid money was tight. All of AID's overseas missions now had at least one population official and in the case of hard-pressed nations such as India, five to ten. Ravenholt moved quickly to allocate funds through nongovernmental organizations such as the International Planned Parenthood Federation. Money went for demographic information, clinic support, training, and contraceptives, including the pill.

The election of a Republican president, Richard Nixon, in 1968 led to the expansion of U.S. foreign assistance for family planning. Throughout the late 1960s and early 1970s, at a time when the Vietnam War was helping make the United States increasingly unpopular in the developing world, the U.S. was mounting and executing a family planning program that probably did more good for poor nations than any other postwar aid effort. Between 1965 and 1980, the United States contributed roughly half of all international assistance for population and family planning. By 1990 the cumulative total of U.S. assistance had reached over $4 billion, with about three-quarters of that paying for actual family planning services and the rest for research and policy development. AID became the world's largest donor of contraceptives, handing out 55 million IUDs and 7.5 billion condoms.

"By promoting the availability and use of modern contraceptive techniques, AID helped slow the pace of population growth in the '60s and '70s," wrote *Washington Post* columnist Hobart Rowen. "It was one of our real foreign aid success stories, notably in Thailand, Indonesia, Mexico, and Bangladesh."[13]

One of the biggest threats to the incipient movement to address rapid population growth was a general antagonism felt by the nations hardest hit toward the nations attempting to help. Developing countries were dissatisfied with the maldistribution of global wealth resulting, in part, from the inequitable terms of trade that existed between the North and South. Discontent on the subject had led to the formation of the Group of 77 nonaligned nations in 1964. It peaked at the Sixth Special Session of the UN General Assembly in March 1974, where the G-77 nations called for a New International Economic Order (NIEO) to, among other things, equalize trade relations and increase aid flows from rich to poor nations.

Anti-Western feelings came to a head in 1974 when the UN convened an international conference in Bucharest, Romania, to address the population issue in the context of national and global development. The conference was beset by a deepening conviction among third world delegates, sharpened by the proclamation of the NIEO, that nothing could be done about population until economic and social conditions were improved. The view was encapsulated in the catchphrase "development is the best contraceptive," which became the informal slogan of the conference. As the final document issued at Bucharest put it more formally, "the basis for an effective solution of the population problem is, above all, socioeconomic transformation."[14]

Adding to the complications was the concerted opposition of two of the strangest bedfellows in global politics: the Catholic Church, which was intensely opposed to the propagation of family planning based on the use of modern contraceptives, and the Communist bloc, which was convinced that capitalism, not population, was the cause of underdevelopment.

Despite the conflicts, the proceedings at Bucharest represented an advance for the incipient global family planning movement. After all the rhetoric was expended, the conferees got down to the business of drafting and adopting by acclamation a blueprint for action that embraced the very premises urged by the Western nations: that a negative relationship exists between population and development; that governments should include strategies to curb population growth in their social and economic plans; that there was a need for international action to support such strategies; and that part of any solution to the population problem was according more rights to women.[15] As two commentators wrote later, the World Population Plan of Action, as it was called, turned out to be a document of "enduring value, which governments, international agencies, and activists could use to legitimize population, family planning, and related programs throughout the third world," and that led to the initiation or expansion of family planning programs in a number of developing countries.[16]

"Despite its wordiness and often hesitant tone," concluded one National Security Council staffer shortly after the conference, the WPPA "contains all the necessary provision for effective population growth control programs at national and international levels."[17]

There was certainly an element of altruism in the U.S. commitment to the task of curbing global population growth through the Kennedy, Johnson, Nixon, Ford, and Carter administrations. American officials recognized that rapid population growth would be a drag on the domestic economies of poor nations and would increase the risk of food shortages. As one National Security Council staff member wrote in a National Security Staff memorandum in 1975: "If significant progress can be made in slowing population growth, the positive impact on growth of GNP and per capita income will be significant."[18]

But the United States was also motivated by self-interest, as the same memorandum made clear: "Whatever may be done to guard against interruptions of supply and to develop domestic alternatives, the U.S. economy will require large and increasing amounts of minerals from abroad, especially from less developed countries. That fact gives the U.S. enhanced interest in the political, economic, and social stability of the supplying countries."[19]

No policy is set in stone, even one that developed a consensus in the U.S. bureaucracy over two decades of work. By 1980 U.S. family planning aid was vulnerable, in part because of its own success. Starting in the late 1960s, record high population growth rates (though not the number of people added to the world's population each year) began to decline. Advances in agricultural technology, notably the green revolution, appeared to avert the threat of famine in developing nations. Back home it was easy for Americans to make the assumption that the population bomb was just about defused. "There was a sense that if you got population programs growing, the problem would be solved, so nobody was concerned anymore," recalls a spokesman for one national environmental organization.[20]

Perhaps more important, a number of influential economists who questioned traditional assumptions about the negative effects of population growth on development were receiving more and more attention as the 1980s began. One way to gauge how the consensus was shifting in favor of this revisionist view is to compare two reports issued by the respected National Academy of Sciences, in which small groups of social scientists examined the same issue: the effect of population growth on economic development.

The first report, issued in 1971, was titled Rapid Population Growth. It provided a ringing endorsement of family planning based on the conclusion that a smaller population would provide significant benefits to a less developed country. Among the seventeen reasons listed: smaller populations would mean greater investments per capita, a higher percentage of people of working age, and less demands on capital to offset the pressure of population on resources and the environment. "Potential output per head will be higher in a stationary than in a growing population," the report concluded.[21]

The second report, issued in 1986, was titled Population Growth and Economic Development. Although it too endorsed family planning, it posited a somewhat weaker association between rapid population growth and economic underdevelopment. The report did concur with the 1971 report that less rapid population growth could have salutary effects. Lower population, by increasing the ratio of capital to labor, would increase levels of per capita income, the authors concluded. Larger families, they judged, would have lower levels of nutrition, schooling, and health per child. But the report also spoke of certain positive ecological effects of population density, and its conclusions, on balance, were more muted than those of the 1971 report. "We reach the qualitative conclusion that slower population growth would be beneficial to economic development for most developing countries," the report said. "There appears to be a legitimate role for population policy, providing its benefits exceed its costs."[22] This subtle difference was to be greatly magnified as demographic revisionism reached a high-water mark after the election of Ronald Reagan to the presidency in 1980.

Reagan's election cleared the way for a significant number of men and women with fundamentally different attitudes on the population issue to replace the occupants of senior government posts.[23] They brought to their jobs two new and complementary perspectives that were destined to have a huge impact on global family planning efforts.

One was a belief in the virtues of classic laissez-faire economics. When they thought about population growth at all, they discounted it as a factor in the development process. Poverty was not a function of population growth but of flawed economics, they believed. The other perspective was brought by a group of hard-core anti-abortionists who sought to dissociate family planning from abortion and, in some cases, targeted all modern birth control methods as well. By the end of the first year of the Reagan presidency, notes former AID population official and Population Action

International president Joseph Speidel, disciples of both schools were scattered through the administration "like raisins in a rice pudding."[24]

The first clear signal that population programs were in jeopardy came within President Reagan's first year in office, when the Office of Management and Budget sought to cut off all support for population activities. The effort failed, but when the final figures were agreed on for 1982, the $345 million requested by the outgoing Carter administration had been cut by over a third, to $211 million. In a harbinger of things to come, zealous administration officials then sought to defund private family planning groups like the Pathfinder Fund and the Planned Parenthood Federation of America, which supported programs that were either providing abortions or abortion referrals with their own money.

Failing that, they defunded one leading population journal—*International Family Planning Perspectives*, published by a spinoff of the PPFA, the Alan Guttmacher Institute—because the journal had run a total of two articles on the subject of abortion. When U.S. AID administrator M. Peter McPherson resisted the move, he was reminded by one leading congressional critic of abortion that Reagan's election "could never have been achieved without the dramatic help of the anti-abortion forces."[25] On yet another front, reluctant AID career officials were forced by senior Reagan appointees to open the door to fringe groups advocating "natural" birth control methods. With a grant supplied by AID the inventors of one, the so-called Billings method, traversed Africa bearing the message that anyone using artificial contraception would "go straight to hell."[26]

In all of this, administration officials were pushed by an increasingly sophisticated lobby that drew on the support of New Right think tanks, Roman Catholics, and Protestant fundamentalists. It championed conservative views on personal morality and women's rights and opposed the growing use of contraceptive sterilization. But its real *raison d'etre* was opposition to abortion. The event that had catalyzed the movement was the Supreme Court's 1973 deci-sion in the case of *Roe v. Wade*, which legalized abortion in the United States. After failing to gain sufficient support for an amendment to the Constitution to ban abortion at home, even with an anti-abortion president in the White House, the move-ment, led by groups like the National Right to Life Committee, the American Life League, and Human Life International, turned to a riper opportunity: abortion abroad.

The gathering discontent of these critics with the international family planning movement and with the abortions they said it was promoting came to a head on the eve of two major events in 1984. The first was the successor to Bucharest, a huge international con-ference on population and development scheduled for Mexico City at the end of July. The second was the Republican National Con-vention, scheduled for Houston two weeks later. As it happened, the imminence of the latter greatly influenced the Reagan admin-istration's approach to the former.

Responding to preconvention election-year pressures from abortion groups, which largely spoke to the administration's own predilections, White House officials agreed to appoint a prolife delegation to the Mexico conference and chose assistant secretary of state James Buckley, director of Radio Free Europe and a former senator and undersecretary of state, to head it. Buckley, a Roman Catholic with strong anti-abortion views, agreed to take the job under one condition: that the administration draft a "re-statement" of U.S. population policy that he could personally sup-port. The document that resulted and that was presented in Mexico caught almost everyone by surprise.

In Mexico Buckley reversed the working premise of the previ-ous five U.S. presidential administrations by announcing that pop-ulation was a "neutral" factor in development, helpful or harmful depending on the economic conditions existing in any given coun-try. "The relationship between population growth and economic development is not a negative one," Buckley proclaimed. "Indeed, both in the American experience and in the economic history of most advanced nations, population growth has been an essential element in economic progress."[27]

It was a view echoed by Reagan himself, who, during a campaign debate a few months later, noted that "the population explosion . . . has been vastly exaggerated . . . overexaggerated. As a matter of fact, there are some pretty scientific and solid figures about how much space there still is in the world and how many more people we can have."[28]

The other American surprise in Mexico was an announcement that in the future funds would be denied to organizations that "support or actively promote abortion as a method of family planning." The announcement was to touch two organizations that stood at the very nerve center of the international family planning network. One was the IPPF, which helped support 120 member programs and a quarter of whose budget was then being supplied by the United States. The other was Family Planning International Assistance, the international arm of Planned Parenthood and one of AID's largest grantees. The two organizations, which together funded a handful of programs that gave advice or referrals on abortion, were cut adrift from the American budget. Over the next several years, more than a dozen other U.S. family planning organizations were forced to disavow abortion to avoid losing U.S. AID funding.

Ironically, the country whose population problem was so severe and whose support for family planning had carried so much weight in Mexico City was also the country that gave credibility in the eyes of many Americans to the Reagan administration's decision to draw the line on abortion. In February 1984, just four months before the Mexico City conference, the public television program NOVA broadcast a disturbing exposé of human rights abuses in China, which ranged from mandatory sterilization and abortion to forced insertions of IUDs, all committed in the name of slowing the country's runaway population growth. Months earlier the Chinese government had replaced senior family planning officials and softened directives to local cadres. But the reforms were obscured by another round of publicity in 1985 as NOVA re-aired its program, and as other TV programs, including "60 Minutes," as well as newspapers, including the *Washington Post*, provided more unsettling accounts of Chinese practices. Soon after, the UNFPA was defunded by the Reagan administration for participating in the management of the Chinese program.[29]

As it happened, the Reagan-Bush years were not without achievement for the family planning movement, though the few gains that were made came in spite of and not because of the policies of the two American administrations. One of the abiding ironies of the Mexico City conference is that by the time the United States had forfeited its own leadership role, the governments of the developing countries themselves had reached a kind of epiphany on the subject of family planning. They came to Mexico not as skeptics and critics, as they had come to Bucharest, but as converts to the notion that slower population growth could make a contribution to economic development. Despite the newly relaxed U.S. view that population was a neutral factor in development, the third world leaders coalesced around the proposition that making family planning services universally available was a matter of "urgency."[30] The result was that at the level of ideology, at least, the opinions expressed by the U.S. delegation were largely consigned to irrelevance.

As one commentator noted later: "Almost every country arrived in Mexico in favor of action against rapid [population] growth. Indeed, there was very little debate on the subject, but also, unfortunately, very little publicity. It was a consensus achieved without conflict, but unnoticed by the hordes of journalists there."[31]

By the end, the conference had added eighty-eight new recommendations to the World Population Plan of Action adopted at

Bucharest. As two other commentators later noted, the participants "departed with a renewed commitment to strengthen population policies and programs."[32]

Another notable development of the 1980s was the extent to which other nations stepped forward to bridge the funding gap created when the Reagan administration curtailed support for the UNFPA and IPPF.[33] The Netherlands, Norway, and Sweden made up most of the loss. One consequence is that today funding for the UNFPA is at an all-time high. The Reagan policy also catapulted Congress into the spotlight, as lawmakers rushed to fill the fiscal breach, appropriating increases that in most years exceeded what the administration had requested. By 1985 the budget for population activities was half again higher than at any time during the Carter administration.[34]

Despite such gains, the overall effect of the Reagan and Bush years was to arrest temporarily the momentum generated through the five previous Democratic and Republican administrations. At home, despite budget increases voted by Congress, the Reagan policy introduced a discordant note into congressional deliberations, ending two decades of consensus on the subject. Abroad, the need for family planning services was growing faster than American aid. Population funding in constant dollars on a per capita basis—that is, per couple of reproductive age in the developing world—actually declined during the Reagan years to the levels of the early 1970s.

By the end of the Reagan years, moreover, the expenditures that were being made were being justified on a substantially narrower basis. Since its inception, the population program within U.S. AID had been devoted primarily, if not exclusively, to demographic goals. The architects of the policy were principally concerned about the effects that rapid growth would have on the economic development, quality of life, and political stability of third world nations and thus believed that using family planning programs to help lower birthrates was in the best interests of rich and poor nations alike. The National Security Council had warned during the Ford administration that the "political consequences of current population factors in the LDCs [less developed countries] . . . are damaging to the internal stability and international relations of countries in whose advancement the U.S. is interested, thus creating political or even national security problems for the U.S."[35] The rationale was strengthened and broadened in the Global 2000 Report to the President, which was issued during the last days of the Carter administration and which warned of the negative environmental consequences of rapid population growth.[36]

Under pressure from the right, such cosmic justifications were jettisoned during the Reagan administration in favor of the narrower though still important goal of improving family welfare—in particular maternal and child health—through greater access to family planning. In addition, effective contraception was promoted to conservative politicians as a means to reduce reliance on abortion. The administration no longer attempted to argue "that population pressures aggravate social, economic, and environmental problems or undermined political stability," wrote Sharon Camp and Craig Lasher in a study of family planning in the 1980s. "The shift . . . took the punch out of U.S. population policy."[37]

Abroad, the consequences of the Reagan administration's attempts to undercut family planning were more severe. Over the next few years the UNFPA was forced to turn down funding requests for dozens of family planning projects. The cuts hit hardest in Africa, where the family planning movement was just beginning to gather momentum and where thirteen programs that the IPPF was on the verge of funding were put on hold. In other countries the sudden cessation of U.S. support for family planning arrested the development of promising population programs.

"It did damage," says one World Bank official of the Reagan policy. "You go to third world countries and talk to finance ministers about population and get a lukewarm reception because of what the United States was saying. For those countries that were sitting on the fence it was the difference between delaying and plunging ahead with family planning."[38]

In the end it may be the lost opportunities that have mattered most. The 1980s were a decade during which considerable advances were possible because of the heightened awareness in developing nations of the benefits of smaller families. But few such advances occurred in the absence of American encouragement and funds.

"For global population efforts, that is, perhaps, the real legacy of the Reagan administration: to have made opposition to population and family planning programs legitimate; to have given opponents full access to the U.S. policymaking process; and to have left the political consensus which once supported these activities badly battered," concluded Camp and Lasher.[39]

There is a final twist to the Reagan and Bush years, wholly unintended by those who helped frame the population policy of the era. Their objective was to lower the global abortion rate. Their strategy for doing so was to separate abortion from family planning by withholding money from family planning organizations that funded or provided abortion services or even counseled on the subject. In fact, some experts believe the policy may have had the consequence of increasing the number of total abortions worldwide. The absence of adequate family planning services makes unintended pregnancies more likely, and unintended pregnancies in particular, experts say, frequently end in abortion.[40]

Even in the years before Reagan and Bush altered U.S. population policy, the time was not ripe to move population issues to the top of the agenda. Although many environmentalists, in particular, believed population growth was the engine of ecological decline, it was too risky to elevate the issue against a backdrop of intensifying abortion politics at home.

"It was on everyone's intellectual radar screen but it was not on everyone's political radar screen. The issue was not a political high-flyer," recalls Douglas Costle, who served as administrator of the Environmental Protection Agency during the Carter administration. "But now it can't be avoided. The best politics ultimately follows the facts, and in this case the facts are catching up with everyone."[41]

With the election of Bill Clinton as president, population has become a priority political item, engaging the interest of top officials in the White House and State Department and rejuvenating the midlevel specialists who have always pressed for a more activist family planning stance.

Within months of taking office, the Clinton administration took steps that amounted to a total reversal of the restrictive policies of the Reagan and Bush administrations. Just two days after his inauguration, Clinton revoked the Mexico City policy, lifting the restrictions that prohibited some family planning organizations from receiving U.S. funding because of abortion-related activities. Within months, the money started flowing: $13.2 million to the IPPF alone as part of a five-year, $75 million commitment by U.S. AID.[42] In another significant move the administration immediately increased funding for population activities to over half a billion dollars, then pledged to press for increases up to $1.2 billion by the year 2000—the American share of the total amount needed to make family planning services available to every woman who wants them. The amount was estimated at $9 billion at a 1989 UN population conference in Amsterdam, where the goal of universal access to family planning was set.[43] That figure has since been revised upward to about $11 billion, with additional increases in subsequent years, to reflect the slowing of progress toward that goal in the late 1980s and early 1990s.

"It's exciting," says Timothy Wirth, the State Department counselor in charge of cross-cutting global issues, including population. "We really have a chance now."[44] Wirth's job itself is one indication of the change of direction at the State Department, which is being reorganized to focus more on global affairs.

Clinton's election "makes a big difference," says Phyllis Piotrow, who directs the Center for Communication Programs at the Johns Hopkins University School of Public Health. "In terms of trying to remove barriers and obstacles created by the last two administrations, I think that it's very important."[45]

The Reagan and Bush administrations struggled to portray population assistance advocates as zealots with a faddish view, says Piotrow. The effect was to raise doubts about the population issue as a serious matter of public policy. "What Clinton has done is to restore the legitimacy of the issue. There's been a total change in tone."[46]

As the third millennium looms there is a heartening convergence of factors that augurs well for ending the world's unprecedented growth in human numbers. The most consequential may be the growing desire on the part of men and women around the world for access to family planning services. Another is the universal awareness that now exists of the magnitude of the population problem, and not only at the level of an individual American presidential administration. Across the institutional spectrum, from national governments in rich and poor nations alike, and in giant multilateral institutions like the UN and the World Bank, there is a recognition that the twenty-first century will pose greater challenges to the human race if population growth is not slowed further.

Perhaps the best grounds for optimism in the current political moment are the unprecedented favorable conditions that now exist worldwide for addressing population issues. For example, for the first time there is no nation—like the United States during the 1980s—or any bloc—like the Communist nations during the 1960s or 1970s—to stand in the way of progress toward that objective. Even religious opposition, while strong at the clerical level in most Catholic countries and in some Islamic nations, has all but disappeared among the rank-and-file faithful. Beyond the diminished *obstacles* to progress is the increased *opportunity* for progress that has been created by the end of the cold war. Freed from the need to concentrate on geostrategic threats to peace, policymakers now have the luxury of turning their attention to the global forces that impinge on the peace and prosperity of nations and the international system as a whole. Central among these threats is the pressure population growth is placing on economic development, food supplies, and the natural environment.

If political leaders are wise enough to capitalize on the opportunity provided by the coming together of this extraordinary constellation of circumstances, the population problem could be solved within two generations. If they are not, providing for the welfare of humanity in the century ahead will be considerably more difficult. Perhaps, in some of the world's poorest regions, it will move beyond the realm of possibility.

Epilogue

Ten o'clock Wednesday morning. An abandoned fruit cart, covered with a blue plastic tarp, stands in a busy marketplace in the lower middle-class Mexico City neighborhood of Tacuva. Ferdinand, a social worker, starts to walk by then stops, goes back, and peels back the tarp. Two youngsters are asleep on a shelf that undergirds the cart. After a minute they scramble out and squint in the hazy sunlight. Grateful to see him, their dirty faces break into broad smiles.

This is a "night out" for the older of the two, seventeen-year-old Juan, who usually sleeps nearby in a burned-out tin hut with the dozen or so others who make up this small community of street kids.

Juan leads Fernando to the others, also still asleep. Two lucky ones lie on battered bare mattresses with springs sprouting. The rest sleep on flattened cardboard boxes. The ground inside the uncovered hut is strewn with litter: old shoes, garbage, rags, bent street signs. A week-old litter of puppies lie on one of the mattresses and as many rangy kittens, probably no older, have also made the hut their home.

A freeway arches overhead. Across the street, above the Center for Faith, Hope and Heaven, a giant neon sign proclaims that "Only Jesus Saves."

With a worried look, Juan shows Fernando an infected finger that will never see a doctor. He is dressed in his only clothes: sneakers, jeans, and a T-shirt bearing the Porsche emblem. The clothes have not been washed for months and smell like it.

Juan has lived here since he was nine. That was when his father beat him and bound him in chains. His father was too poor to support a large family, so Juan started life on his own. The years since have been mired in meaninglessness.

For food, he and the others run errands and fetch water for the merchants who run food stalls nearby. In return they get scraps, the leftovers at the end of the day. For recreation, they hang out near the hut, watching a world go by that barely touches them. Small tin cans of glue, rigged with plastic spouts for sniffing, are constant companions to blunt the pain and boredom. Another companion is a bottle of "Leon," pure alcohol with a sugarcane stick, which the boys pass around. Juan got it at the liquor store. He doesn't explain how. Sometimes beer substitutes. As they drink, they talk.

"I talk about how bad I feel to live here and how hungry and cold I am. And I talk about the police. I'm afraid of the police." Periodically the police conduct raids. He says they kick him in the groin and take him away for a week or two. Then he's back until the next time.

Juan made it through elementary school but can't prove it. His certificate was taken away when he was placed in a reformatory for eighteen months for being with a group of older boys who raped a twenty-two-year-old woman.

He points to a series of scars on his right arm inflicted when he tried to kill himself with a jagged piece of glass two years ago. A year before that he tried to hang himself. He says he won't try again, because Fernando told him life was worth living.

"If you know how to live, life is beautiful," he says. "The world is my friend," echoes bright graffiti etched on a wall at Covenant House, the home where Fernando works and where he would like Juan to come live. But for Juan, it is too late. At seventeen, the habit of dissoluteness is too ingrained. He says he would like to do what his father does—drive a bus—but he knows he will never have the chance.

"I get high because people look down on me. So life doesn't seem that beautiful after all."

He once went into the mission across the street, run by Christian evangelicals, but was unhappy because, not being Catholic, they did not worship the Virgin Mary. "The Virgin can help me. I pray that God and the Virgin will help little by little by helping me stop using drugs."

He thinks of going home. "When I was little I followed my father around like a puppy. He wants me to go to a rehab center but he won't let me come home." Money is scarce, and his stepmother doesn't want any of it spent on him.

He met a girl once, on a subway, on one of his rare trips out of the neighborhood. He liked her, but he's under no illusions. "I'll never be able to get married because I'll never have a job. I'll be here till I die. Where else would I go?"

If Juan is lucky he will live to be forty, maybe forty-five. That's about the life span for kids who grow up on the streets. He is one of thousands of boys and girls, victims of urban poverty that overcrowding has made worse, who have no home but the streets. Some live in manholes, some in abandoned houses; some huddle beneath blankets along subway tracks near grates that spew warm air. The government says there are only one thousand of them. Covenant House says there may be fifty times that number.

"It's a political question," says Fernando. "The Mexican government wants the world to think it's a first world community.

The number of kids on the street shows how bad off things really are."

Salvation has not reached across the street from the mission. The world of the Porsche is as remote as the stars. "For them," says Fernando, "there is no future."

I met Juan, whose real name I have not used, one chilly morning in January 1993, shortly after starting the research on this book. The magnitude of his physical and spiritual deprivation left a deep impression. Buried in the anonymity of an urban slum, he is perhaps as invisible as any member of the human race can be. Innumerable times since that January morning, I have considered how difficult it must be for people living in more comfortable circumstances to comprehend the conditions that have defined his unhappy world and extinguished his small hopes.

In a sense, this book is about Juan. He is a reminder of what happens when population growth outstrips economic performance, which is the case in so many poor nations scattered through Africa, Asia, and Latin America. Even if population growth were drastically curtailed, there would still be boys like Juan, since the circumstances that have led him to the streets are not the product of population growth alone. But if population growth is not curtailed at a faster pace there will be many more like him. The tragedy of that possibility is demonstrated by Juan's life. It is expressed more poignantly in the bright, engaging smile that, despite his circumstances, Juan managed to bestow on a passing stranger from a faraway place. Such sparks of life should be better tended by the world community.

There is no secret about what needs to be done. Economic development, which will help reduce the demand for large families, will be one important component of a comprehensive strategy to reduce fertility and further slow rates of population growth in developing countries like Mexico. Another will be narrowing the inequities between the sexes that are prevalent in many developing nations. As one journalist summarizes the requirements: "Emancipate women. Educate them. Help them space their pregnancies. Give their children health care. Allow them options beyond motherhood."[1] The investment that promises the biggest short-term payoff is simply making sure that safe and effective family planning methods are made universally available.

The simple truth is that rapid population growth is one of the few solvable problems in an otherwise complicated world. Four decades of experience with family planning have made it abundantly clear what programs and methods work best. The experience of family planning agencies in countries from Thailand to Bangladesh has provided valuable, transferable lessons that are even now being incorporated into the practice of countries that were late to set up population programs. New contraceptive or abortion technologies, like the abortion drug RU-486, may make an eventual contribution to lower fertility. But even with existing methods, the task of attaining population stabilization is both affordable and achievable.

"Family planning is one thing we know how to do well so let's get on with it and rejoice," says Malcolm Potts, who teaches public health at the University of California at Berkeley. "Just provide services in a respectful way, listen to what people want, provide good geographically, culturally, and economically accessible services, and fertility falls. That's what the data show. If you give people access to contraceptives and abortion they practically stop having children."[2]

As Potts notes, rapid population growth is no longer a problem looking for a solution but a solution looking for resources.[3] It was the resources of the industrialized nations that helped lower deathrates in the developing world half a century ago, contributing to the population explosion that has occurred there since. The idea of investing the modest resources now needed to lower birthrates has appealing symmetry. More to the point, such an investment would be the consummate act of enlightened self-interest on the part of wealthy nations which, in the absence of such support, will not long remain isolated from the daunting consequences of rapid global population growth.

Notes

Unless otherwise specified, country population data and data on national family planning programs are derived from the following sources:

United Nations, Department for Economic and Social Information and Policy Analysis, *World Population Prospects: The 1992 Revision* (New York, 1993).

World Population Data Sheet of the Population Reference Bureau, Inc. (Washington, D.C.: Population Reference Bureau, 1993).

John A. Ross, W. Parker Mauldin, and Vincent C. Miller, *Family Planning and Population: A Compendium of International Statistics* (New York: United Nations Population Fund and The Population Council, 1993).

INTRODUCTION

1. Alexander de Sherbinin, "Spotlight: Algeria," *Population Today 20*, November 1992, 11.

2. Richard Gardner, *Negotiating Survival: Four Priorities After Rio* (New York: Council on Foreign Relations Press, 1992), 19–20.

3. Remarks by President William Clinton, Drexel University, Philadelphia, 20 April 1992.

4. "Nothing Is Unthinkable," *The Lancet* 15, September 1990, 659.

5. Mark Sagoff, "Doing the Numbers: Demographic Trends and Global Population," in *Philosophy and Public Policy* 13, Fall 1993, 5.

6. Malcolm Potts, "Unmet Demand for Family Planning," *Interdisciplinary Science Reviews* 18, 4.

7. The U.N. Long-Range Population Projections: What They Tell Us (Washington, D.C.: Population Reference Bureau, 1992).

8. *Africa Region Population Projections, 1992–1993* (Washington, D.C.: The World Bank, 1992), 126.

9. John Cleland, James Phillips, Sajeda Amin, and G. M. Kemal, *Determinants of Reproductive Change in Bangladesh* (Washington, D.C.: The World Bank, 1994).

10. World Health Organization, *The Current Global Situation of the HIV/AIDS Pandemic* (Geneva, 1 July 1993); World Health Organization, The *HIV/AIDS Pandemic: 1993 Overview* (Geneva, 1993).

11. The World Bank, *Effective Family Planning Programs* (Washington, D.C., 1993), 14. Even in the worst-hit countries, AIDS will reduce population growth by no more than one percentage point, the Bank reports. See also United Nations, Department of Economic and Social Information and Policy Analysis, *World Population Prospects: The 1992 Revisions* (New York, 1993), 57.

12. Hugh O'Haire, "AIDS and Population: Think Again," *Populi* 20, December 1993/January 1994, 8–11.

13. Interview with Rafael Mazin and Armando Peruga, Washington D.C., 11 January 1994.

14. "The Future of Africa," *Population Newsletter* (United Nations: Department of International Economic and Social Affairs, Population Division), December 1991, 1.

15. Shiro Horiughi, "World Population Growth Rate: Why Declines Stalled in the 1980s," *Population Today* 21, June 1993, 6.

16. Royal Society of London and the U.S. National Academy of Sciences, "Population Growth, Resource Consumption, and a Sustainable World," Joint Statement issued 26 February 1992.

17. Jessica Tuchman Mathews, "Redefining Security," *Foreign Affairs* 68, Spring 1989, 164.

18. United Nations, United Nations High Commissioner for Refugees, *The State of the World's Refugees 1993: The Challenge of Protection* (New York: Penguin, 1993).

19. Telephone interview with Bruce Wilcox, 29 November 1993.

20. Paul Ehrlich, *The Population Bomb* (New York: Ballantine Books, 1968); Donella H. Meadows, Dennis L. Meadows, Jorgen Randers, and William W. Behrens III, *The Limits to Growth: A Report for the Club of Rome Project on the Predicament of Mankind* (New York: New American Library, 1972).

21. Interview with Philander Claxton, Washington, D.C., 4 February 1994.

22. U.S. Department of Commerce, Economics and Statistics Administration, Bureau of the Census, "Nation's Population Projected to Grow by 50 Percent During Next 60 Years, Census Bureau Reports," (Washington, D.C., 4 December 1992).

23. See Monique Miller, "U.S. Population Growth and the Wildlands Vision," in David Clarke Burks, ed., *Place of the Wild: A Wildlands Anthology of Original Essays*, in press. Periodic information on the implications of population growth in the United States is provided in *Clearinghouse Bulletin*, published by Carrying Capacity Network, Washington, D.C. See also Robert McConnell, "An American Laboratory: Population Growth and Environmental Quality in California," in *Focus* (Carrying Capacity Network) 3, 1993.

24. Paul Kennedy, *Preparing for the Twenty-First Century* (New York: Random House, 1993), 24.

25. Telephone interview with Marten Van Heuven, 5 January 1994.

26. Howard LaFranchi, "Forging New Ties Across the Mediterranean," *Christian Science Monitor*, 27 January 1993, 1.

27. Stanley Hoffman, "A UN Volunteer Military Force—Four Views," *New York Review of Books* XL, 24 June 1993.

28. Telephone interview with John Steinbruner, 22 September 1993.

29. Gregory Foster, et. al., "Global Demographic Trends to the Year 2010: Implications for U.S. Security," *Washington Quarterly*, Spring 1989, 5.

30. United Nations, United Nations Population Fund, *Population, Resources and the Environment: The Critical Challenge* (New York, 1991), 56.

31. International Labor Organization, *Economically Active Population 1950–2025: Estimates and Projections, Vol. 5, World Summary* (Geneva, 1986).

32. Quoted in Don Hinrichsen, "The Need to Balance Population with Resources: Four Case Studies," *Populi* 18, 1991, 37.

33. Thomas Homer-Dixon, "On the Threshold: Environmental Changes as Causes of Acute Conflict," *International Security* 16, Fall 1991, 76–116. See also "Desperate Departures: The Flight of Environmental Refugees," *Toward the 21st Century*, Number 4 (Washington, D.C.:, The Population Institute, 1992).

34. George D. Moffett III, "Middle East's Cup Runneth Dry," *Christian Science Monitor*, 8 March 1990, 10–11. Other articles in a *Christian Science Monitor* series on the Middle East water crisis appeared 13 March, 14 March, and 16 March 1990. See also Rebert Engelman and Pamela LeRoy, *Sustaining Water: Population and the Future of the Renewable Water Supplies* (Washington, D.C.: Population Action International, 1993); Peter Gleick,

"Water and Conflict," and Miriam R. Lowi, "West Bank Water Resources and the Resolution of Conflict in the Middle East," in *Environmental Change and Acute Conflict*, Occasional Paper Number 1 (American Academy of Arts and Sciences and University of Toronto, September 1992); and Joyce Starr, "Water Wars," *Foreign Policy* 82, Spring 1991, 25ff.

35. Homer-Dixon, "On the Threshold of Environmental Changes," 97.

36. See Chapter 3 for a detailed accounting of the views of the "optimists" and "pessimists."

37. United Nations/Institut National d'Etudes Demographic, *Consequences of Rapid Population Growth in Developing Countries*, Expert Group Meeting, New York, 23–26 August 1988 (New York: Taylor and Francis, 1991), 369.

38. Interview with Norman Myers, New York, 23 September 1993. See Barbara Tuchman, *The March of Folly: From Troy to Vietnam* (New York: Alfred A. Knopf, 1984).

39. *Population, Resources and the Environment*, 77.

40. *Consequences of Rapid Population Growth*, 368.

CHAPTER ONE

1. Interview with Mohamed Sid-Ahmed, Cairo, 11 May 1993.

2. United Nations, Department of Economic and Social Affairs, Population Division, *Population Growth and Policies in Megacities: Cairo* (New York, 1990), 1; *1992 Information Please Almanac* (Boston: Houghton-Mifflin, 1992).

3. The term is used in Anthony Giddens, *Modernity and Self-Identity: Self and Society in the Late Modern Age* (Stanford: Stanford University Press, 1991).

4. Robert Schiffer, *The Exploding City: An Unforgettable Journey Through Nine Great Cities* (New York: St. Martin's Press, 1990), 3.

5. Lester Brown and Jodi Jacobson, *The Future of Urbanization: Facing the Ecological and Economic Constraints*, Worldwatch Paper No. 77 (Washington, D.C.: Worldwatch Institute, May 1987), 5.

6. See Jay Axelbank, "The Crisis of the Cities," *Populi* 15, December 1988, 28–35. The five-volume report was issued by the Institut d'Estudis Metropolitans de Barcelona.

7. United Nations, Department of International Economic and Social Affairs, Population Division, *World Urbanization Prospects: Estimates and Projections of Urban and Rural Populations and of Urban Agglomerations 1990* (New York, 1991), 21.

8. Ibid., 24.

9. Schiffer, *Exploding City*, 7.

10. United Nations, *World Urbanization Prospects*, 199–206.

11. Isberto Ramon, "Asia: Environmental Pollution the Price Paid for Economic Growth," in *Metropolis 2000: Big Cities, Bigger Problems*, Inter Press Service, Special News Service, No. 22, 9–22 December 1990, 12.

12. "Third World Metropolises Are Becoming Monsters," *Der Spiegel*, reprinted in *World Press Review*, October 1989, 24.

13. World Health Organization, "The Urban Crisis: Will Megacities Lead to Megacrisis?," *WHO Features*, No. 156 (Geneva, May 1991), 2.

14. Population Action International, "Cities: Life in the World's 100 Largest Metropolitan Areas" (Washington, D.C., 1990).

15. Interview with Saskia Sassen, Washington, D.C., 30 July 1993.

16. Cited in Sharon Camp, "Urbanization: Megacities Appearing All Over the World," in op. cit. *Metropolis 2000*, 18.

17. Winthrop Carty, "Towards an Urban Bias," in Global Edition, *Earthwatch*, Number 43, 4th Quarter 1991, 13.

18. Kennedy, *Preparing for the Twenty-First Century*, 26.

19. Interview with Saskia Sassen.

20. Cited in Robin Wright, "L.A. Riots Called Symptom of Worldwide Urban Trend," *Los Angeles Times*, 25 May 1992, A-7.

21. Sa'ad Eddin Ibrahim, "A Sociological Profile," in Abdulaziz Saqqaf, *The Middle East City: Ancient Traditions Confront a Modern World* (New York: Paragon House Publishers, 1987), 209.

22. Ibid., 223.

23. Carol Berger interview with Naguib Mahfouz, Cairo, 13 May 1993.

24. Interview with Mohammed Auda, Cairo, 7 May 1993.

25. Theroux, Peter, "Clamorous Heart of Egypt: Cairo," *National Geographic*, April 1993, 44.

26. United Nations, Department of International Economic and Social Affairs Population Division, *Population Growth and Policies in Megacities: Cairo* (New York, 1990), 22.

27. Chris Hedges, "Industrious Egypt Is Choking Its People to Death," *New York Times*, November 26, 1993, A-4.

28. Ibrahim, "A Sociological Profile," 224.

29. Interview with Mahmoud Sheriff, Cairo, 11 May 1993.

30. *Population Growth and Policies in Megacities: Cairo*, 16.

31. Interview with Milad Hana, Cairo, 9 May 1993.

32. Lowe, Marcia, *Shaping Cities: The Environmental and Human Dimension*, Worldwatch Paper No. 105 (Washington, D.C.: Worldwatch Institute, October 1991), 5.

33. Schiffer, *Exploding City*, 14.

34. Axelbank, "The Crisis of the Cities," 33.

35. Interview with Sobri Abdel Hakim, Cairo, 12 May 1993.

36. Population Action International, "Cities."

37. Interview with Mohammed Auda.

38. Interview with Tahseen Basheer, Cairo, 12 May 1993.

39. Ibid.

40. Interview with Carol Berger, Cairo, 12 May 1993.

41. Background interview, Cairo, 11 May 1993.

42. Interview with Mohammed Auda.

43. Interview with Hassan El-Geretly, Cairo, 12 May 1993.

44. Telephone interview with Michael Cohen, 24 February 1994.

45. United Nations, United Nations Development Programme, *Development for the Urban Future* (New York, 1988).

46. *Population Growth and Policies in Megacities: Cairo*, 27.

47. Interview with Sobri Abdel Hakim.

48. Dennis A. Rondinelli and John D. Kasarda, "Job Creation in Third World Cities," in John D. Kasarda and Allan M. Powell, eds., *Third World Cities: Problems, Policies, and Prospects* (Newbury Park: Sage Publications, 1993), 112.

49. Alan Gilbert and Josef Gugler, *Cities, Poverty and Development: Urbanization in the Third World* (Oxford: Oxford University Press, 1992), 256.

50. Ibid., 252.

51. Rondinelli and Kasarda, "Job Creation in Third World Cities," 112.

52. Gilbert and Gugler, *Cities, Poverty and Development*, 244.

53. Ibid., 251. See also Rondinelli and Kasarda, "Job Creation in Third World Cities," 113.

54. Gilbert and Gugler, *Cities, Poverty and Development*, 250.

55. Interview with Heba Handoussa, Cairo, 10 May 1993.

56. Interview with Ali Shulkani, Cairo, 12 May 1993.

57. *Development for the Urban Future*, 5.

58. Eugene Linden, "Megacities," *Time*, 11 January 1993, 38.

59. *Development for the Urban Future*, 7.

60. Raj Mangal Prasad and Christine Furedy, "Small Businesses from Urban Wastes—Shoe Renovation in Delhi," *Environment and Urbanization* 4, October 1992, 59.

61. Jac Smit and Joe Nasr, "Urban Agriculture for Sustainable Cities: Using Wastes and Idle Land and Water Bodies as Resources," *Environment and Urbanization* 4, October 1992, 141ff.

62. Lyrics by Ahmed Adawiya.

CHAPTER TWO

1. Cited in McOwiti O. Thomas, "Upwardly Mobile in Machakos," *Panoscope* 35, April 1993.

2. Interview with Donald Thomas, Nairobi, 9 August 1993.

3. Sharon Camp, "Population Pressure, Poverty and the Environment," in Carol Rae Hansen, ed., *The New World Order: Rethinking America's Global Role* (Flagstaff: Arizona Honors Academy Press, 1992), 376–8.

4. Paul Harrison, *The Greening of Africa: Breaking Through in the Battle for Land and Food* (London: Paladin Grafton Books, 1987), 26.

5. *Three Essays on Population* (New York: Mentor Books, 1963), 59.

6. Peter Hendry, *Food and Population: Beyond Five Billion* (Washington, D.C.: Population Reference Bureau, Inc., August 1991), 3.

7. Paul Harrison, *The Third Revolution: Environment, Population and a Sustainable World* (London and New York: I. B. Tauris/Penguin Books., Ltd, 1992), 43. See also Hendry, *Food and Population*, 5–10; World Bank, *Poverty and Hunger: Issues and Options for Food Security in Developing Countries* (Washington, D.C., 1986), 23; Harrison, *The Greening of Africa*; Robert Repetto, *Population, Resources, Environment: An Uncertain Future* (Washington, D.C.: Population Reference Bureau, Inc., July 1987), 14–23; World Bank, *Sub-Saharan Africa: From Crisis to Sustainable Growth* (Washington, D.C., 1989). For an optimistic assessment see Dennis Avery, *Global Food Progress, 1991* (Indianapolis: Hudson Institute, 1991). For a highly pessimistic view see Henry W. Kendall and David Pimentel, "Constraints on the Expansion of the Global Food Supply," (Washington, D.C.: Union of Concerned Scientists, 5 August 1993).

8. Telephone interview with Dennis Avery, 30 July 1993.

9. Per Pinstrup-Andersen, "Solving World Hunger Will Require a New Vision and Renewed Investment in Agricultural Research and Development," *Backgrounder* (Washington, D.C.: International Food Policy Research Institute, January 1993). According to the IFPRI, "the number of malnourished (underweight) children throughout the developing regions of the world increased from 166 million to 188 million between 1975 and 1990."

10. Per Pinstrup-Anderson, "Solving World Hunger."

11. Cited in *International Food Policy Research Institute, 1992 Report* (Washington, D.C., 1992), 7. Continent-wide, food self-sufficiency ratios dropped in Africa from 98 percent in 1972–1974 to 86 percent in 1980 and are projected to drop to 71 percent by the year 2008, as noted in A. A. Aidoo, "Women and Food Security: The Opportunity for Africa," *Development* 12, 1988, 56–62.

12. Telephone interview with Stephen Vosti, 12 July 1992.

13. Wilhelm Adel, *Agricultural Fluctuations in Europe from the 13th to 20th Centuries*, trans. Olive Ordish (New York: St. Martin's Press, 1978); and B. H. Slicher van Bath, *The Agrarian History of Western Europe, A. D. 500–1850*, trans. Olive Ordish (New York: St. Martin's Press, 1963).

14. Ibid., 238.

15. See Keith Schneider, "Scientific Advances Lead to Era of Surplus Around the World," *New York Times*, 9 September 1986, C-1.; Richard Critchfield, "An Old Hand Launches a Green Revolution in Africa," *International Herald Tribune*, 27 March 1987, 6; Orville L. Freeman, "Meeting the Food Needs of the Coming Decade: Agriculture vs. the Environment," *The Futurist*, November–December 1990, 15–21; World Commission on the Environment and Development, *Our Common Future* (Oxford and New York: Oxford University Press, 1987); and Kennedy, *Preparing for the Twenty-First Century*, 65–81.

16. Schneider, "Scientific Advances."

17. Paul Lewis, "Food Production and the Birth Rate Are in a New Race," *New York Times*, 10 May 1992, E-4.

18. Telephone interview with Lester Brown, 30 July 1993.

19. Lester R. Brown, Christopher Flavin, and Hal Kane, *Vital Signs 1992: The Trends That Are Shaping Our Future* (New York and London: W. W. Norton and Company, 1992), 24.

20. *International Food Policy Research Institute Report 1992*, 7–9.

21. Repetto, *Population, Resources and Environment*, 18.

22. Interview with Lester Brown.

23. Hossain, Mahabub, *Nature and Impact of the Green Revolution in Bangladesh*, Research Report 67 (Washington, D.C.: International Food Policy Research Institute, July 1988).

24. Interview with Helmut Hess, Dhaka, 23 March 1993.

25. Interview with Stephen Vosti.

26. Interview with Dennis Avery.

27. Ibid.

28. Interview with Lester Brown.

29. Telephone interview with Robert Chandler, 28 July 1993.

30. Interview with Stephen Vosti.

31. Telephone interview with Eileen Kennedy, 13 December 1993.

32. Scott Pendleton, "Farm Productivity Must Surge to Meet the World's Needs," *Christian Science Monitor*, 21 October 1992, 9.

33. Joachim Von Braun, "Underrated Agriculture: Declining Aid, Increasing Need," *Backgrounder* (Washington, D.C.: International Food Policy Research Institute, January 1993).

34. Telephone interview with Joachim Von Braun, 27 July 1993.

35. Robert O. Blake, Memorandum to Members and Advisers, Committee on Agricultural Sustainability for Developing Countries, 12 November 1993, A-2, A-3.

36. Background interview, 7 August 1993.

37. Harrison, *The Greening of Africa*, 334.

38. *Sub-Saharan Africa: From Crisis to Sustainable Growth*, 8–9.

39. *International Food Policy Research Institute Report 1992*, 9.

40. *Sustaining Water*, 30.

41. See, for example, Sally Ethelston, "Agriculture in Egypt: 'Burdens of the Past, Options for the Future,' " unpublished manuscript, Georgetown University, 1984, 31.

42. Quoted in Clive Ponting, *A Green History of the World: The Environment and the Collapse of Great Civilizations* (New York: Penguin Books, 1991), 76.

43. World Resources Institute, "New Data Reveal Startling Soil Degradation Around the World," Press release, 24 March 1992. See also United Nations, Food and Agriculture Organization, "Soil Loss Accelerating Worldwide," 13 July 1993.

44. Paul R. Erlich, Anne H. Ehrlich, and Gretchen C. Daily, "Food, Security, Population, and Environment," in *Population and Development Review* 19, March 1993, 3.

45. Interview with Joachin Von Braun.

46. Interview with Dennis Avery.

47. Lester R. Brown, et al., *State of the World 1993* (New York: W. W. Norton, 1993), 12.

48. United Nations, Food and Agriculture Organization, *Agriculture: Toward the Year 2000*, revised version (Rome, 1987), 66.

49. United Nations, Food and Agriculture Organization, "Soil Less Accelerating Worldwide," 2.

50. Alexandratos Nikos, ed., *World Agriculture Toward 2000: An FAO Study* (New York: Belhaven, 1988), 79.

51. Cited in Donald L. Plucknett, "The Global Agricultural Research System: Geared to the Needs of an Expanding Population," Paper presented at the World Food Production Conference, Rio de Janeiro, Brazil, 6–9 November 1989, 9–10.

52. John Seabrook, "Tremors in the Hothouse," *New Yorker*, 19 July 1993, 31ff.

53. Deborah Erikson, "Hot Potato," *Scientific American* 26, September 1990, 160.

54. Joan Hailton, "A Storm Is Brewing Down on the Farm," *Business Week*, 14 December 1992, 98.

55. Rosie Mestel, "Altered Vegetable States," *Discover* 14, January 1993, 45.

56. Anderson, Clifton E., "The Biotechnology Revolution: Who Wins and Who Loses?" in Howard F. Didsbury, Jr., *The Years Ahead: Perils, Problems, and Promises* (Bethesda: World Future Society, 1993), 143–156.

57. Interview with Lester Brown.

58. Kerri Wright Plantais and Michael P. Collinson, "Biotechnology and the Developing World," *Finance and Development* 29, 29 March 1992, 34.

59. Laurent Belsie, "Biotechnology Promises Fresh Gains," *Christian Science Monitor*, 28 October 1992, 12.

60. James Ellis, "Can Biotech Put Bread on Third World Tables?" *Business Week*, 14 December 1992, 100.

61. Ibid.

62. Interview with Alvin Young, Washington, D.C., 7 July 1993.

63. Telephone interview with Andrew Kimbrell, 7 July 1993.

64. Seabrook, "Tremors in the Hothouse," 34.

65. Interview with Andrew Kimbrell.

66. Pamela Weintraub, "The Coming of the High-Tech Harvest," *Audubon* 94, July/August 1992, 92–94.

67. The concern is expressed in United Nations, Food and Agriculture Organization, "Extinction of Plant Species Accelerating" (Rome, 23 March 1992), 4.

68. Interview with Alvin Young.

69. Interview with Dennis Avery.

70. Telephone interview with Clifton Anderson, 6 July 1993.

71. Ibid.

72. Harrison, *The Greening of Africa*, 27–45, 80–97.

73. Alberto Valdes and Maurice Schiff, "A Synthesis of the Economies in Developing Countries," in *The Political Economy of Agricultural Pricing Policy*, vol. 4 (Baltimore: Johns Hopkins University Press, 1992), 15.

74. Robert S. McNamara, "The Challenges for Sub-Saharan Africa," Sir John Crawford Memorial Lecture, Washington, D.C., 1 November 1985.

75. R. Stephen Brent, "Aiding Africa," *Foreign Policy* 80, Fall 1990, 135.

76. Repetto, *Population, Resources, Environment*, 38–39; Harrison, *The Greening of Africa*, 80–97.

77. *International Food Policy Research Institute Report 1992*, 15.

78. Aidoo, "Women and Food Security."

79. Mbaari Kinya, *Environment and Energy Issues as They Affect*

Women in Embu District, Kenya, Women, Environment and Population Project, United Nations Research Institute for Social Development, September 1992, 30.

80. The World Bank, *Kenya: The Role of Women in Economic Development,* a World Bank Country Study (Washington, D.C.: May 1989), xiv, 12.

81. *Sub-Saharan Africa: From Crisis to Sustainable Growth,* 9.

82. Interview with Lester Brown.

83. Interview with Idriss Jazairy, Washington D.C., 24 November 1992.

84. Telephone interview with Paul Harrison, 27 July 1993.

85. Interview with Gideon Mutiso, Nairobi, 9 August 1993.

86. Interview with Donald Thomas.

87. Brent, "Aiding Africa," 128.

88. Background interview.

89. Interview with Stephen Vosti.

90. Telephone interview with Robert Brinkman, 7 July 1993.

CHAPTER THREE

1. Interview with Norman Schwartz, Flores, Guatemala, 11 September 1993.

2. Interview with Alfredo Mendez, Guatemala City, 9 September 1993.

3. Ponting, *A Green History of the Earth,* 81; see also Wilbur E. Garrett, "La Ruta Maya," *National Geographic,* October 1989, 424ff.

4. See Richard E. Bilsborrow and Pamela E. DeLargy, "Land Use, Migration, and Natural Resource Deterioration: The Experience of Guatemala and the Sudan," in Kingsley Davis and Mikhail Bernstam, eds., *Resources, Environment, and Population: Present Knowledge, Future Options* (New York and Oxford: Oxford University Press, 1991), 125–147.

5. For a discussion of the history of the population debate see Nathan Keyfitz, "Population Theory and Doctrine: A Historical Survey," in William Petersen, ed., *Readings in Population* (New York: Macmillan, 1972); Charles C. Mann, "How Many Is Too Many?" *The Atlantic* 271, February 1993, 47–67; E. P. Hutchinson, *The Population Debate: The Development of Conflicting Theories up to 1900* (Boston: Houghton Mifflin, 1967).

6. Quoted in Hutchinson, *The Population Debate,* 13.

7. Nathan Keyfitz, "Population and Development within the Ecosphere: One View of the Literature," Reprint RR-91-14 (Laxenburg, Austria: International Institute for Applied Systems Analysis, August 1991), 4–5.

8. Quoted in Hutchinson, *The Population Debate,* 17.

9. Ibid., 34.

10. For the text of Malthus's seminal essay, see Philip Appleman, ed., *Thomas Robert Malthus: An Essay on the Principle of Population—Text, Sources and Background, Criticism* (New York: W. W. Norton, 1976), 15ff.

11. Quote from *Gentleman's Magazine*, 1835, cited in John Maynard Keynes, *Essays in Biography* (New York: Horizon Press, 1951), 110.

12. John Stuart Mill, *Principles of Political Economy* (1848), quoted in Appleman, *Thomas Robert Malthus*, 153.

13. William Godwin, *Of Population: An Inquiry Concerning the Power of Increase in the Numbers of Mankind* (1820), quoted in ibid., 145.

14. Quoted in Mann, "How Many Is Too Many?" 50.

15. Karl Marx, *Capital* (1867), quoted in Appleman, *Thomas Robert Malthus*, 159–60.

16. Friedrich Engels, *Outlines of a Critique of Political Economy* (1844), quoted in ibid., 148–149.

17. Marie Jean Antoine Nicholas Caritat, Marquis de Condorcet, *The Future Progress of the Human Mind* (1795), quoted in ibid., 8.

18. Dennis Hodgson, "Orthodoxy and Revisionism in American Demography," *Population and Development Review 14*, December 1988, 546–547.

19. Kingley Davis, "Population and Resources: Fact and Interpretation," in Davis and Bernstam, eds., *Resources, Environment, and Population*, 10.

20. Donella Meadows, et al., *The Limits To Growth*. See also Donella H. Meadows, Dennis L. Meadows, Jergen Randers, *Beyond the Limits: Confronting Global Collapse, Envisioning a Sustainable Future* (Post Mills, Vermont: Chelsea Green, 1992).

21. Donella Meadows, remarks delivered at the Woodrow Wilson International Center for Scholars, Washington, D.C., 13 April 1992.

22. See Teitelbaum, "The Population Threat," *Foreign Affairs* 71, Winter 1992–93, 71–72.

23. See Alvin Hansen, *Full Recovery or Stagnation* (New York: W. W. Norton, 1938) and Alvin Hansen, *Fiscal Policies and Business Cycles* (New York: W. W. Norton, 1941).

24. John Maynard Keynes, "President Roosevelt's Gold Policy," *The New Statesman and Nation*, 20 January 1934, reprinted in Donald Moggridge, ed., *The Collected Writings of John Maynard Keynes*, vol. XXI, *Activities 1931–1939: World Crises and Policies in Britain and America* (London: Macmillan/Cambridge University Press, 1982), 316. Also John Maynard Keynes, *The General Theory of Employment, Interest and Money* (New York: Harcourt, Brace, 1936), 318.

25. "Rapid Growth of Family Units Is Spur to Business in U.S.," *U.S. News & World Report*, 2 June 1950, 656.

26. David Osterfeld, remarks delivered at the Cato Institute, 12 November 1993. See David Osterfeld, *Prosperity Versus Planning: How Government Stifles Economic Growth* (New York: Oxford University Press, 1992).

27. Ibid.

28. Telephone interview with Ben Wattenberg, 14 May 1992. See Ben Wattenberg, "Less Pop in Population Explosion?: Hardly an Explosion," *Washington Times*, 27 May 1992, G-1.

29. John Tierney, "Betting the Planet," *New York Times Magazine*, 2 December 1990, 51ff. The debate between the optimists and pessimists is also captured in Norman Myers and Julian Simon, *Scarcity or Abundance?: A Debate on the Environment* (New York: W. W. Norton, forthcoming). A history of the debate in popular magazines is found in John R. Wilmoth and Patrick Ball, "The Population Debate in American Popular Magazines, 1946–90," *Population and Development Review* 18, December 1992, 631–668.

30. Ehrlich, *The Population Bomb*. See also Paul R. Ehrlich and Anne H. Ehrlich, *The Population Explosion* (New York: Simon and Schuster, 1990).

31. Ibid, prologue.

32. Telephone interview with Paul Ehrlich, 15 September 1993. Unless otherwise indicated, subsequent quotes from Ehrlich are drawn from this interview.

33. Telephone interview with Samuel Preston, 17 November 1993.

34. Ehrlich, *The Population Bomb*, prologue.

35. Telephone interview with Julian Simon, 16 September 1993. Unless otherwise indicated, subsequent quotes from Simon are drawn from this interview. See also Julian L. Simon, *Population Matters: People, Resources, Environment, and Immigration* (New Brunswick: Transaction Publishers, 1990); Julian L. Simon and Herman Kahn, *The Resourceful Earth* (New York: Basil Blackwell, 1984); and Julian L. Simon, *The Ultimate Resource* (Princeton: Princeton University Press, 1981).

36. Julian Simon, "Resources, Population, Environment: An Oversupply of False Bad News," *Science* 208, 27 June 1980, 1431–37.

37. Mann, "How Many Is Too Many?" 48.

38. Telephone interview with Dennis Hodgson, 18 November 1993.

39. Quoted in George F. Will, "Chicken Littles," *Washington Post*, 31 May 1992, C-7.

40. Telephone interview with Nathan Keyfitz, 20 September 1993. See Keyfitz, *Population and Development within the Ecosphere*; Nathan Keyfitz, "Influence of Human Reproduction on Environment," Paper presented to the New York Academy of Science, Research Triangle Park, NC, 21–24

May 1993; and Nathan Keyfitz, *Genuine Interdisciplinary Study Is Possible* (Laxenburg, Austria: International Institute for Applied Systems Analysis, 11 August, 1993).

41. Telephone interview with Bruce Wilcox, 17 November 1993.

42. Nathan Keyfitz, *Are There Ecological Limits to Population?* Working Paper 93–16 (Laxenburg, Austria: International Institute for Applied Systems Analysis, April 1993), 4.

43. Interview with Nathan Keyfitz.

44. Interview with Samuel Preston.

45. Warren Sanderson, *Economic-Demographic Simulation Models: A Review of Their Usefulness for Policy Analysis*, Working Paper RR-80-14 (Laxenburg, Austria: International Institute for Applied Systems Analysis, 1980).

46. Interview with Nathan Keyfitz.

47. Michael Teitelbaum and Jay Winter, "The Missing Links: The Population-Environment Debate in Historical Perspective," in Gayl D. Ness, William D. Drake, and Steven Brechin, *Population-Environment Dynamics: Ideas and Observations* (Ann Arbor: University of Michigan Press, 1993).

48. Telephone interview with Michael Teitelbaum, 10 December 1993.

49. John Horgan, "Profile: Paul Karl Feyerabend—The Worst Enemy of Science," *Scientific American*, May 1993, 36–37.

50. Interview with Bruce Wilcox.

51. Nick Eberstadt, "Population and Economic Growth," *Wilson Quarterly*, Winter 1986, 100–101.

52. Interview with Michael Teitelbaum.

53. Interview with Nathan Keyfitz.

54. Joel E. Cohen, "How Many People Can Earth Hold?" *Discover* 13, November 1992, 116.

55. United Nations, United Nations Population Fund, *Population, Resources and the Environment: The Critical Challenges* (New York, 1991), 118.

56. Telephone interview with Robert Repetto, 31 August 1993.

57. Interview with Julian Simon.

58. Interview with Sharon Camp, Washington, D.C., 19 January 1993. Writes Joel Cohen: "When other factors in human productivity are already taxed to the point of severely diminishing returns, one more human being may represent one more perennially empty stomach, one more soul stunted before it can realize its share of the glory of being a human being." Op. cit., Cohen, "How Many People Can Earth Hold?" 118.

59. Paul Harrison, *The Third Revolution*, 39.

60. UNFPA, *State of the World Population 1992*, 29–30.

61. Background interview, 25 October 1993.

62. Royal Society of London and the U.S. National Academy of Sciences, "Population Growth, Resource Consumption, and a Sustainable World."

63. Union of Concerned Scientists," World's Leading Scientists Issue Urgent Warning to Humanity," 18 November 1992.

64. "1993 'Science Summit' on World Population: A Joint Statement on Population by 56 of the World's Scientific Academies," October 1993.

65. Repetto, *Population, Resources, Environment: An Uncertain Future*, 23.

66. "Sharon L. Camp Responds," *Conscience*, Autumn 1993, 10.

67. Cited in William Booth, "Tropical Forests Disappearing at Faster Rate," *Washington Post*, 9 September 1991, A-10.

68. According to the UN Population Fund, "By the year 2030, 80 percent of the world's projected population of more than 8 billion people are expected to be living in tropical forest countries. . . . Ecuador's population is projected to increase from 10.9 million to 24 million before it attains zero growth in about a century's time; Cameroon's from 12 million to 67 million; Cote d'Ivoire's from 12 million to 83 million; Madagascar's from 12 million to 49 million; Nigeria's from 112 million to 500 million; Myanmar's from 43 million to 97 million; India's from 871 million to 1.7 billion; Indonesia's from 188 million to 345 million; and Vietnam's from 68 million to 168 million." UNFPA, *Population, Resources and Environment: The Critical Challenges*, 45.

69. Ibid., 63. Environmental refugees in Africa, Asia, and Latin America now number an estimated 10 million, according to the UN Population Fund.

70. Harrison, *The Third Revolution*, 199.

71. Lester R. Brown, Christopher Flavin, and Hal Kane, "Vital Signs 1992: *The Trends That Are Shaping Our Future* (New York: W. W. Norton, 1992), 30. See also Lester Brown, "Postmodern Malthus: Are There Too Many of Us to Survive?" *Washington Post*, 18 July 1993, C-3.

72. Robert Engelman and Pamela LeRoy, *Sustaining Water*. For other sources on diminishing water resources see Introduction, note 34.

73. Robert Engelman and Pamela LeRoy, "Water Shortages May Threaten One in Three People by 2025," Population Action International, 8 November, 1993, 2.

74. Engelman and LeRoy, *Sustaining Water*, 18.

75. Ibid., 36.

76. Brown, et al., *Vital Signs*, 60.

77. *America in the 21st Century*, 19.

78. Mark Sagoff, "Population and Nature: Sorting Out the Impact of Population Growth," *Conscience*, Autumn 1993, 22.

79. Ibid., 23.

80. Futures Group estimates based on Asian Development Bank, *Interim Report for Vehicular Emissions Control Planning in Metro Manila* (October 1991).

81. Interview with John Freymann, Washington, D.C., 15 October 1993.

82. Telephone interview with Robert S. McNamara, 5 May 1992. See Robert S. McNamara, "Time Bomb or Myth: The Population Problem," *Foreign Affairs*, June 1984.

83. *Tropical Rain Forests: A Vanishing Treasure* (Washington, D.C.: Sierra Club, 1990), 1, 12.

84. Maria Conception Cruz, Carrie A. Meyer, Robert Repetto, and Richard Woodward, *Population Growth, Poverty, and Environmental Stress: Frontier Migration in the Philippines and Costa Rica* (Washington, D.C.: World Resources Institute, 1992), 53.

85. Interview with Alfredo Mendez. See also Richard E. Bilsborrow and Paul W. Stupp, *The Effects of Population Growth on Agriculture in Guatemala*, Carolina Population Center Papers, Number 88–24, (Chapel Hill, September 1988), 16–17.

86. Background interview, 9 September 1993.

87. Interview with Helmut Hess, Dhaka, 23 March 1993.

88. Telephone interview with Richard Bilsborrow, 8 September 1993.

89. Interview with Norman Schwartz.

90. *Population Growth, Poverty, and Environmental Stress*, (p. 69) notes, for example, that incentives to cattle ranching have been removed. Brazil and other Amazon Basin nations have recognized the homelands of indigenous peoples, a move that has protected forest land and slowed the rate of deforestation. Also see *Worldwatch* 117.

91. *America in the 21st Century*, 20.

92. Interview with Norman Schwartz.

93. Ponting, *Green History of the World*, chapter 17.

94. Telephone interview with Robert Engelman, 11 January 1993.

CHAPTER FOUR

1. Donaldson, *Nature Against Us*, 117.

2. Telephone interview with Shanti Conli, 19 January 1994.

3. *Population Picks and Pans: The Population Crisis Committee's 1991 Selection of the Ten Countries Worldwide Making the Most and Least Progress in*

Family Planning (Washington, D.C., Population Crisis Committee, 1991), 9–10.

4. *Kenya Demographic and Health Survey, 1993*, Preliminary Report (Columbia, Maryland: Macro International, Inc., 1993).

5. *Population Picks and Pans*, 2.

6. United Nations, United Nations Population Fund, *Meeting the Population Challenge* (New York: undated), 11.

7. Telephone interview with Werner Fornos, 4 February 1993.

8. Peter J. Donaldson and Amy Ong Tsui, *The International Family Planning Movement* (Washington, D.C.: Population Reference Bureau, Inc., November 1990), 5.

9. Ellen Jamison, Peter Johnson and Richard Engels, *World Population Profile: 1987* (Washington, D.C.: U.S. Department of Commerce, Economics and Statistics Administration, Bureau of the Census, December 1987), 13. See also World Health Organization, *Steep Decline in World Fertility Rates: Contraceptive Use up Sharply* (Geneva, 24 June 1992), 2.

10. The World Bank, *Population and the World Bank: Implications from Eight Case Studies* (Washington, D.C., 1992). According to the Bank, "Between two-thirds and three-fourth of this fertility decline [in eight case studies in Asia, Africa, and Latin America] has been due to increased use of modern contraceptive methods. Most of the remainder is accounted for by increasing age of marriage."

11. *Access to Affordable Contraception: 1991 Report on World Progress Toward Population Stabilization* (Washington, D.C.: Population Crisis Committee, 1991).

12. Interview with Philander Claxton, 3 February 1994.

13. World Health Organization, *Steep Decline in World Fertility Rate*, 3.

14. "A Watershed of Ideas," *People* 11, December 1984, 4–5.

15. Steven W. Sinding and Sheldon J. Segal, "Birth-Rate News," *New York Times*, 19 December 1991, A-31.

16. John Bongaarts, "The Fertility Impact of Family Planning Programs," Paper prepared for the IPPF Family Planning Congress, New Delhi, October 1992, 14–15. See also Population Council, "Impact of Family Planning Programs in Developing Countries Is Assessed in New Study by Population Council Researchers" (New York, 24 January 1991).

17. For a detailed description of fertility transition in Thailand, see John Knodel, Aphichat Chamratrithirong, and Nibhon Debavalya, *Thailand's Reproductive Revolution* (Madison: University of Wisconsin Press, 1987); and Anthony Bennet, Carl Frisen, Peerasit Kamnuansilpa, and John McWilliam, *How Thailand's Family Planning Program Reached Replacement*

Level Fertility: Lessons Learned, Population Technical Assistance Occasional Paper No. 4 (Arlington, Va.: Dual and Associates, Inc., 9 November 1990).

18. Knodel, et al., *Thailand's Reproductive Revolution*, chapter 3.

19. Interview with John Knodel, Bangkok, 17 March 1993.

20. Tefft, Sheila, "Family-Planning Efforts Succeed in Thailand," *Christian Science Monitor*, 8 July 1992, 11.

21. The discussion of the evolution of the Thai government's interest in family planning is drawn from United Nations, Department of International Economic and Social Affairs, *Integrating Development and Population Planning in Thailand* (New York, 1991).

22. Ibid., 19.

23. Ibid., 5.

24. Interview with John Baker, Bangkok, 19 March 1993.

25. Knodel, et al., *Thailand's Reproductive Revolution*, 124.

26. Ibid., 124–137.

27. The "flow of resources" thesis is discussed in John C. Caldwell, *Theory of Fertility Decline* (New York: Academic Press, 1982).

28. Knodel, et al., *Thailand's Reproductive Revolution*, 142.

29. Interview with Peter Donaldson, Bangkok, 18 March 1993.

30. Knodel, et al., *Thailand's Reproductive Revolution*, 187.

31. Background interview, 11 May 1993.

32. Interview with Peter Donaldson.

33. Miguel Trias, Untitled paper presented at the Lome Conference on Service Delivery, 1 June 1990, 6. See also W. Parker Mauldin and John A. Ross, "Family Planning Programs: Efforts and Results, 1982–89," *Studies in Family Planning* 22, November–December 1991, 350–367.

34. Interview with John Bongaarts, 17 July 1992.

35. Tefft, "Family Planning Efforts Succeed in Thailand."

36. *Population and the World Bank*, 52.

37. World Bank, *Effective Family Planning Programs* (Washington, D.C., 1993), 56.

38. Teitelbaum, "The Population Threat," 71.

39. Julian Simon, "China's Family-Planning by Coercion," *Washington Post*, 10 March 1993, A-19.

40. Shanti R. Conli and Sharon L. Camp, *China's Family Planning Program: Challenging the Myths*, Country Series #1 (Washington, D.C.: Population Crisis Committee, 1992).

41. Trias, "Lome Conference," 1.

42. William Warren, "Mechai—Thailand's Ubiquitous Family Planner," *Reader's Digest*, January 1978, 96–100. See also Bennet, et al., *How Thailand's Family Planning Program Reached Replacement Level*, 37, 81.

43. Background interview with U.S. foreign service officer.

44. Warren, "Mechai," 98.

45. Background interview with U.S. foreign service officer.

46. Knodel, et al., *Thailand's Reproductive Revolution*, 175.

47. Richard Cornelius and John Novak, "Contraceptive Availability and Use in Five Developing Countries," *Studies in Family Planning* 14, December 1983, 302–317.

48. Bennet, et al., *How Thailand's Family Program Reached Replacement Level*, 75.

49. Judith Bruce, "Fundamental Elements of the Quality of Care: A Simple Framework," *Studies in Family Planning* 21, March–April 1990, 65.

50. Siti Pariani, David M. Herr, and Maurice D. Van Arsdol, "Continued Contraceptive Use in Five Family Planning Clinics in Surabaya, Indonesia," Paper presented at the annual meeting of the American Public Health Association, New Orleans, 19–22 October 1987, cited in op. cit., World Bank, *Effective Family Planning Programs*, 43.

51. Anrudh Jain, "Fertility Reduction and the Quality of Family Planning Services," *Studies in Family Planning* 20, January–February 1989, 10–16.

52. *Population and the World Bank*, 33–34.

53. Ibid., 34.

54. Ruth Simmons and James F. Phillips, "The Integration of Family Planning with Health and Development," in Robert J. Lapham and George B. Simmons, *Organizing for Effective Family Planning Programs* (Washington, D.C.: National Academy Press, 1987), 185–212. Sallie Craig Huber and Phillip Harvey, "Family Planning Programmes in Ten Developing Countries: Effectiveness of Mode of Service Delivery," *Journal of Biosocial Science 21*, July 1989, 267–77.

55. Knodel, et al., *Thailand's Reproductive Revolution*, 44.

56. World Bank, *Effective Family Planning Programs*, 78.

57. "The Reproductive Revolution: New Survey Findings," *Population Reports*, Series M, Number 11, December 1992, 16.

58. World Bank, *Effective Family Planning Programs*, 78.

59. Bruce, "Fundamental Elements of the Quality of Care," 76.

60. Sidney Ruth Schuler, E. Noel McIntosh, Melvyn C. Goldstein, and Badri Raj Pande, "Barriers to Effective Family Planning in Nepal," *Studies in Family Planning* 16, September–October 1985, 260–270.

61. John C. Caldwell and Pat Caldwell, "What Does the Matlab Fertility Experience Really Show?" *Studies in Family Planning* 3, September–October 1992, 308.

62. Ibid., 294.

63. Lily P. Kak and Marjorie Brahms Signer, *The Introduction of Community-Based Family Planning Services in Rural Mali: The Kitibougou Family Health Project*, Working Paper No. 2 (Washington, D.C.: Centre for Development and Population Activities, 1993).

64. Ibid., 9.

65. Interview with Peggy Curlin, Washington, D.C., 10 March 1993.

66. Population Action International, "1990 Report on Progress Towards Population Stabilization," Briefing Paper #23 (Washington, D.C., 1991).

67. Dorothy L. Nortman, Jorge Halvas, and Aurora Rabago, "A Cost-Benefit Analysis of the Mexican Social Security Administration's Family Planning Program," *Studies in Family Planning* 15, January–February 1986, 1ff.

68. Jacqueline Darroch Forrest, Susheela Singh, "Public Sector Savings Resulting from Expenditures for Contraceptive Services," *Family Planning Perspectives* 22, January–February 1990, 6–15.

69. Cited in Donaldson and Tsui, *The International Family Planning Movement*, 30.

70. *The Tata Steel Family Welfare Story: Benefits for Company and Community* (Washington, D.C.: Population Reference Bureau, Inc., March 1989).

71. Nafis Sadik, *The State of World Population, 1992* (New York: United Nations Population Fund, 1992), 7.

72. World Bank, "Classification of Developing Countries by Per Capita GDP and Total Fertility Rate, 1991," Data Files (Washington D.C., 1991).

73. Background interview, 29 May 1993.

74. Interview with Charles Pill, Washington, D.C., 15 October 1993.

75. Interview with Thomas Goliber, Washington, D.C., 15 October 1993.

76. World Bank, *East Asian Miracle: Economic Growth and Public Policy: A World Bank Policy Research Report* (Oxford and London: Oxford University Press, 1993), 193.

77. Nancy Birdsall, David Ross, and Richard Sabot, "Underinvestment in Education: How Much Growth Has Pakistan Foregone?" Paper presented at the Ninth Annual General Meeting of the Pakistan Society of Development Economists, Islamabad, January 1993, 30.

78. World Bank, *East Asian Miracle*, 195–196.

79. Telephone interview with Martin Vaessen, 18 May 1992.

80. Telephone interview with Duff Gillespie, 20 May 1992.

81. Napaporn Havanon, John Knodel, Werasit Sittitrai, *The Impact of Family Size on Wealth Accumulation in Rural Thailand*, Report No. 3 (Bang-

kok: Institute of Population Studies, Chulalongkorn University, May 1990).

82. Chai Podhisita, Napaporn Havanon, John Knodel, and Werasit Sittitrai, "Women's Work and Family Size in Rural Thailand," *Asia-Pacific Population Journal* 5, June 1990, 31–52.

83. John Knodel, Napaporn Havanon, and Werasit Sittitrai, "Family Size and the Education of Children in the Context of Rapid Fertility Decline," *Population and Development Review* 16, March 1990, 31–62.

84. John Knodel, letter to the author, 18 January 1994.

85. W. Parker Mauldin and John A. Ross, "Family Planning Programs: Efforts and Results, 1982–89," *Studies in Family Planning* 22, November–December 1991, 350ff.

86. Donaldson and Tsui, *The International Family Planning Movement*, 33–34.

87. See, for example, Kua Wongboosin and Vipan Prachuabmoh Ruffolo, "Future of Thailand's Population Policy: Potential Directions," Paper presented at the Annual Meeting of the Population Association of America, Cincinnati, 1–3 April 1993.

88. Interview with John Baker.

89. Interview with John Knodel.

90. Telephone interview with Ann Way, 2 May 1993.

91. Conli and Speidel, *Global Population Assistance*, 5–7.

92. Steven W. Sinding, "Getting to Replacement: Bridging the Gap Between Individual Rights and Demographic Goals," Paper presented at the International Planned Parenthood Federation Family Planning Congress, 23–25 October 1992, New Delhi, 7.

93. "1990 Report on Progress Towards Population Stabilization."

94. Population Resource Center, "Executive Summary: Unmet Need and Demand for Contraceptives 1990–2000" (Princeton, undated).

95. Conli and Speidel, *Global Population Assistance*, 5–7. See also World Bank, *Effective Family Planning Programs*, 83–86.

96. Ibid., 70–71. See also Maureen Lewis and Genevieve Kenney, "The Private Sector and Family Planning in Developing Countries," Policy, Planning and Research, Working Paper Series No. 96, Population and Human Resources Department, World Bank (Washington, D.C., September 1988); "Paying for Family Planning," *Population Reports*, Family Planning Programs, Series J., No. 39, November 1991; "Self-Sufficiency in CSM Programs," *Social Marketing Forum* 116, Spring 1989; World Bank, "Pricing and Cost-Recovery Experience in Family Planning Programs," Staff Working Papers, Number 684, Population and Development Series Number 9 (Washington, D.C., 1985).

97. Telephone interview with Dan Lissance, 24 February 1993.

98. Philip D. Harvey, "To Maximize Contraceptive Prevalence Keep Prices Low," *DKT International* 3, August 1993, 3.

99. Interview with Graciela Duce, Mexico City, 3 February 1993.

100. Adrian Lajous, "Mexico Shifts Position, Cuts Its Growth Rate," *Forum for Applied Research and Public Policy*, Summer 1991, 18–20.

101. Interview with Manual Urbina, Mexico City, 2 February 1993.

102. Ibid.

103. Jodi Jacobson, *Women's Reproductive Health: The Silent Emergency*, Worldwatch Paper No. 102 (Washington, D.C.: Worldwatch Institute, June 1991), 46.

104. Nafis Sadik, *Investing in Women: The Focus of the 1990s* (New York: United Nations Population Fund, undated), 8.

105. United Nations Population Fund, *Meeting the Population Challenge* (New York, undated), 21. See also "Adolescent Sexual Activity and Childbearing in Latin American and the Caribbean: Risks and Consequences," (Washington, D.C.: Population Reference Bureau, Inc., 1992); National Research Council, *Social Dynamics of Adolescent Fertility in Sub-Saharan Africa* (Washington, D.C.: National Academy Press, 1993); United Nations, Department of International Economic and Social Affairs, "Adolescent Reproductive Behavior: Evidence from Developing Countries" (New York, 1989), 42.

106. Sadik, *Investing in Women*, 5.

107. Telephone interview with Sidney Ruth Schuler, 6 April 1993.

108. Interview with Alfonso Lopez Juárez, Mexico City, 28 January 1993.

109. Interview with Susan Rich, 16 February 1994.

110. Interview with Peggy Curlin.

111. Cynthia Lloyd, "What Is the Family (And Who Does the Planning)?" *Populi* 8, April 1993, 10.

112. Interview with Alfonso Lopez Juárez.

113. Telephone interview with Suzanne Kindervatter, 13 April 1993.

114. Ibid.

115. Interview with Peggy Curlin.

116. Malcolm Potts, "Network," *Family Health International* 13, August 1992.

117. Ibid.

118. Therese McGinn and Azara Bamba, "Male Knowledge, Use and Attitudes Regarding Family Planning in Burkina Faso," *International Family Planning Perspectives* 15, September 1989, 87.

119. "Men—New Focus on Family Planning Programs," *Population Reports*, Series J., No. 33, November–December 1986, 23. See also Karen

Oppenheim Mason and Anju Malhotra Taj, "Differences Between Women's and Men's Reproductive Goals in Developing Countries," *Population and Development Review* 13, December 1987, 611–638.

120. Interview with Godwin Mzenge, Nairobi, 6 August 1993.

121. Mark A. Uhlig, "In Mexico, Machismo Slows Family Planning," *New York Times*, 7 November 1990, A-16.

122. Interview with Godwin Mzenge.

123. Background interview with U.S. AID official, 17 May 1992.

124. Telephone interview with Judith Bruce, 14 April 1993.

125. David Scott Clark, "Mexican Men Get the Message About Limiting Family Size," *Christian Science Monitor*, 8 July 1992, 11.

126. Background interview with UNFPA official.

127. John A. Ross and Elizabeth Frankenberg, *Findings from Two Decades of Family Planning Research* (New York: The Population Council, 1993), chapter 9.

128. *Expanding Access to Safe Abortion: Key Policy Issues* (Washington, D. C.: Population Action International, September 1993), 1.

129. Ibid., 2.

130. Ibid.

131. Donaldson and Tsui, *The International Family Planning Movement*, 36.

132. Ross and Frankenberg, *Findings from Two Decades of Family Planning Research*, 65.

133. Telephone interview with J. Joseph Speidel, 27 January, 1994.

CHAPTER FIVE

1. Quoted in Cameron Barr, "Female Empowerment Leads to Fewer Births," *Christian Science Monitor*, 8 July 1992, 14.

2. Sadik, *Investing in Women*, 3.

3. Interview with Kim Streafield, Dhaka, 27 March 1993.

4. Ruth Dixon-Mueller, *Population Policy and Women's Rights: Transforming Reproductive Choice* (Westport: Praeger, 1993), x.

5. Betsy Hartmann, *Reproductive Rights and Wrongs: The Global Politics of Population Control* (New York: Harper and Row, 1987), xii.

6. Three helpful introductions to the gender perspective are Dixon-Mueller, Hartmann, and Sadik, all previously cited. See also Jodi Jacobson, *Gender Bias: Roadblock to Sustainable Development*, Worldwatch Paper No. 110 (Washington, D.C.: Worldwatch Institute, 1992); Jacqueline Pitanguy and Rosalind Petchesky, "Women and Population: A Feminist Perspective," *Conscience*, Autumn 1993, 5–7; "Country Rankings of the Status of

Women: Poor, Powerless, and Pregnant," Briefing Paper No. 20 (Washington, D.C.: Population Crisis Committee, June 1988). See also Proceedings of the UN Expert Group Meeting on Population and Women, Gaborone, Botswana, 22–26 June, 1992; Adrienne Germain, "Population Control and Women's Health: Balancing the Scales" (New York: International Women's Health Coalition, June 1989).

7. Telephone interview with Carmen Barroso, 30 September 1993. See also: Carmen Barroso, "Women's Health: Towards an Agenda for the Nineties," Paper prepared for the 18th National Council for International Health, Washington, D.C., 23 June 1991.

8. Hartmann, *Reproductive Rights and Wrongs*, 88.

9. Ibid., 69.

10. World Bank, Population and the World Bank, 33–34.

11. Hartmann, *Reproductive Rights and Wrongs*, 66.

12. See Jacobson, *Gender Bias*.

13. Telephone interview with Jodi Jacobson, 4 October 1993.

14. Ibid.

15. Telephone interview with Cynthia Lloyd, 12 April 1993.

16. Sharon L. Camp, "Global Population Stabilization: A 'No Regrets' Policy," *Conscience* xiv, Autumn 1993, 7.

17. Telephone interview with Nahid Toubia, 30 November 1993.

18. Ibid.

19. Interview with Sajeda Amin, Dhaka, 27 March 1993.

20. Interview with Shamina Islam, Dhaka, 29 March 1993.

21. Ibid.

22. Elizabeth King, *Educating Girls and Women: Investing in Development* (Washington, D.C.: World Bank, 1990), 14.

23. *Closing the Gender Gap: Educating Girls* (Washington, D.C.: Population Action International, 1994).

24. Bonnie K. Jay, et al., "Bangladesh Women's Health Coalition," *Quality/Calidad/Qualite* 3 (New York: Population Council, 1991), 3.

25. Telephone interview with Gabrielle Ross, 14 April 1993.

26. Interview with Nahid Choudhury, Dhaka, 30 March 1993.

27. Interview with Mufaweza Khan, Dhaka, 23 March 1993.

28. Interview with Peggy Curlin, Washington, D.C., 20 March 1993.

30. Interview with Mufaweza Khan.

31. Interview with Muhammad Yunus, Dhaka, 27 March 1993.

32. Susan Greenhalgh, "Women in Informal Enterprise: Empowerment or Exploitation," Research Division Working Paper No. 33 (New York: Population Council, 1991).

33. "Dr. Muhammed Yunus of the Grameen Bank Talks About His

Unique Institution to the *Daily Star*, " [Dhaka] *Daily Star Weekend Magazine*, 11 December 1992, 9.

34. Interview with Muhammed Yunus.

35. Interview with F. H. Abed, Dhaka, 29 March 1993.

36. Molly Moore, "Banking on Bangladesh's Destitute Women," *Washington Post*, 16 August 1992, A-1.

37. Interview with F. H. Abed.

38. Sidney Ruth Schuler, Dominique Meekers, and Syed Hashemi, "The Impact of Women's Participation in Credit Programs on Family Planning in Rural Bangladesh," Working Paper #3 (Dhaka: Development Research Centre, Jahangirnagar University, September 1992), 17.

39. Ibid., 17.

40. Telephone interview with Judith Bruce, 14 April 1993.

41. Interview with F. H. Abed.

42. Interview with Syed Hashemi, Dhaka, 24 March 1993.

43. Interview with Zarine Rahman Khan, Dhaka, 27 March 1993.

44. Interview with Sajeda Amin.

45. Interview with Cynthia Lloyd. See Cynthia B. Lloyd, "Family and Gender Issues for Population Policy," Paper presented at the UN Expert Group Meeting on Population and Women, Gaborone, Botswana, 22–26 June 1992.

46. Greenhalgh, "Women in the Informal Enterprise," cited in ibid., 26.

47. Interview with Cynthia Lloyd.

48. Ibid.

49. W. P. Handwerker, "Women's Power and Fertility Transition: The Cases of Africa and the West Indies," *Population and Environment* 13, Fall 1991, 55–78.

50. For example, see Donaldson, *Nature Against Us*, 152–54, on South Korea.

51. Handwerker, "Women's Power and Fertility Transition."

52. Telephone interview with Virginia Abernethy, 6 April 1993.

53. James Phillips, Ruth Simmons, Michael Koenig, and J. Chakraborty, "Determinants of Reproductive Change in a Traditional Society: Evidence from Matlab, Bangladesh," *Studies in Family Planning* 19, November–December 1988, 313–34.

54. World Bank, *Population and the World Bank*, 40.

55. Interview with Napaporn Havanon, Bangkok, 22 March 1993.

56. *Manorama Yearbook, 1992* (Thiruvananthapuram, Karala: Malayala Manorama, 1992), 601. See P. K. Nayer, "Karala Women in Historical and Contemporary Perspective," in E. Mahadevan, ed., *Women and Population*

Dynamics: Perspectives from Asian Countries (New Delhi: Sage Publications, 1989), 205–220.

57. "Women's Development Key to MCH/FP," *Journal of Population and Health Studies* 7, December 1987, 19–38.

58. Interview with Manual Urbina, Mexico City, 2 February 1993.

59. *Kenya Demographic and Health Survey*, 12.

60. United Nations, Department of International Economic and Social Affairs, Population Division, *Fertility Behavior in the Context of Development: Evidence from the World Fertility Survey* (New York, 1986).

61. Lawrence Summers, "Investing in All the People: Educating Women in Developing Countries," Paper presented at the World Bank Annual Meeting, Washington, D.C., 1992.

62. Boom Mo Chung, et al., *Psychological Perspectives: Family Planning in Korea* (Seoul: Hollym Corporation Publishers for Korean Institute for Research in the Behavioral Sciences, 1972).

63. Stephen Viederman, "Pursuing the Links Between Education and Fertility," *Populi* 5, 1978, 50–53.

64. Nancy Birdsall, "Social Development Is Economic Development," Paper presented to the delegates of the Social Committee, United Nations General Assembly, 19 October 1992.

65. Telephone interview with Elizabeth King, 30 November 1993. See also Zeba Sathar and Karen O. Mason, "Why Female Education Affects Reproductive Behavior in Urban Pakistan," Research Report No. 89–148, Population Studies Center, University of Michigan (Ann Arbor, July 1989).

66. Cited in Sadik, *Investing in Women*, 22.

67. Interview with Judith Bruce.

68. Interview with J. Joseph Speidel.

69. Cited in Barr, "Female Empowerment Leads to Fewer Births."

70. Quoted in ibid.

71. John Ward Anderson and Molly Moore, "Born Oppressed," *Washington Post*, 14 February 1992, A-48.

72. Fred Arnold, "Sex Preference and Fertility: What Is the Link?" *Asia-Pacific Population and Policy*, April 1987.

73. Sadik, *Investing in Women*, 4.

74. Arnold, "Sex Preference and Fertility."

75. Yagya B. Karki, "Sex Preference and the Value of Sons and Daughters in Nepal," *Studies in Family Planning* 19, May–June 1988, 169–78.

76. Karen Oppenheim Mason, "The Impact of Women's Social Position on Fertility in Developing Countries," in J. M. Stycos, ed., *Demography as an Interdiscipline* (New Brunswick: Transaction Publishers, 1989), 100–107.

77. United Nations, United Nations International Children's Emer-

gency Fund, *The State of the World's Children 1991* (New York: Oxford University Press, 1992), 5.

78. Interview with John Baker.

79. Susan Cochrane and K. C. Zachariah, *Infant Mortality as a Determinant of Fertility: The Policy Implications*, Staff Working Papers, No. 556 (Washington, D.C.: The World Bank), 1985.

80. United Nations, Secretariat, "Interrelationships Between Child Survival and Fertility," *Population Bulletin of the United Nations*, No. 25 (New York, 1988), 27–50.

81. J. N. Srivastava, "Impact of Child Mortality on Family Size Desires and Family Planning Practices Among White Collar Workers," *Journal of Family Welfare* 37, 1991, 19.

82. Cochrane and Zachariah, *Infant Mortality as a Determinant of Fertility*.

83. "Healthier Mothers and Children Through Family Planning," *Population Reports*, Series J, No. 27, May–June 1984, J663–J667. The evidence is partially disputed by John Bongaarts, "Does Family Planning Reduce Infant Mortality?" *Population and Development Review* 14, March 1988, 188ff.

84. Cochrane and Zachariah, *Infant Mortality as a Determinant of Fertility*.

85. Interview with Peter Donaldson. On the same point, see Thomas Merrick, "Social Development, Program Effort and Fertility Transitions," Paper presented at the Experts Group Meeting on Family Planning, Health and Family Well-Being, Bangalore, 26–30 October 1992. Writes Merrick: "A lot has been learned . . . with most of the evidence pointing to synergies rather than competition between the 'supply' and 'demand' factors. . . . Fertility declines most rapidly in countries with high scores on both sets of indicators."

86. Interview with Judith Bruce.

87. Ibid.

88. "The Reproductive Revolution: New Survey Findings," *Population Reports*, Series M, Number 11, December 1992, 2.

89. Interview with Malcolm Potts.

90. Robert Lapham and W. Parker Mauldin, "The Effects of Family Planning on Fertility: Research Findings," in Robert Lapham and G. B. Simmons, eds., *Organizing for Effective Family Planning Programs* (Washington D.C.: National Academy Press, 1987), 647–680.

91. Steven Sinding, "Getting to Replacement."

92. Interview with Abbas Bhuiya, Dhaka, 27 March 1993.

CHAPTER SIX

1. In 1993, a group of one hundred international scholars, government officials, and representatives of private voluntary organizations cited "world population growth" second after "environmental issues" as the issue that would dominate the twenty-first century. Among possible measures to reduce population growth, a "change [in] the Vatican's position" was ranked as one of the most important. The surveys were part of the Millennium Project co-sponsored by the Futures Group and the United Nations University.

2. Interview with Paul Burgess, Washington, D.C., 14 May 1992.

3. For Latin America as a whole, the contraceptive prevalence rate (CPR) is 58 percent compared to 46 percent for Asia, not including China, and 21 percent for Africa.

4. "IPPF/Western Hemisphere Region Public Response Guide" (New York: International Planned Parenthood Federation), 2.

5. "Fortalecimiento del Mexico Secular," *Excelsior*, June 1991, 9.

6. Mary Beth Weinberger, "Changes in the Mix of Contraceptive Methods During Fertility Decline: Latin America and the Caribbean," Paper presented at the Seminar on Fertility Transition in Latin America, Buenos Aires, 3–6 April 1990, 3, 12–13.

7. Ibid., 17.

8. "Mexico National Abortion Opinion Survey," Report presented to the Population Crisis Committee, undated, SPF #138xx.

9. Cited in Jodi L. Jacobson, *The Global Politics of Abortion*, Worldwatch Paper No. 97 (Washington, D.C.: Worldwide Institute, July 1990), 29.

10. Stanley K. Henshaw and Jane Silverman, "The Characteristics and Prior Contraceptive Use of U.S. Abortion Patients," *Family Planning Perspectives* 20, July–August 1988, 158–68.

11. "The Reproductive Revolution," 22.

12. Peter Gumbel, "Italy's Birthrate, the World's Lowest, Is a Vexing Anomaly," *Wall Street Journal*, 18 June 1993, A-1. See also Susan Kalish, "Spotlight: Italy," *Population Today* 21, April 1993, 11.

13. Shanti Conli and Sharon L. Camp, *India's Family Planning Challenge: From Rhetoric to Reality*, Country Studies Series No. 2 (Washington, D.C.: Population Action International, 1992), 14.

14. Interview with James Ross, Dhaka, 30 March 1993. See also R. B. N. Sinha, "Attitudes of Hindus and Muslims towards Family Planning," *Journal of Family Welfare*, June 1991, 47ff.

15. Quoted in Julia Michaels, "Brazilians Face Population Dilemma," *Christian Science Monitor*, 8 July 1992, 13.

16. Interview with Bruce Harris, Mexico City, 29 January 1993.

17. Joseph Chamie, *Religion and Fertility: Arab Christian-Muslim Differentials* (Cambridge and New York: Cambridge University Press, 1981).

18. Interview with Joseph Chamie, New York, 27 January 1993.

19. *Population Picks and Pans 1992* (Washington, D.C., Population Action International, 1992), 15.

20. Susan Pick de Weiss, Lucille C. Atkin, James N. Gribble, and Patricia Andrade-Palos, "Sex, Contraception, and Pregnancy Among Adolescents in Mexico City," *Studies in Family Planning* 22, March–April 1991, 74–82.

21. "IPPF/WHR Public Response Guide."

22. Interview with Susan Pick de Weiss, Mexico City, 1 February 1993.

23. Interview with Frances Kissling, Washington, D.C., 11 January 1993.

24. Calvin Goldscheider and William D. Mosher, "Religious Affiliation and Contraceptive Usage: Changing American Patterns, 1955–82," *Studies in Family Planning* 19, January–February 1988, 48ff. Also Calvin Goldscheider and William D. Mosher, "Patterns of Contraceptive Use in the United States: The Importance of Religious Factors," *Studies in Family Planning* 22, March–April 1991, 102ff.

25. Telephone interview with Sylvia Marcos, 29 January 1993.

26. Interview with Sonia Ochoa Delgado, Huixquilucan, Mexico, 2 February 1993.

27. Interview with Susan Pick de Weiss.

28. Untitled manual, p. 10.

29. Sidney Ruch Schuler and Syed M. Hashemi, "Islamic Ideology, Contraception and the Emergence of Women in Bangladesh," Working Paper #4 (Dhaka: Development Research Centre, Jahangirnagar University), 6–7.

30. N. J. Austrian, "Modernization, Legal Reforms and the Place of Women in Muslim Developing Countries," Doctoral dissertation, Southern Illinois University at Carbondale, 1987.

31. R. H. Chaudhury, "Hindu-Muslim Differential Fertility: How Much Religious and How Much Socio?" *Social Action* 34, July–September 1984, 251–73.

32. Interview with Paul Burgess.

33. Discussion of the evolution of the Roman Catholic view of contraception and family planning is drawn largely from Francis X. Murphy, "Catholic Perspectives on Population Issues II," *Population Bulletin* 35 (Washington, D.C.: Population Reference Bureau, Inc., February, 1981); *The Evolution of an Earthly Code: Contraception in Catholic Doctrine* (Washing-

ton, D.C.: Catholics for a Free Choice, undated); and John T. Noonan, Jr., *Contraception: A History of its Treatment by the Catholic Theologians and Canonists* (Cambridge, Mass: Belnap Press/Harvard University Press, 1986).

34. *Evolution of an Earthly Code*, 1.

35. Murphy, *Catholic Perspectives*, 9.

36. Ibid.

37. *Evolution of an Earthly Code*, 4.

38. Murphy, *Catholic Perspectives*, 11.

39. Ibid., 12.

40. *Evolution of an Earthly Code*, 10.

41. Thomas A. Shannon, "Ethical Dilemmas in Population Policy," *Conscience* VII, March–April 1986, 3.

42. Ibid.

43. Interview with Father Francis Murphy, Annapolis, Maryland, 19 January 1993.

44. *Evolution of an Earthly Code*, 16.

45. Xavier Rynne, "Caves of the Vatican," *New York Review of Books*, 12 August 1993, 49.

46. Murphy, *Catholic Perspectives*, 24.

47. Kenneth L. Woodward, et al., "New Rules for an Old Faith," *Newsweek*, 30 November 1992, 71.

48. "Jean-Marie Guenois, "The Encyclical Is Ready!" *The Catholic World Report*, July 1993, 34–35.

49. Murphy, *Catholic Perspectives*, 8.

50. Background interview, Mexico City, 29 January 1993.

51. Joseph Gallagher, "Rome's Birth-Control Conceptions Flunk Real World Test," *National Catholic Reporter* 28, 14 September 1992.

52. For elaborate explanations of the dissenting view, see Charles E. Curran, *Faithful Dissent* (Kansas City: Sheed and Ward, 1986), and Philip S. Kaufman, *Why You Can Disagree and Remain a Faithful Catholic* (Bloomington, Ind.: Meyer-Stone Books, 1989).

53. Interview with Sheik Mohammad Sayyid Tantawi, Cairo, 10 May 1993.

54. Habib Bourghiba, address delivered 25 December 1962, quoted in *Population and Development in Tunisia* (Tunis: Ministry of the Family and Improvement of the Status of Women, Republic of Tunisia, 1984).

55. Caryle Murphy, "Iran Promoting Birth Control in Policy Switch," 8 May 1992, A-7.

56. Telephone interview with Aziza Hussein, 10 May 1992.

57. Interview with Sheikh Mohammad Sayyid Tantawi.

58. From the Prophet's sayings, quoted in Abdel Rahim Omran, *Family*

Planning in the Legacy of Islam (New York and London: Routledge, 1992), 31.

59. Egyptian Ministry of Waqfs and Ministry of Information, Education and Communication Center, *Islam's Attitude Towards Family Planning* (Cairo, 1992), 19.

60. Omran, *Family Planning in the Legacy of Islam*, 117.

61. Ibid., 253.

62. Interview with Sheikh Mohammad Sayyid Tantawi.

63. Interview with Abdel Omran, Washington, D.C., 14 May 1992.

64. Interview with Sheikh Mohammad Sayyid Tantawi.

65. "Italian Woman's Death in Birth Revives Debate on Abortion Laws," *Washington Times*, 30 January 1993.

66. Ibid.

67. Interview with Thomas Merrick, Washington, D.C., 22 January 1993.

68. Cited in interview with Ricardo Blancarte, 28 January 1993.

69. Among frequent references to the cultures of life and death is Pope John Paul II, Farewell Remarks, Stapleton Airport, Denver, 15 August 1993, cited in *Origins* 23, 26 August 1993, 200.

70. David Clark Scott, "Mexico Finalizes Restoration of Ties to Catholic Church," *Christian Science Monitor*, 28 September 1992, 7; Tim Golden, "Mexico Ending Church Restraints After 70 Years of Official Hostility," *New York Times*, 28 December 1991, A-1.

71. Background interview, 28 January 1993.

72. Elaine Burns, "Mexico's Abortion Debate Flares," *The Guardian*, 6 February 1991.

73. Katherine Ellison, "Mexico's Growing Population Attracts Abortion Fight," *Miami Herald*, 31 August 1992.

74. Interview with Alfonso Lopez Juárez, Mexico City, 28 January 1993.

75. Background interview, 2 February 1993.

76. Interview with Manual Urbina.

77. Interview with Edgar Gonzales, Mexico City, 2 February 1993.

78. Ibid.

79. *El Universal* (Mexico City), 5 November 1991, 14.

80. Ellison, "Mexico's Growing Population Attracts Abortion Fight."

81. Interview with Alfonso Lopez Juárez.

82. James Brooke, "Peru's Church Battles a Contraception Plan," *New York Times*, 16 November 1990, A-9.

83. Population Action International, "*Humanae Vitae* at 25 Years: The Catholic Church and International Family Planning Efforts," 2.

84. On the Polish situation, see Reed Boland, "Eastern Europe: Shifting Policies," *Populi* 20, March 1993, 7.

85. *Population Picks and Pans* 1992, 31.

86. Lualhati Bost, "Contraceptive Use in the Philippines: Political Forces Contributing to the Levels of Use and Effectiveness of Methods," Paper presented at the Conference on Demographic Transition in Southeast Asia, Hanoi, 13–14 April 1992, 12, 15.

87. Terence H. Hull, "Government and Society in Southeast Asian Family Planning Programs: The Cases of Indonesia, Vietnam and the Philippines," Paper presented at the 1991 Annual Meeting of the Population Association of America, Washington, D.C., 21–23 March 1991, 25.

88. Bost, "Contraceptive Use in the Philippines," 13.

89. William Branigin, "Manila, Catholic Church Split on Family Planning," *Washington Post*, 18 August 1993, A-28.

90. The memorandum cited is U.S. National Security Council, "Implications of Worldwide Population Growth for U.S. Security and Overseas Interests," NSSM 200, December 10, 1974.

91. Bost, "Contraceptive Use in the Philippines," 10. See also Jim Kennett, "Church and State Go Head-to-Head Over Philippine Family Planning," *Family Planning World*, March–April 1993.

92. Background interview with UNFPA official, 26 January 1993.

93. Mark Hertzgaard, "Hands That Rock the Cradle," *The Independent on Sunday*, 25 April 1993, 16.

94. Ibid., 15–16.

95. Interview with Frances Kissling.

96. Interview with Graciela Duce.

97. Interview with Francis Murphy.

CHAPTER SEVEN

1. Dwight D. Eisenhower, *Waging Peace, 1956–1961* (Garden City: Doubleday, 1965), 504.

2. The early history of the birth control and family planning movements is drawn from the following sources: Hartmann, *Reproductive Rights and Wrongs*, chapters 5 and 6; Francis X. Murphy, *Catholic Perspectives; Encyclopedia Britannica*, 15th edition (Chicago, 1975). Of particular value throughout the chapter has been Phyllis Tilson Piotrow, *World Population Crisis: The United States Response* (New York: Praeger, 1973) and Peter Donaldson, *Nature Against Us*.

3. Murphy, *Catholic Perspectives*, 11.

4. Hartmann, *Reproductive Rights and Wrongs*, 93.

5. John Ensor Harr and Peter J. Johnson, *The Rockefeller Conscience: An American Family in Public and in Private* (New York: Charles Scribner's Sons, 1991), 432.

6. Piotrow, *World Population Crisis*, 37–38.

7. William H. Draper, Jr., interview by Jerry N. Ness, 11 January 1972, Harry S. Truman Library, Independence, Mo., May 1974, 59–60.

8. Ibid., 60.

9. Ibid., 62.

10. Interview with Julia Henderson, Sarasota, Fl., 11 December 1993. All subsequent quotes from Henderson are drawn from this interview.

11. Piotrow, *World Population Crisis*.

12. Ibid., 125.

13. Hobart Rowen, "Clinton Must Focus on Overpopulation," *Washington Post*, 14 March 1993, A-1.

14. United Nations, Department of Economic and Social Affairs, Population Division, *The Population Debate: Dimensions and Perspectives*, vol. 1, *Papers of the World Population Conference*, Bucharest, 1974 (New York, 1985).

15. See Jason L. Finkle and Barbara B. Crane, "The Politics of Bucharest: Population, Development, and the New International Economic Order," *Population and Development Review* 1, September 1975, 87–114; Ian Pool, "From Bucharest to Mexico: The Politics of International Population Conferences," *New Zealand Population Review*, April 1985, 52–63; Paul Demeny, "Population on the World Agenda, 1984: A View from Bucharest," speech reprinted in *Population and Development Review* 10, 1984, 353–359.

16. Jason L. Finkle and Barbara B. Crane, "Ideology and Politics at Mexico City: The United States at the 1984 International Conference on Population," *Population and Development Review* 11, March 1985, 21.

17. National Security Council, "Implications of Worldwide Population Growth," 95.

18. Ibid., 6.

19. Ibid., 43.

20. Interview with Nancy Wallace, Washington, D.C., 13 May 1992.

21. National Academy of Sciences, *Rapid Population Growth: Consequences and Policy Implications*, 2 vols. (Baltimore, Md.: Johns Hopkins University Press, 1971).

22. *Population Growth and Economic Development: Policy Questions* (Washington, D.C.: National Academy Press, 1986), 90–91.

23. A thorough discussion of the Reagan years is found in Sharon L. Camp and Craig R. Lasher, *International Family Planning Policy—A Chron-*

icle of the Reagan Years, Unpublished manuscript (Washington: Population Crisis Committee, February 1989); and Michael S. Teitelbaum, "The Population Threat."

24. Interview with J. Joseph Speidel.

25. Camp and Lasher, *International Family Planning Policy,* 38.

26. Ibid., 40–41.

27. *Policy Statement of the United States of America at the International Conference on Population* (Second Session), Mexico, D. F., 6–13 August 1984. See Finkle and Crane, "Ideology and Politics at Mexico City"; and Pool, "From Bucharest to Mexico."

28. Camp and Lasher, *International Family Planning Policy,* 27.

29. See Michael Weisskopf, "Abortion Policy Tears at Fabric of China's Society," *Washington Post,* 7 January 1985, A-1, A-20; "China's Birth Control Policy Drives Some to Kill Baby Girls," *Washington Post,* 8 January 1985, A-1, A-10; "Shanghai's Curse: Too Many Fight for Too Little," *Washington Post,* 6 January 1985, A-1, A-30.

30. Finkle and Crane, "Ideology and Politics at Mexico City," 1.

31. Pool, "From Bucharest to Mexico," 57.

32. Finkle and Crane, "Ideology and Politics at Mexico City," 21.

33. Camp and Lasher, *International Family Planning Policy,* 101.

34. For the current contributions of the twenty major international donors, see Conli and Speidel, *Global Population Assistance.* Among developed nations, Norway alone has met and surpassed internationally agreed upon targets, both for family planning aid and overall development assistance, according to the report.

35. National Security Council, "Implications of Worldwide Population Growth," 10.

36. Council on Environmental Quality, *The Global 2000 Report to the President* (Washington, D.C.: Government Printing Office, 1980).

37. Camp and Lasher, *International Family Planning Policy,* 74.

38. Interview with Ishrat Husain, Washington, D.C., 11 March 1993.

39. Camp and Lasher, *International Family Planning Policy* 6.

40. See, for example, Stanley Henshaw, "Induced Abortion: A World Review," *Family Planning Perspectives* 22, March–April 1990, 76–89.

41. Telephone interview with Douglas Costle, 25 January 1993.

42. For the measures undertaken by the Clinton administration, see Steven A. Holmes, "Clinton Seeks to Restore Aid for Family Planning Abroad," *New York Times,* 1 April 1993, A-1; John M. Goshko, "Planned Parenthood Gets AID Grant," *Washington Post,* 23 November 1993, A-12; Steven Greenhouse, "U.S. to Spend More on Birth Control," *New York Times,* 23 January 1994, 9. See also Statement by Timothy Wirth, U.S.

Representative to the Second Preparatory Committee for the International Conference on Population and Development at the Preparatory Meeting, 11 May 1993; Statement by Timothy Wirth, United States Representative to the Second Session Preparatory Committee for the International Conference on Population and Development, Closing Statement, 21 May 1993.

43. International Forum on Population in the Twenty-First Century, "Amsterdam Declaration: A Better Life for Future Generations," 6–9 November 1989.

44. Telephone interview with Timothy Wirth, 27 January 1994.

45. Telephone interview with Phyllis Piotrow, 29 January 1994.

46. Ibid.

EPILOGUE

1. Hertzgaard, "Hands That Rock the Cradle," 16.

2. Telephone interview with Malcolm Potts, 7 December 1993.

3. Malcolm Potts and Allan Rosenfield, "The Fifth Freedom Revisited II: The Way Forward," *The Lancet* 336, 24 November 1990, 1295.

Suggestions for Further Reading

Adel, Wilhelm. *Agricultural Fluctuations in Europe from the 13th to 20th Centuries*, trans. Olive Ordish. New York: St. Martin's Press, 1978.

Avery, Dennis. *Global Food Progress, 1991*. Indianapolis: Hudson Institute, 1991.

Bennet, Anthony, Carl Frisen, Peerasit Kamnuansilpa, and John McWilliam. *How Thailand's Family Planning Program Reached Replacement Level Fertility: Lessons Learned*. Population Technical Assistance Occasional Paper No. 4. Arlington, Va.: DUAL and Associates, Inc., 9 November 1990.

Bilsborrow, Richard E., and Paul W. Stupp. *The Effects of Population Growth on Agriculture in Guatemala*. Carolina Population Center Papers, Number 88–24. Chapel Hill, September 1988.

Birdsall, Nancy, ed. *The Effects of Family Planning Programs on Fertility in the Developing World*. World Bank Staff Working Paper 677. Washington, D.C., 1985.

Brown, Lester, et. al. *State of the World, 1993: A Worldwatch Institute Report on Progress Toward a Sustainable Society*. New York: W. W. Norton, 1993.

Brown, Lester R., Christopher Flavin, and Hal Kane. *Vital Signs 1992: The Trends That Are Shaping Our Future*. New York: W. W. Norton, 1992.

Brown, Lester, and Jodi Jacobson. *The Future of Urbanization: Facing the

Ecological and Economic Constraints. Worldwatch Paper No. 77. Washington, D.C.: Worldwatch Institute, May 1987.

Bulatao, Rodolfo, A, and Ann Elwan. *Fertility and Mortality Transition: Patterns, Projections, and Interdependence.* World Bank Staff Working Paper 681. Washington, D.C., 1992.

Caldwell, John C. *Theory of Fertility Decline.* New York: Academic Press, 1982.

Chamie, Joseph. *Religion and Fertility: Arab Christian-Muslim Differentials.* Cambridge and New York: Cambridge University Press, 1981.

Cleland, John, and J. Hobcraft, eds. *Reproductive Change in Developing Countries: Insights from the World Fertility Survey.* New York and Oxford: Oxford University Press, 1985.

Cleland, John, James Phillips, Sajeda Amin, and G. M. Kemal. *Determinants of Reproductive Change in Bangladesh.* Washington, D.C.: The World Bank, 1994.

Closing the Gender Gap: Educating Girls. Washington, D.C.: Population Action International, 1994.

Conli, Shanti R., and Sharon L. Camp. *China's Family Planning Program: Challenging the Myths.* Country Series #1. Washington, D.C.: Population Action International, 1992.

———. *India's Family Planning Challenge: From Rhetoric to Action.* Washington, D.C.: Population Action International, 1992.

Conli, Shanti R., and J. Joseph Speidel. *Global Population Assistance: A Report Card of the Major Donors.* Washington, D.C.: Population Action International, 1993.

Cruz, Maria Conception, Carrie A. Meyer, Robert Repetto, and Richard Woodward. *Population Growth, Poverty, and Environmental Stress: Frontier Migration in the Philippines and Costa Rica.* Washington D.C.: World Resources Institute, 1992.

Curran, Charles E. *Faithful Dissent.* Kansas City: Sheed and Ward, 1986.

Davis, Kingsley, and Mikhail Bernstam, eds. *Resources, Environment, and Population: Present Knowledge, Future Options.* New York and Oxford: Oxford University Press, 1991.

Demeny, Paul. *Demography and the Limits to Growth.* New York: Population Council, 1989.

Didsbury, Howard F., Jr. *The Years Ahead: Perils, Problems, and Promises.* Bethesda, Md.: World Future Society, 1993.

Dixon-Mueller, Ruth. *Population Policy and Women's Rights: Transforming Reproductive Choice.* Westport, Conn.: Praeger, 1993.

Donaldson, Peter J. *Nature Against Us: The United States and the World Population Crisis, 1965–1980.* Chapel Hill: University of North Carolina Press, 1990.

Donaldson, Peter J., and Amy Ong Tsui. *The International Family Planning Movement.* Washington, D.C.: Population Reference Bureau, Inc., November 1990.

Ehrlich, Paul. *The Population Bomb.* New York: Ballantine Books, 1968.

Ehrlich, Paul R., and Anne H. Ehrlich. *The Population Explosion.* New York: Simon and Schuster, 1990.

Engelman, Robert, and Pamela LeRoy. *Sustaining Water: Population and the Future of Renewable Water Supplies.* Washington, D.C.: Population Action International, 1993.

The Evolution of an Earthly Code: Contraception in Catholic Doctrine. Washington, D.C.: Catholics for a Free Choice, undated.

Fisher, Julie. *The Road from Rio: Sustainable Development and the Nongovernmental Movement in the Third World.* Westport, Conn.: Praeger, 1993.

Gardner, Richard. *Negotiating Survival: Four Priorities After Rio.* New York: Council on Foreign Relations Press, 1992.

Gilbert, Alan, and Josef Gugler. *Cities, Poverty and Development: Urbanization in the Third World.* Oxford: Oxford University Press, 1992.

Greenhalgh, Susan. *Women in Informal Enterprise: Empowerment or Exploitation.* Research Division Working Paper No. 33. New York: Population Council, 1991.

Gupte, Pranay. *The Crowded Earth: People and the Politics of Population.* New York: W. W. Norton and Company, 1984.

Hansen, Carol Rae, ed. *The New World Order: Rethinking America's Global Role.* Flagstaff: Arizona Honors Academy Press, 1992.

Hardin, Garrett. *Living within Limits: Ecology, Economics, and the Population Taboo.* New York: Oxford University Press, 1993.

Harrison, Paul. *The Greening of Africa: Breaking Through in the Battle for Land and Food.* London: Paladin Grafton Books, 1987.

———. *The Third Revolution: Environment, Population and a Sustainable World.* London and New York: I. B. Tauris/Penguin Books., Ltd, 1992.

Hartmann, Betsy. *Reproductive Rights and Wrongs: The Global Politics of Population Control.* New York: Harper and Row, 1987.

Hendry, Peter. *Food and Population: Beyond Five Billion*. Washington, D.C.: Population Reference Bureau, Inc., August 1991.

Hossain, Mahabub. *Nature and Impact of the Green Revolution in Bangladesh*. Research Report 67. Washington, D.C.: International Food Policy Research Institute, July 1988.

Hunger Project. *Ending Hunger: An Idea Whose Time Has Come*. New York: Praeger, 1985.

Hutchinson, Edward P. *The Population Debate: The Development of Conflicting Theories up to 1900*. Boston: Houghton Mifflin Co., 1967.

Jacobson, Jodi L. *Gender Bias: Roadblock to Sustainable Development*. Worldwatch Paper No. 110. Washington, D.C.: Worldwatch Institute, 1992.

————. *The Global Politics of Abortion*. Worldwatch Paper No. 97. Washington, D.C.: Worldwatch Institute, July 1990.

Kennedy, Paul. *Preparing for the Twenty-First Century*. New York: Random House, 1993.

Kasarda, John D., and Allan M. Powell, eds. *Third World Cities: Problems, Policies, and Prospects*. Newbury Park, Calif. Sage Publications, 1993.

Kaufman, Philip S. *Why You Can Disagree and Remain a Faithful Catholic*. Bloomington, Ind.: Meyer-Stone Books, 1989.

King, Elizabeth. *Educating Girls and Women: Investing in Development*. Washington, D.C.: World Bank, 1990.

Knodel, John, Aphichat Chamratrithirong, and Nibhon Debavalya. *Thailand's Reproductive Revolution*. Madison: University of Wisconsin Press, 1987.

Lapham, Robert J., and George B. Simmons. *Organizing for Effective Family Planning Programs*. Washington, D.C.: National Academy Press, 1987.

Lowe, Marcia. *Shaping Cities: The Environmental and Human Dimension*. Worldwatch Paper No. 105. Washington, D.C.: Worldwatch Institute, October 1991.

Meadows, Donella H., Dennis L. Meadows, Jorgen Randers, and William Behrens III. *The Limits to Growth: A Report for the Club of Rome Project on the Predicament of Mankind*. New York: New American Library, 1972.

Meadows, Donella H., Dennis L. Meadows, and Jergen Randers. *Be-*

yond the Limits: Confronting Global Collapse, Envisioning a Sustainable Future. Post Mills, Vt.: Chelsea Green, 1992.

Murphy, Francis X. *Catholic Perspectives on Population Issues II*. Washington, D.C.: Population Reference Bureau, Inc., February 1981.

Myers, Norman, and Julian Simon. *Scarcity or Abundance?: A Debate on the Environment*. New York: W. W. Norton, 1994.

National Research Council. *Contraception and Reproduction: Health Consequences for Women and Children in the Developing World*. Washington, D.C.: National Academy Press, 1989.

———. *Population Growth and Economic Development: Policy Questions*. Washington, D.C.: National Academy Press, 1986.

———. *Rapid Population Growth: Consequences and Policy Implications*. 2 vols. Baltimore: Johns Hopkins University Press, 1971.

Ness, Gayl D., William D. Drake, and Steven Brechin. *Population-Environment Dynamics: Ideas and Observations*. Ann Arbor: University of Michigan Press, 1993.

Noonan, John T. *Contraception: A History of Its Treatment by the Catholic Theologians and Canonists*. Cambridge, Mass.: Belknap Press/Harvard University Press, 1986.

Omran, Abdel Rahim. *Family Planning in the Legacy of Islam*. New York and London: Routledge, 1992.

Osterfeld, David. *Prosperity Versus Planning: How Government Stifles Economic Growth*. New York: Oxford University Press, 1992.

Petersen, William, ed. *Readings in Population*. New York: Macmillan, 1972.

Piotrow, Phyllis. *World Population Crisis: The United States Response*. New York: Praeger, 1977.

Ponting, Clive. *A Green History of the World: The Environment and the Collapse of Great Civilizations*. New York: Penguin Books, 1991.

Population Picks and Pans: The Population Crisis Committee's 1991 Selection of the Ten Countries Worldwide Making the Most and Least Progress in Family Planning. Washington, D.C.: Population Crisis Committee, 1991.

Population Picks and Pans 1992. Washington, D.C.: Population Action International, 1992.

Ramphal Shridath. *Our Country, the Planet: Forging a Partnership for Survival*. Washington, D.C.: Island Press, 1992.

Repetto, Robert. *Population, Resources, Environment: An Uncertain Fu-*

ture. Washington, D.C.: Population Reference Bureau, Inc., July 1987.

Ross, John A., and Elizabeth Frankenberg. *Findings from Two Decades of Family Planning Research*. New York: The Population Council, 1993.

Saqqaf, Abdulaziz. *The Middle East City: Ancient Traditions Confront a Modern World*. New York: Paragon House Publishers, 1987.

Schiffer, Robert. *The Exploding City: An Unforgettable Journey Through Nine Great Cities*. New York: St. Martin's Press, 1990.

Segal, Sheldon J., and Amy Ong Tsui. *Demographic and Programmatic Consequences of Contraceptive Innovations*. New York: Plenum Press, 1989.

Simon, Julian. *Population Matters: People, Resources, Environment, and Immigration*. New Brunswick, Conn.: Transaction Publishers, 1990.

———. *The Ultimate Resource*. Princeton, N. J.: Princeton University Press, 1981.

Simon, Julian, and Herman Kahn. *The Resourceful Earth*. New York: Basil Blackwell, 1984.

Stycos, J. M., ed. *Demography as an Interdiscipline*. New Brunswick, Conn.: Transaction Publishers, 1989.

United Nations Population Fund. *Investing in Women: The Focus of the 90s*. New York, undated.

———. *Meeting the Population Challenge*. New York, undated.

———. *Population, Resources and the Environment: The Critical Challenges*. New York, 1991.

———. *The State of the World Population* 1993. New York, 1993.

United Nations, Food and Agriculture Organization. *Agriculture Toward 2000*. Revised version. Rome, 1987.

van Bath, B. H. Slicher. *The Agrarian History of Western Europe A.D. 500–1850*, trans. Olive Ordish. New York: St. Martin's Press, 1963.

Weeks, John Robert. *Population: An Introduction to Concepts and Issues*. 5th ed. Belmont, Calif.: Wadsworth Publishing Co., 1992.

Wilson, Yates. *Family Planning on a Crowded Planet*. Westport, Conn.: Greenwood, 1983.

World Bank. *Effective Family Planning Programs*. Washington, D.C., 1993.

————. *Population and the World Bank: Implications from Eight Case Studies.* Washington, D.C., 1992.

————. *Population Growth and Policies in Sub-Saharan Africa.* Washington, D.C., 1986.

————. *Poverty and Hunger: Issues and Options for Food Security in Developing Countries.* Washington, D.C., 1986.

————. *Sub-Saharan Africa: From Crisis to Sustainable Growth.* Washington, D.C., 1989.

World Commission on the Environment and Development. *Our Common Future.* Oxford and New York: Oxford University Press, 1987.

Index

Abed, F. H., 205, 206, 211
Abernethy, Virginia, 211–12
Abortion, 142, 180–82, 186,
  193–94, 196, 200–1, 284
  Catholics and, 231–32, 239, 245,
    252, 254
  New Right, and U.S. population
    policy, 282–84, 288, 289
  religious restrictions limiting
    access to, 237
  RU-486, 182, 296
Adolescents, 238
  family planning targeted at,
    173–77
Africa, 127, 173
  abortion in, 193–94
  agriculture and food supply in,
    64–65, 67–68, 70, 76–77, 83,
    88–96
  demographic transition in, 10,
    14
  family planning in, 287
  infant mortality in, 219
  migration from, 18
  population projections for, 8

sub-Saharan, see Sub-Saharan
  Africa
urbanization in, 31
see also specific geographic areas
Agency for International
  Development (U.S. AID), 84,
    198–99, 200, 275–77, 282, 284,
    286, 289
Agriculture, 33–34, 42–43, 59–60,
  61–96
  biotechnology, 81–88
  compost, 63
  crop rotation, 68–69
  cultivating new land, 78–81
  environmental damage, effect of,
    76
  erosion, 78, 80
  family planning, link with, 76–77
  fertilizer, 68, 69, 72, 74, 75
  foreign aid, 75, 84
  green revolution, 69–73, 74, 78,
    92, 106, 108, 110, 113, 280
  imports, 75, 80
  industrialization and, 69
  small farmers, 62–63, 90–92

343

Agriculture (*cont.*)
  soil degradation, 77–78
  technology and, 66–74, 78,
    81–88, 92–94, 104, 108, 110,
    113, 280
  terracing, 62
  urban bias, 33, 89
  water for, 43, 56, 62–63, 72,
    73–74, 77, 79, 81
  see also specific geographic areas
AIDS, 11–12, 157, 177, 245
Air pollution, 38, 127, 128–29,
  172
Algeria, 1–2, 18, 240
American Birth Control League
  (ABCL), 266, 267
Amin, Sajeda, 194, 209
Anderson, Clifton, 88
Antigua, 211
Aquino, Corey, 258–59
Asia, 273
  agriculture in, 69, 70
  infant mortality in, 219
Auda, Mohammed, 37, 43
Augustine, St., 242
Avery, Dennis, 67, 73, 78–79, 87

Baker, John, 146–47, 167, 219
Bangladesh:
  abortion in, 200–1
  family planning in, 11, 152, 169,
    171–72, 191, 212, 239–40, 277
  family size in, 212–13
  fertility in, 142, 212
  green revolution in, 71–72
  infant and child mortality in, 199,
    202, 216
  migration from, 20
  population projections for, 197
  women's empowerment as
    population approach in,
    184–87, 194–209

women's status in, 194–96,
    208–9, 218
Bangladesh Rural Advancement
  Committee (BRAC), 185, 187,
    204, 205, 207, 208
Bangladesh Women's Health
  Coalition (BWHC), 199, 200,
    201
Barbados, 211
Barroso, Carmen, 190
Basheer, Tahseen, 44–45, 46–47,
    48–49, 50
Bentham, Jeremy, 264
Bhuiya, Abbas, 223
Bilsborrow, Richard, 132
Biodiversity, 86, 87
Biotechnology, 81–88
Birth control, see Contraceptives;
    Family planning programs
Birth control pills, 139, 142, 154,
    155, 156, 231, 276
Birth Control Review, 266
BKK Credit Program, 204
Bolivia, 181, 235
Bongaarts, John, 143–44, 151
Borlaug, Norman, 78
Botswana, 140
Bourghiba, Habib, 247
Boyer, Herbert W., 81
Brazil, 55, 85, 127, 257
  deforestation in, 130, 133
  family planning in, 158, 231,
    257
Brent, R. Stephen, 90, 94
Brinkman, Robert, 95
Brown, Lester, 70, 71, 74, 83, 92
Bruce, Judith, 179, 207, 216, 221
Buckley, James, 283
Burgess, Paul, 241
Burkina Faso, 64–65
Bush administration, 285, 286, 288,
    290

Cairo, Egypt, 25–28, 31, 34–60
  "City of the Dead," 2, 51–53, 246
  food supply in, 42–43
  housing in, 27, 39–42, 43
  physical decentralization efforts,
    54–55
  pollution in, 38–39
  population density, 26, 37
  population growth, 26, 37, 60
  population projections, 37
  sanitation in, 34, 44
  sewer systems in, 34, 38–39, 50
  squatter communities in, 2, 31,
    51–53, 246
  traffic in, 38, 50, 53
Cairo Family Planning Association,
  248
Calcutta, India, 30–31, 32
Cameroon, 90
Camp, Sharon, 187–88, 287, 288
Canada, 181
Carlyle, Thomas, 103
Carter administration, 282, 287
Catholicism and family planning,
  225–32, 234, 235–38, 241–46,
  252–61, 282, 291
  abortion, 231–32, 239, 245, 252,
    254
  history of, 241–44
  political power of the Church,
    252–61, 268, 273, 275, 278
  practices of Catholics, 228–32,
    245, 246, 260–61
  Second Vatican Council (1963),
    243–44
Chamie, Joseph, 235
Chandler, Robert, 74
Chen, Marty, 217
China, 84, 127
  abortion in, 181, 190
  agriculture in, 60, 90
  decentralization efforts, 55

deforestation in, 117
family planning in, 8, 140, 142,
  144, 152–53, 178, 190, 284–85
fertility in, 142
infanticide, female, 217–18
population projections for, 153
Choudhury, Nahid, 199–200, 201
Cities, 234
  civil order fragmented in, 34
  decentralization efforts, 54–55
  mega-cities, 30, 33
  migration to, 16, 29, 31
  population growth concentrated
    in, 15, 28–30
  squatters in, see Squatters
  super-cities, 30
  see also specific cities
Claxton, Philander, 143
Cleveland, Harlan, 274
Climate change, 66, 110
Clinton administration, 289–90
Club of Rome, 17, 105–6
Cohen, Joel, 121
Cohen, Michael, 53–54
Cohen, Stanley R., 81
Colombia, 142, 171, 236, 239
Communism, 105, 278
Concerned Women for Family
  Planning, 201–3
Condoms, 154, 156–57, 171–72,
  177, 179, 232, 264
Condorcet, Marie Jean, 102, 104,
  113
Conli, Shanti, 140
Contraceptives, 2–3, 11, 139, 142
  choice of, 143, 155–57, 189,
    194
  discontinuance of due to poor
    quality, 189
  history of use of, 263–64
  price sensitivity of, 172
  supplies of, 170

Contraceptives (*cont.*)
  use of, *see* Family planning
    programs
  see also Family planning
    programs; *names of specific
    contraceptives; names of specific
    geographic areas*
Contraceptive social marketing
  (CSM) programs, 170–72
Costa Rica, 130, 133
Costle, Douglas, 289
Crime, urban, 34, 43
Cuba, 140
Curlin, Peggy, 160, 175, 177, 202

Davis, Kingsley, 105
Decentralization of population,
  54–55
Deforestation, 18, 98–99, 117, 125,
  130–35
  see also specific geographic areas
Delhi, India, 59
Demographic debate, 21–22, 102–21
Demographic transition, four-stage,
  10–11, 13, 66, 139–40
de Weiss, Susan Pick, 236, 238
Diaphragm, 264
DMPA, 155
DNA Plant Technology, 88
Donaldson, Peter, 140, 149, 150,
  220–21
Draper, William H., Jr., 270–71,
  275
Duce, Graciela, 261

Easterlin, Richard, 112
Eberstadt, Nick, 120
Echeverria-Alverez, Luis, 173
Economic and social development:
  population growth and, 4, 5, 11,
    13, 105, 112, 123, 162–65,
    220–23, 278, 280–81, 295

status of women and, *see* Women,
  status of
Ecuador, 85
Education:
  decreased family size and high
    costs of, 148, 149, 229
  family planning combined with,
    177
  for men, 179
  for women, 5, 142, 177, 194, 195,
    198–99, 202–3, 213–16, 223,
    240, 296
Egypt, 84
  agriculture in, 55–56
  Cairo, see Cairo, Egypt
  family planning in, 2–3, 58, 142,
    171, 209, 249
  foreign aid to, 50, 53
  population growth in, 2, 251
  unemployment in, 35, 39, 47,
    57–59
  women's status in, 209
Ehrlich, Paul, 17, 108–15, 117
Eisenhower, Dwight D., 262, 270,
  271
El-Geretly, Hassan, 52–53
el Mouelhy, Mawaheb, 2–3
El Salvador, 231
Employment:
  lack of, *see* Unemployment and
    underemployment
  opportunities for women, 142,
    177, 202, 211, 215, 240
Energy, 66, 98–99
  fossil fuel consumption,
    127–28
Engelman, Robert, 134
Engels, Friedrich, 103, 104
Environmental degradation, 18,
  97–135
  conflict resulting from, 20
  demographic debate, 102–21

fossil fuel consumption and, 127–28
government policy and, 130–35
historically, 101–2
studies of population growth and, 123–24
value assigned to resources, 118–19
warnings about, 124–25
see also specific geographic areas
Essay on the Principle of Population (Malthus), 65, 102
Ethiopia, 94–95
Eugenicists, 266–67
Europe, 18, 128, 231
Exploding City, The (Schiffer), 29

Family Planning International Assistance, 284
Family planning programs, 2, 4, 5, 11, 136–83, 220–23, 268–91, 296
abortion and, see Abortion
adolescents, targeting, 173–76
agricultural production and, 76–77
Catholicism and, *see* Catholicism and family planning
choice of contraceptives, 143, 155–57, 189, 194
choice of sources, 157
cost of, 161
decentralization of services, 153–55
financial incentives, 191–92
funding for, 170, 269, 274–90
impetus for, 105, 267–77
latent demand for, 150
media messages, 138, 151, 157–58, 179–80
men as target of, 177–80
national support for, 151–53

"natural" methods of, 227–29, 235, 237, 243, 246, 282
parallel programs to empower women, *see* Women, status of
preference for sons and, 216–18
religion and, *see* Religion and family planning
sensitivity of client needs, 158–60
slowdown in fertility decline, overcoming, 168–69
successful, characteristics of, 153
worldwide support and acceptance for, 140–42
see also Contraceptives; *names of specific geographic areas*
Family size, 140, 182–83, 192, 193–94
desirability of smaller, 11, 145, 147, 148, 149, 183, 186–87
preference for sons and, 216–17
small family norm, 11, 14, 139
see also specific geographic areas
Farming, *see* Agriculture
Fertility, 15, 139–44
countries with continued high levels of, 110–11
family planning to reduce, *see* Family planning programs
high GNP and low, 162
infant mortality and, 142, 166, 219–20, 233
preference for sons and, 216–17, 218, 233
replacement level, 8, 9, 10, 14, 139, 140, 141, 166, 167, 168, 180
status of women and, 186–88, 194–95, 197, 223
see also specific geographic areas
Feyerabend, Paul Karl, 119
Fiji, 142
FINCA program, 205

Fisheries, 118
Food supply, *see* Agriculture
Ford administration, 287
Ford Foundation, 269
Fornos, Werner, 141
France, 263, 264, 273
Freymann, John, 129
Fruits of Philosophy, The (Knowlton), 264–65
Fulbright, J. William, 275
Fundamentalists:
    Muslim, *see* Muslim fundamentalists
    Protestant, 282
Futures Group, 128–29

Gardner, Richard, 274
Ghana, 158, 194
Gillespie, Duff, 164
Global warming, 110
Godwin, William, 103
Goliber, Thomas, 163
Gonzales, Edgar, 255
Grameen Bank (Bangladesh), 204, 205, 206, 208
Great Britain, 9, 127, 264, 273
Greenhalgh, Susan, 210
Green revolution, *see* Agriculture, green revolution
Gregory IX, Pope, 242
Gregory X, Pope, 242
Guatemala, 99, 162–63
    deforestation in, 98–101, 125, 130–33, 135
    environmental degradation in, 98–101, 125, 130–33, 135

Haiti, 125
Hakim, Sobri Abdel, 43, 55
Hana, Milad, 41, 42
Handoussa, Heba, 56–59
Hansen, Alvin, 106–7

Harris, Bruce, 234
Harrison, Paul, 65, 76, 92, 122–23
Hartmann, Betsy, 192, 265
Hashemi, Syed, 206, 207–8, 239–40
Havanon, Napaporn, 213
Henderson, Julia, 272–73, 274
Hendry, Peter, 66
Hess, Helmut, 72, 132
Hinduism, 233, 240
Hodgson, Dennis, 114
Hoffman, Stanley, 18
Housing, 31–33, 234
    in Cairo, 29, 39–42, 43
Humanae Vitae, 244, 245, 246
Hussein, Aziza, 248

Ibn Abdullah, Jabir, 250
Ibrahim, Saad Eddin, 35, 36
Imperial Chemical Industries, 84
India, 55, 110, 127, 213
    family planning in, 141–42, 143, 156, 161, 171, 272–73, 276
    female sterilization in, 156, 161
    fertility in, 14, 142, 156
    green revolution in, 70–71
    infant mortality in, 219–20
    migration to, 20
    status of women in, 205, 217
Indonesia, 90
    family planning in, 152, 156, 191, 248, 277
    fertility in, 14, 111, 142, 168
    infant mortality in, 220
    population projections for, 14–15
    status of women in, 204
Industrialization, 29, 69, 141
Infanticide, female, 217–18
Infant mortality, 159, 183
    in Bangladesh, 199, 202, 216
    fertility and, 142, 166, 219–20, 233

International Board of Plant
Genetic Diversity, 86
International Fund for Agricultural
Development (IFAD), 92
International Planned Parenthood
Foundation (IPPF), 258, 284,
286, 287, 289
International Rice Research
Institute (IRRI), 73
International Union for the
Conservation of Nature, 123
International Women's Health
Coalition, 200
Iran, 127, 141, 233, 248
Islam, 232–33, 237, 238–40, 241,
246–51, 291
see also Muslim fundamentalists
Islam, Shammima, 197–98
Italy, 181, 232
IUD, 139, 142, 153, 154, 155, 156,
190, 276, 284
Ivory Coast, 194

Jacobson, Jodi, 192, 193
Jakarta, Indonesia, 30, 55, 59
Japan, 116, 128, 268, 270
Jazairy, Idriss, 92
Jobs, see Employment;
Unemployment and
underemployment
John Paul II, Pope, 225–26, 232,
241, 244, 257
John XXIII, Pope, 243
Johnson, Lyndon B., 276

Karachi, Pakistan, 32
Kennedy, Eileen, 75
Kennedy, John F., 271, 273–74,
275
Kennedy, Paul, 33
Kenya, 60, 78, 214
agriculture in, 61–64, 80, 91

family planning in, 141, 152, 158,
176–77
fertility in, 141
Kerala, India, 213
Keyfitz, Nathan, 116–20
Keynes, John Maynard, 107
Khan, Mufaweza, 201–3
Khan, Zarine Rahman, 209
Kimbrell, Andrew, 85–86
Kindervatter, Suzanne, 177
King, Elizabeth, 215
Kinya, Mbaari, 91
Kissling, Frances, 236, 260
Knodel, John, 144–45, 148, 149,
167
Knowlton, Charles, 264–65
Koran, 246, 248, 249, 250
Kuznets, Simon, 112

Lapham, Robert, 222
Lasher, Craig, 287, 288
Latin America, 10
abortion in, 232
family planning in, 140, 159,
230–32, 239
infant mortality in, 219
landholding patterns in, 131–32
status of women in, 205
urbanization of, 31
Limits to Growth, The (Club of
Rome), 17, 105–6, 119
Lloyd, Cynthia, 193, 210–11
Lopez Juárez, Alfonso, 174, 175,
254, 256

McNamara, Robert, 89, 130
McPherson, M. Peter, 282
Mahfouz, Naguib, 36
Malawi, 90
Malaysia, 157
Mali, 159–60, 194
Malnutrition, 66, 77

Malthus, Thomas, 6, 65–66, 68–69, 102–4, 108, 121, 264

Manila, Philippines, 30, 32, 39, 128–29

Mann, Jonathan, 113

Marcos, Sylvia, 237

Marriage, delaying age of, 175, 215, 223

Marx, Karl, 103, 104

Maternal and child health services, *see* Reproductive health services

Maternal mortality rates, 201

Matthews, Jessica Tuchman, 16

Mauldin, W. Parker, 166, 222

Meadows, Donella, 106

Media promotion of family planning, 138, 151, 157–58, 179–80

Meekers, Dominique, 206

Men as target of family planning, 177–80

Mendez, Alfredo, 100

Merrick, Thomas, 252

Mexfam, 174, 175, 254, 256

Mexico, 127, 226
agriculture in, 69–70, 90
family planning in, 161, 172–76, 179–80, 226, 236, 252–53, 277
female literacy in, 214
fertility in, 111, 173
religion and family planning in, 224–32, 237–38, 244–45, 252–56, 261

Mexico City, Mexico, 30, 31, 39, 172, 292–95
traffic in, 38, 172

Middle East, 127, 214–15, 219

Migration to cities, 16, 29, 31

Mill, John Stuart, 103

Moi, Daniel Arap, 152, 191

Monsanto, 84

Moore, Hugh, 270

Moore, Stephen, 114

Morocco, 141

Mubarak, Hasni, 50, 58

Murphy, Francis X., 242, 243, 261

Muslim fundamentalists, 248, 251
in Egypt, 28, 42, 46–49, 54, 59

Mutiso, Gideon, 93–94

Myers, Norman, 23

Mzenge, Godwin, 178

Nasser, Gamal Abdel, 27, 49, 58

National Academy of Sciences, 124, 269, 280

National Population Council (Mexico), 173

Neo-Malthusians, 264–65

Nepal, 76, 218, 233

Nigeria, 9, 175, 178

Nixon, Richard, 275, 277

NORPLANT, 155

Omran, Abdel, 251

Oral contraceptives, 139, 142, 154, 155, 156, 231, 276

Osterfeld, David, 107, 108

Owen, Robert Dale, 265

Pakistan, 220, 240
family planning in, 142, 163–64, 171, 269, 276

Panama, 231

Paul VI, Pope, 244

Pendleton, Scott, 75

Peru, 181, 235, 257

Philippines, 90, 257–58

Pill, Charles, 162–63

Pinstrup-Andersen, Per, 67

Piotrow, Phyllis, 275, 290

Pius XI, Pope, 242–43

Pius XII, Pope, 243

Place, Francis, 264

Planned Parenthood, 267, 269, 271, 284

Poland, 257

Pollution, 105–6

air, 38, 127, 128–29, 172

water, 38, 126–27

Ponting, Clive, 134

Population Action International, 141

Population Bomb, The (Ehrlich), 17, 108–9, 113

Population Council, 269

Population growth:

economic and social development and, *see* Economic and social development, population growth and

world, *see* World population growth

see also specific geographic areas

Population momentum, 8, 153, 182

Potts, Malcolm, 177, 222, 296

Preston, Samuel, 118–19

Pro-Vida, 255–56

Puerto Rico, 231

Ramos, Fidel, 258

Ravenholt, Dr. Remiert T., 276, 277

Reagan administration, 258, 281–88, 290

Religion and family planning, 224–61

Catholicism, *see* Catholicism and family planning

cultural values, religion's influence on, 237–39

Hinduism, 233, 240

Islam, 232–33, 237, 238–40, 241, 246–51, 291

relationship between, 234–36

self-imposed restrictions, 237

see also specific geographic areas

Repetto, Robert, 122, 124–25

Replacement level fertility, 8, 9, 10, 14, 139, 140, 141, 166, 167, 168, 180

Reproductive health services, 221

family planning provided along with, 157, 199–201, 202

Rockefeller, John D., III, 268–69

Rockefeller Foundation, 268–69

Roe v. Wade, 283

Romania, 181

Ross, Gabrielle, 200

Ross, James, 233

Ross, John, 166

Rowen, Hobart, 277

Royal Academy of London, 124

RU-486 ("abortion pill"), 296

Rusk, Dean, 17

Ruttan, Vernon, 81

Rwanda, 78, 80, 157

Sadat, Anwar, 27

Sagoff, Mark, 128

Salas, Rafael, 274

Salinas de Gortari, Carlos, 253

Sanger, Margaret, 265–68

Sanitation, 33, 34, 44

San Salvador, El Salvador, 59

Sao Paulo, Brazil, 30, 32, 43

Sassen, Saskia, 32, 34

Saudi Arabia, 75, 141

Schiffer, Robert, 29, 30–31

Schuler, Sidney Ruth, 174, 206, 239–40

Schwartz, Norman, 99–100, 132–33

Security:

rapid population growth and, 19, 287

terrorism, see Terrorism

Serrano Limon, Jorge, 256

Sewer systems, 33, 34, 38–39, 50

Sheriff, Mahmoud, 39

Shulkani, Ali, 59
Sid-Ahmed, Mohamed, 25–28
Simon, Julian, 108, 111–15, 121, 122
Sinding, Steven, 143, 222
Singapore, 75
    family planning in, 140, 141, 166
South Korea, 10, 23–24, 55
    family planning in, 140, 142, 157, 163–64, 191, 213
    fertility in, 211, 213
    opportunities for women in, 213
Soviet Union, former, 127, 128
Speidel, Joseph, 216, 281–82
Squatters, 31–33, 59, 131, 132, 134
    in Cairo, 2, 31, 51–53, 246
Sri Lanka, 142, 214
Steinbruner, John, 19, 21
Sterilization, 191, 231
    female, 142, 155, 156, 161, 191, 231
    forced, 143, 190, 284
    male, 158, 178, 179
    religious restrictions limiting access to, 237
Stevenson, Adlai, 274–75
Streatfield, Kim, 188
Sub-Saharan Africa, 80, 140
    AIDS in, 12
    demographic transition in, 14

Taiwan, 211, 213
    family planning in, 16, 140
Tantawi, Mohammed Sayeed, 246–51
Tanzania, 12, 60, 91, 219
Tapia, Marta, 175–76
Technology, 16, 112–13, 129
    agricultural, *see* Agriculture, technology and
    future population growth and reliance on, 121–24

Teitelbaum, Michael, 119
Terrorism, 28, 46–47, 54
Thailand, 222
    abortion in, 181
    agriculture in, 90
    family planning in, 136–39, 140, 144–50, 151, 153–55, 157–58, 164–68, 222, 277
    replacement fertility in, 10, 13, 166, 167
Thomas, Donald, 64, 94
Toubia, Nahid, 193, 194
Traffic, 38, 50, 53, 172
Trias, Miguel, 153
Truman, Harry S, 271
Tunisia, 157, 168, 240
Turkey, 142, 158, 240

Uganda, 12
Unemployment and underemployment, 19–20, 39, 234
    in Egypt, 35, 39, 47, 57–59
United Kingdom, 9, 127, 264, 273
United Nations, 271, 272, 273–74, 278
UN Conference on Environment and Development (UNCED) in Rio, 1992, 258–60
UN Conference on Women, 1985, 189
UN Development Programme, 54
UN Population Commission, 271–72
UN Population Fund (UNFPA), 122, 258, 274, 285, 286
United States, 127
    contraceptive use in, 276
    energy use, 128
    family planning movement in, 265–71
    fertility in, 142

population policy, 258, 262–63,
269–71, 273–77, 279–90
population projections for, 17
U.S. AID, *see* Agency for
International Development
U.S. Food and Drug
Administration (FDA), 82
Urbanization, *see* Cities
Urbina, Manual, 173

Vaessen, Martin, 164
Valdes, Alberto, 89
Van Heuven, Marten, 18
Vasectomy, 158, 178, 179
Viederman, Stephen, 215
Viravaidya, Mechai, 153–55
Von Braun, Joachim, 75–76, 78
Vosti, Stephen, 68, 73, 74, 94–95

Water, 20, 77, 126–27
for agriculture, 43, 56, 62–63, 72,
73–74, 77, 79, 81
desalinization of, 73–74, 126
Water pollution, 38, 126–27
Wattenberg, Ben, 108, 121
Way, Ann, 168
Wetlands, 126
Wilcox, Bruce, 16, 117, 120
Winter, Jay, 119
Wirth, Timothy, 289–90
Woman Rebel, 266
Women, status of, 184–223, 234,
238–39, 265, 295–96
agricultural reforms to benefit,
91, 95
in developing world, 177–78,
194–96

education, 5, 142, 177, 194, 195,
198–99, 202–3, 213–16, 223,
240, 296
employment opportunities, 142,
177, 202, 211, 215, 240
improvement of status, and
fertility, 186–88, 194–95,
197–223, 240
infanticide, female, 217–18
preference for sons, 216–18
reproductive health services, *see*
Reproductive health services
small business loans for, 185–86,
203–8
see also specific geographic areas
World Bank, 53–54, 89–90
World population growth, 2, 5, 6–9,
17–18, 115–16, 143, 290–91
agriculture and, *see* Agriculture
concentration of, 15, 28–30
demographic debate, 21–22,
102–21
environmental degradation and,
see Environmental degradation
post-World War II recognition
and interest in slowing, 267–90
trends and projections, 6–9, 13,
15–16, 19, 24, 122, 129–30
World Population Plan of Action,
278–79, 285–86

Young, Alvin, 85, 86–87
Yunus, Muhammed, 203–5, 211

Zaire, 12, 80, 89
Zambia, 80, 89
Zimbabwe, 91, 140, 152, 159, 179